THE CONSEQUENCES OF DETERMINISM

From the reviews of *A Theory of Determinism*:

'Professor Honderich provides a treatise that is learned, logical and humane and may convince us that Determinism is both true and tolerable. In the process he provides a theory of the nature of minds and brains that helps us to solve many problems . . . It will be evident that this is a very serious book, from which much can be learned.'

J. Z. Young in *Brain*

'a big book on a grand theme . . . The book is wide-ranging and weaves in with the theory of determinism a powerful theory of the mind . . . J. L. Austin remarked that determinism was "a name for nothing clear, that has been argued for only incoherently." It may have been true then, but it is certainly not true now.'

Justin Broackes in *The Sunday Times*

'it seems undeniable that this book revivifying what many philosophers had considered a "dead problem", and rescuing it from unclarity and impasse, constitutes a major philosophical breakthrough.'

Jane O'Grady in the *Literary Review*

'deals with topics which are of crucial importance in a number of related areas of philosophy . . . anyone interested in the subjects tackled cannot fail to be stimulated by it.'

Andrew Jack in *Mind*

'Honderich's achievement is impressive, in its scope and detail, and in the relentless thoroughness with which he pursues his project . . . He offers a wealth of helpful suggestions, disposes of many flawed views that have been proposed, and elevates the level of debate in this most important area of philosophical inquiry.'

Richard Schacht in *Inquiry*

THE CONSEQUENCES
OF DETERMINISM

A Theory of Determinism
Volume 2

TED HONDERICH

CLARENDON PRESS · OXFORD

Oxford University Press, Walton Street, Oxford OX2 6DP
Oxford New York Toronto
Delhi Bombay Calcutta Madras Karachi
Petaling Jaya Singapore Hong Kong Tokyo
Nairobi Dar es Salaam Cape Town
Melbourne Auckland
and associated companies in
Berlin Ibadan

Oxford is a trade mark of Oxford University Press

Published in the United States
by Oxford University Press, New York

© Ted Honderich 1988

First published in hardback as Part 3 of
A Theory of Determinism: The Mind, Neuroscience, and Life-Hopes
This paperback edition first published 1990

British Library Cataloguing in Publication Data
Honderich, Ted
A theory of determinism.
1. Determinism. Free will. Determinism & free will
I. Title II. Mind and brain III. The consequences of determinism
123
ISBN 0–19–824282–4 v. 1
ISBN 0–19–824283–2 v. 2

Library of Congress Cataloguing in Publication Data
Honderich, Ted.
[Theory of determinism (1990)]
A theory of determinism/Ted Honderich.
Includes bibliographical references.
Contents: v. 1. Mind and brain — v. 2. The consequences of determinism.
1. Neuropsychology. 2. Determinism (Philosophy) I. Title.
QP360.H665. 612.8—dc20 89–28934
ISBN 0–19–824282–4 (v. 1)
ISBN 0–19–824283–2 (v. 2)

Typeset by Pentacor Ltd,
High Wycombe, Bucks
Printed in Great Britain by
Biddles Ltd, Guildford & King's Lynn

To Bee, Janet, John, Kiaran,
Pauline, and Ruth

Acknowledgements

The following, to whom I am most grateful, commented on some or all of the last draft of this book: Prof. Sir Alfred Ayer, Prof. Colin Blakemore, Dr Malcolm Budd, Dr Kerry Greer, Dr W. D. Hart, Ms Cynthia Macdonald, Mr Derek Parfit, Prof. Christopher Peacocke, Ms Nicola Lacey, Mr Derek Matravers, Mr Wayne Norman, Prof. Anthony O'Hear, Prof. Timothy Sprigge, Prof. Euan Squires, Dr Anthony Sudbery, Ms Patricia Walsh, Prof. J. Z. Young, and an anonymous reader for the Oxford University Press.

The following, to whom I am also very grateful, commented on a previous draft, or on writings which issued directly in the book: Prof. Donald Davidson, Prof. Daniel Dennett, Prof. Sir John Eccles, Prof. Paul Fatt, Dr Gertrude Falk, Dr Vivette Glover, Prof. Alastair Hannay, Prof. Benjamin Libet, Mr David Lloyd-Thomas, Mr John Mackie, Mr Peter Morriss, Mr Nicholas Nathan, Dr Carlos Nino, Prof. Hilary Putnam, Ms Janet Radcliffe Richards, Mr Richard Rawles, Prof. David Sanford, Prof. Amartya Sen, Mr Peter Smith, Prof. Stephen Stich, Prof. Patrick Wall, Prof. V. M. Weil, Dr. Edgar Wilson.

I have also benefited from questions, objections, and stoicism on the part of postgraduates and undergraduates at University College London—particularly in a seminar on the manuscript in 1986—and stalwarts who turned up to guest lectures and meetings of philosophy societies in British, American, and Canadian universities.

I also thank, although we have had our differences, my teachers, past colleagues, and colleagues at University College London, including, first of all Prof. Jerry Cohen for our many spirited encounters, and also Prof. Ayer, Prof. Myles Burnyeat, Prof. Stuart Hampshire, Dr Peter Downing, Dr John Watling, Prof. Bernard Williams and Prof. Richard Wollheim.

Mr John Allen and Mr John Spiers, librarians at University College London, were most helpful.

Typing was done with forbearance by Ms Catherine Backhouse, Ms Dinah Perry, and Ms Wendy Robbins.

Editorial work for the paperback edition was very ably and amiably assisted by Ms Helen Betteridge.

Contents

Contents

Introduction

What are the consequences of a conceptually satisfactory theory of our ongoing lives, above all our deciding and acting, in terms of causal and other necessary connections? What are the consequences, that is, of a theory of ourselves which locates us within the natural world rather than apart from it? What are the consequences, again, of a theory of our lives which *eschews* explanations, if they can be called such, which are intrinsically mysterious, explanations having to do with Free Will? Such mysterious explanations include within themselves a certain proposition, on reflection a striking one. It is that *every* fact about a person, including every fact about brain and Central Nervous System, and character and personality, and thought and feeling, might have been exactly as it was before and at the moment when the person understood something, or hoped, or decided, or acted, and nevertheless the understanding, hoping, deciding or acting might never have occurred. That was a possibility in reality, not merely something that can be thought without contradiction.

To put the same question in a last and the most familar philosophical way, what follows from a *determinist* theory of our existence?

I have in mind, as philosophers generally have, a theory which is deterministic in a strong way. Many theories of our existence, including Freud's, whatever else is to be said of them, can be, and often are, taken in the strong deterministic way. The same question of consequences arises, as it turns out, about certain widely accepted outlooks or theories which are less deterministic, or indeed partly indeterministic and wholly consistent with a common interpretation of Quantum Theory. It arises, for example, about what is sometimes called naturalism, or the scientific vision of ourselves, which may combine micro-indeterminism with macro-determinism. (Dennett, 1984 Searle, 1984, Lect. 6) Philosophers have given more attention to this question of consequences than to two prior ones, those of the conceptual adequacy and of the truth of determinism. Expressed differently, and as generally, it is the question of what we are to make of our lives if or since determinism is true.

It has given rise to two traditions, each seeming to be as strong now, in 1990, as it has been in past centuries. The answer given in one tradition is that if determinism is true, we are not free. Determinism and freedom are incompatible, irreconcilable. Almost always, in this tradition, out of the conviction that we *are* free, or out of the deep desire to be so, it is also concluded that determinism is not true. The answer to the question of the consequences of determinism given in the second tradition is that the truth of determinism does not or would not touch our freedom. We are free despite its truth, as many say, or as some say, because of it. Determinism and freedom are compatible, reconcilable.

My great hope for this book, and my greatest claim for it, is that it resolves the problem of the consequences of determinism. At least it gives the fundamentals or outline of the reolution. It resolves the problem not by succeeding where there must be no hope of succeeding, where whole declamatory lecture-halls of philosophers, as audacious or arrogant as I, and certainly more able, have failed. That is, it does not succeed by establishing that one or the other of the two traditions is correct. It is part of the resolution of the problem that both are mistaken. Their fundamental propositions are false.

The problem, as remarked, is the one most considered by philosophers, at least since Thomas Hobbes's *Liberty and Necessity* of 1646. It has almost always been considered a certain way. The question has been asked whether, if determinism is true, we are free in such a way that we are morally responsible for our actions. One tradition answers no, the other yes. To that question has occasionally been attached another closely related moral issue, that of the justification of punishment.

To proceed in this way is not to come into close touch with the true subject of the consequences of determinism. It is to leave out a lot of that subject, most of it. P. F. Strawson's 'Freedom and Resentment' (1962) rightly directed philosophers away from moral responsibility (although with the official aim of returning to it) to another part of the general question. It has to do not with feelings of moral approval and disapproval with respect to someone's decision or action, which is in fact the subject-matter of the question of moral responsibility, but with what may be called *personal* feelings, of which resentment and gratitude are two. However, there are more parts to the question of consequences, and they require attention as much. Indeed, in my view, one of these can be said to demand attention more than either the given moral disapproval and approval or personal feelings. It is the question of how determinism stands to what can be called our *life-hopes*. It is with respect to this above all that a theory of determinism appears to be most challenging. It can be, as it has been to many, including myself, a black thing.

The first chapter of the book begins a consideration of life-hopes, personal feelings, and moral disapproval and approval, and also additional consequences of determinism. One, which has hitherto been misplaced and isolated in philosophical discussions, and thus been misconceived, has to do with knowledge. The fifth and sixth matters considered in an initial way in the chapter have to do with morality, but not moral responsibility. They are the matter of right action and principles, and the matter of the general moral standing of persons.

It is my contention that a broad fact established in the seventh chapter, having to do with our common attitudes and responses in the matter of determinism and life-hopes, determinism and personal feelings, and so on, is fully sufficient to provide a refutation of the propositions fundamental to the two traditions of Incompatibilism and Compatibilism. Those propositions are elicited by means of a brief historical survey carried foward in the second chapter. it is indeed the conclusion of the second chapter that both traditions consist in provable error.

The third chapter completes the inquiry into determinism and life-hopes, personal feelings, knowledge, moral responsibility, actions and principles, and the general moral standing of agents. It gives my resolution of the problem of the consequences of determinism. It is also a resolution, as already indicated, of the problem of consequences raised as much by widely held near-determinist theories of the mind which assert or contemplate indeterminism at the micro-level, by way of Quantum Theory, but none the less accept or tend to accept macrodeterminism, a determinism which certainly includes what are commonly called neural events. This principal conclusion of the book may not be right, as I am confident it is, but very certainly it is not more of the same. It is not one more attempt to have one of those two so overridden and wearied nags, Incompatibilist or Compatibilist, plod at last into the winner's enclosure. They are both put out to pasture.

The fourth chapter does not carry the fundamental argument onward, but applies it in connection with a final consequence of determinism, its consequence for an array of institutions, practices, and habits in our societies. Among these but only one of seven, although it is given most attention, is punishment. If there has been an insufficient awareness of the range of consequences of determinism, there has also been an insufficient awareness of the extent of what can properly be regarded as this last one of those consequences, having to do with the array of institutions, practices, and habits. Reflection here finally issues in a consideration of determinism and politics.

It would be satisfactory to conclude this introduction by saying that my aim in what follows has been no more than to advance truth, or, even, to advance truth and do myself some good by doing so. Whatever can be said along those lines, something needs to be added. Philosophy in general does seem one of the intellectual endeavours which most gives rise to kinds of assertiveness, combativeness, and dismissiveness. The latter traits, as it seems, are pervasive, not a lot less noticeable when they are officially disavowed. (Nozick, 1981) Philosophers cannot but seem to be *advocates*—learned or not so learned counsel. I do not mean that they do not believe in their briefs, but rather that they certainly press them. The truth may be owed to the subject-matters of philosophy, which are such that the facts in them do not in the end speak for themselves, or speak still more uncertainly than elsewhere. Whatever the explanation of this truth about philosophers and philosophy, I cannot claim to have risen far enough above it.

The present volume is a reprinting of the third part of my *A Theory of Determinism: The Mind, Neuroscience, and Life-Hopes*. It stands on its own, a completed account of the consequences of determinism. As remarked earlier, it has to do with the consequences of any strong determinist theory, such as the one expounded in the companion volume, *Mind and Brain*, which consists in the first and second parts of *A Theory of Determinism: The Mind, Neuroscience, and Life-Hopes*. It may be of interest to indicate something of the contents of that volume.

In its first part, *Mind and Brain* considers the question of whether there does exist a conceptually satisfactory determinist theory of our lives. Is there a clear and explicit, complete, and in general a conceptually adequate theory of our ongoing lives, mostly notably our decisions and actions, in terms of causal or other necessary connections? Such connections, called nomic or lawlike connections to distinguish them from logically necessary connections rooted in words and other symbols, are pervasive in the natural world, and fundamental to it. They are connections not between words but in reality. They are the cement of the universe.

In the second half of this century, and perhaps before, it has been replied, and perhaps more often thought, that there is no such theory. *Mind and Brain* gives the answer that there is. It does so by providing one. This is the main endeavour of the first of its two parts.

However well supported or confirmed, what is ordinarily called a theory remains at least in some way tentative, not advanced or taken as a settled truth, or at any rate not something on a level with *simple* truths. A theory is not a report of observations, but a deeper account of them. Our relation to the atomic theory, or the theories of evolution or gravity or of reciprocal synapses, is not our relation to the simple truths that things have weight or hearts, or that they fall, or change together. Still, the fundamental fact for us about any theory, however conceptually satisfactory, is the fact of how it stands to reality. What reason can we have for accepting it?

Hence the second question addressed in the book, in its second part, is whether the theory of determinism expounded in it is well supported. There is reason to think so. If it cannot be said to be proved true, it cannot be said to be proved false either. Certainly I believe the determinism of the book, at any rate the main lines of it, or, to speak a bit more carefully, I take it to have the strength, say, of the theory of evolution. It is, in my feeling about it, no speculation. To concede that belief in the theory goes somewhat beyond the evidence and is consistent with some hesitation and diffidence is perhaps not to allow greatly more than that the belief in question, like a great deal else, indeed everything of interest, is not a matter of sense-experience or simple logical necessity.

To return to the first question, that of the existence of a conceptually satisfactory determinist theory of our ongoing lives, the view that there was none was taken near the mid-century by two of the most acute of philosophers, J. L. Austin (1956, p. 131) and P. F. Strawson (1962, p. 187). Neither of them, it is worth saying, was moved to his conclusion by the sorts of *feeling*—one is tempted to say *mere* feeling—including spirituality and residual religiousness, noticeable enough among opponents of determinism. Neither was dedicated to the preservation of the human mystery. They have not remained alone in their scepticism. David Pears, despite being a remover of barriers in the way of a determinist theory, takes us to lack a theory that works. (1973, p. 110) A. J. Ayer is of a similar mind. (1984c, p. 3) Such opponents of determinism as Stuart Hampshire and Anthony Kenny, although concerned to refute determinism, also have doubts as to its conceptual adequacy. (Hampshire, 1965, 1972a; Kenny, 1975, 1978; cf. Watson, 1982, p. 9; Trusted, 1984, p. 138; W.H. Davis, 1971, p. vii)

It would be difficult for sceptics to imagine and clarify, let alone defend, a general line of argument or a principle of inquiry which would issue in the conclusion that a conceptually satisfactory determinist theory is *impossible*. Indeed, the scepticism of Austin, Strawson, and others is properly to be taken as a lesser if a substantial thing, a claim as to just the *absence*, and the likelihood of a continued absence, of such a determinist theory.

It is one thing to declare or more likely to presuppose that Free Will, the Faculty of the Will, the Self-Conscious Mind, or what I may seem to speak of in speaking of my self, are pieces of metaphysical excess, or even nonsense, or that our choices and decisions are quite clearly effects, or that our behaviour is lawlike, or that the brain is a machine or the biological instantiation of certain formal systems. It is another thing to set out a determinist theory which is explicit, complete, and at a proper level of specificity. To do the latter thing is to do no less than set out a philosophy of mind and action. To do so is necessarily to deal with three problems: the relation between neural and mental events, the antecedents of those events, and the nature of action. Each of these can reasonably be taken to generate further conceptual problems. There is also a prior problem, yet more general than the three mentioned, which is the nature of necessary or nomic connection.

As it seems to me, then, the given scepticism as to the likelihood of a conceptually adequate determinism of the given kind has had as its best ground a true perception of the *largeness* of the enterprise, and a true awareness that it has not been succeeded in, or even much attempted. Determinism as an account of our existence, when it has not been presupposed, has been talked of rhetorically, briskly defined in formal ways, remarked on as the basis of one or another model of the mind, had its truth affirmed or denied on the basis of premises distant from the subject-matter, and had its human consequences assiduously contemplated and disputed. It has not been much *expounded*.

The first chapter of *Mind and Brain* is given over to the prior problem in any satisfactory exposition of determinism, that of causal and other nomic connections. It gives an independent account of these. The second, third, and fourth chapters, together with the first, comprise a philosophy of mind and action. The second has to do with simultaneous mental and neural events, the psychoneural relation. It presents a first part of a new theory of that relation, the Union Theory, which supplants Identity Theories of mind and brain. The third chapter concerns the explanation of mental events, their antecedents. It examines the conceptual viability of Free Will—indeterminist thoughts and theories of mental events—and also completes the Union Theory. The fourth chapter gives an account of the nature of actions and their explanation. The three hypotheses advanced in these chapters are, with the prior account of nomic connection, the principal parts of the determinist theory advanced. The theory is, in certain reasonable senses, complete and specific.

It is distinct, certainly, from other determinisms. It is distinct from, although consonant with, determinist theories of absolute generality, having to do with all that exists. Newton and LaPlace come here, and, to the discomfiture of many contemporary physicists, Einstein. My interest is not in the whole universe—or how determinism works in physics (Earman, 1986)—but ourselves. A part of what will be said is of relevance to LaPlacean or universal determinism, but that is not our subject. To set aside other things which *are* of similar limited scope but none the less irrelevant, the theory of this book is distinct from deterministic Freudianism and similar congeries of ideas.

To linger a moment with the example of Freud, it has sometimes been thought by philosophers, as it was by Hampshire, that psychoanalysis is 'the new positive science of human conduct', and that it is to be taken as providing the principal challenge to human freedom, that above all with which freedom must be shown to be compatible. (1959, p. 255) My own persistent attitude in this matter is close enough to one once tartly expressed by Bernard Williams. 'To say that a view of human freedom is compatible with scientific advance because it is compatible with developments in psychoanalysis is much like saying that a material is uninflammable because it doesn't burst into flames when one shines an electric torch on it.' (1960, pp. 41–2) Whatever else of a more tolerant sort is to be said of Freudianism (MacIntyre, 1971b), it is not the theory of the book and plays no part at all in it.

Nor is the theory to be identified with various determinisms other than the universal kind and the Freudian. It is not a *weak* determinism that involves something less or looser than causal and nomic connection properly conceived. It is different in kind from any view that involves so-called causally sufficient conditions, or so-called complete causes, that merely probabilify and do not necessitate their effects. Again, it is of course not a *partial* determinism, which limits its causes to certain levels or items, perhaps *events* somehow conceived, and allows that when *persons* or *agents* perform their acts of volition or whatever, this is not a matter of ordinary cause and effect.

The theory is not, to use again a certain description in a way now common, a model of the mind, or the brain, or both. It is not, that is, a middle-level speculation as to the organization or function of either mind or brain or both—where many such speculations at this moment of history are computer-based conceptions issuing in characterizations of the brain as a semantic engine, an information-processing system, and so on. The theory does not conflict with such models of how mind or brain work, but rather is logically prior to them. It is best regarded, perhaps, in so far as its relation to such models is concerned, as establishing certain fundamental constraints on their formulation— constraints given by the three hypotheses and associated propositions. The theory is of the nature of mind and brain, including the fundamental principles of their operation. Finally, with respect to various overviews or taxonomies of determinisms, it is clear that an attempt to put the determinism of the book into the three or four categories of determinism supplied by one philosopher (Popper, 1982b), would do great damage either to it or the categories. Nor does it fit easily into other taxonomies. (Ayers, 1968; Trusted, 1984)

Reassuringly, the theory is not a world apart from everything. It has inexplicit historical antecedents, above all in Hume's splendid Sections 1 and 2, Part 3, Book 2, of *A Treatise of Human Nature*. The theory in its several parts approximates to a number of views in the contemporary philosophy of mind, views on brain and mind, or action, or on lesser subjects, these being at least tacitly determinist in nature. It is identical, I think, with no set of these views—and not identical either, incidentally, with my own previous writings on the subject. I have changed my mind about important issues. It is approximate, too, to certain ruling presuppositions in contemporary neuroscience.

To return to the second question, that of the truth of the theory, it will be clear already that its three hypotheses are properly if briefly described as claims of fact, to be settled in part by empirical evidence. They differ somewhat among themselves in this respect, but none purports to be merely a logically necessary or conceptual truth, in no need of empirical confirmation. Despite philosophy's proper pre-occupation with the unempirical, it would be wholly wrong to suppose that such factual claims have not in fact been part of philosophy, or are not such now. No philosophical journal is without them, or what immediately presupposes them. It is sometimes said or implied that such claims ought not to be within philosophy, roughly on the ground that questions of fact are properly the business of scientists. There are excellent reasons for dissenting, and thus for supposing that the ongoing history of philosophy does not involve a kind of general trespass on science. The main reason, to restrict ourselves to claims about the relation between mental and neural events, and the explanation of those events, and the explanation of actions, is that such claims do, despite their factual nature, raise conceptual issues. They raise issues fundamental to philosophy and to be resolved only by methods and ways of reflection that are most developed within philosophy. To say so is not to embrace just the anti-scientism, arguable as it can seem, that supposes there actually are two ways of understanding, the subjective and the objective. (Cf. T. Nagel, 1986, p. 9, Davidson, 1980e, p. 216) Science is such as to give it a right to judgement on the claims in question. So too is philosophy.

Something else quite simple is more important than the possibility that the determinist theory of the book would be more properly advanced by a philosopher or a scientist. It is that any adequate treatment of the fundamental question must be subject to both philosophical and scientific constraints. It must aspire to both philosophical and scientific virtues. That is not to say that any adequate treatment of the question must in part be a piece of science, but it goes some small way in that direction. There are writings on determinism and freedom that must be allowed philosophical respectability, and which very notably lack the other respectability, as there are writings whose neurophysiology, psychology, computer science, or Quantum Theory must be taken as authoritative, but whose departures into vagueness and looseness, indeed flights of fancy, are philosophically unsatisfying, or breath-taking, or close to absurd.

The fifth chapter of the book is largely given over to a survey of directly relevant neuroscience. It gives a certain summation as of the year 1988 of the sciences that fall under that heading, a summation for philosophical and like readers. In so doing, it gives an assessment of the body of empirical evidence that is most important to the book's theory, and to any similar determinism, and also most important to opposition to them. There is no other evidence so important, in any other science, any body of knowledge, any set of propositions whatever. There is no evidence so important to the questions of the mind-brain relation, the explanation of mental and neural events, and the explanation and nature of actions. My confidence that the theory advanced here is well confirmed is not wholly, but it is in the main, owed to this evidence.

It will come as an irritation to some readers, and a relief to others, that despite what has just been said, the book is no piece by a handmaiden of science. If it is no piece of anti-scientism in the sense mentioned above, it is certainly no piece of scientism, which is to say dismissive of all that is not science. (Cf. P. F. Strawson, 1985, p. 67; Mackie, 1976, p. 169) Nor does it have in it the odd dream of philosophy's being succeeded by 'neurophilosophy'. (P. S. Churchland, 1986) Also, I have found it impossible to believe that the evidence for determinism which is provided by neuroscience is overborne by the familiar, obscure, and too often merely magisterial considerations of a philosophical kind drawn from something else commonly accorded pride of place, which is physics, and in particular Quantum Theory. The fifth chapter, if it finds support for the theory of the book in neuroscience, also argues against the idea, certainly not uncommon among scientists, that any determinism is refuted by Quantum Theory. One of my several reasons is that the subject-matters of the first part of the book—the psychoneural relation, the psychobehavioural relation, and so on—are under the very eye of neuroscience. They are not near to being under the eye of physics.

Neuroscience is in fact touched not at all, or barely, by indeterminist ideas drawn from Quantum Theory. It is also true that the incorporation of an interpretation of Quantum Theory into indeterminist pictures of the mind produces something very approximate to incoherence and contradiction.

Finally, with respect to the truth of determinism, philosophers as distinct from scientists have advanced a considerable number of what they take to be refutations. Some of these are in fact considered in the four chapters (1–4) which are primarily concerned to expound and clarify. This is so since many objections are of a mixed character. The sixth chapter *Mind and Brain* is concerned with a set of related objections of roughly an epistemological kind.

1

Two Families of Attitudes, and Dismay and Intransigence

Of what consequence is the likely truth of determinism, or of theories akin to it, including a number of near-determinisms, to our thoughts and feelings about our individual prospects, thoughts and feelings we have in contemplating our futures? Of what consequence, secondly, is determinism to our feelings about other persons who affect our lives well or badly? That is, of what consequence is it to our appreciative and our resentful feelings, these being non-moral feelings? Thirdly, how does it stand to our claims of knowledge, our confidence of laying hold of truth? Of what consequence is it, fourthly, to our holding ourselves and others morally responsible for things, or crediting ourselves and others with moral responsibility—which is to say of what consequence to certain feelings on our part of moral approval and disapproval? Of what consequence is it, fifthly, to the general moral standing or worth of persons, their standing over time or indeed in their whole lives, and, sixthly, to judgements of the rightness or wrongness of particular actions and of kinds of actions? Finally, how does determinism stand to certain large and encompassing institutions, practices, and habits, including punishment by the state? These go a considerable way to making our societies what they are. They contribute to their nature.

All these questions are pressing, but the most pressing, or at any rate one which is as pressing as any other, is the first, that of consequences of the theory of determinism for an individual's engaged outlook on his or her own coming life, his or her own future. It is not a question which has been discussed, at least explicitly, in connection with any determinism. On the contrary, there has in the truly vast literature on determinism and freedom been a persistent concentration on the upshot of determinism for moral responsibility, for our holding others and ourselves responsible for particular actions, and crediting others and ourselves with such responsibility. What is arguably most significant, then, has been overlooked or avoided.

This is a yet larger fact than the typical failure to locate the question of knowledge, our third question, in this context. Arguably it is with respect to our conception of our own future lives that a determinism is most challenging to us, least tolerable. Determinism can be a black thing, as many have attested. It can, as in the case of Mill, and as he said, weigh on our existence like an incubus. (1924 (1873), p. 118) It did so for a time on mine. That it is our conception of our own prospects which perhaps is most sensitive to a determinism is in accord with a considerable fact, no doubt in some ways a disagreeable one. It is the fact whose nature is disputable, whose rationality and tolerability will continue to have attention in various ways (Parfit, 1984, Pt.1), the fact that we are not in the first instance moral agents, concerned in an impartial way with ourselves and others. We are first of all self-interested, concerned with ourselves and with those to whom we are connected.

To leave out life-hopes and knowledge in considering the consequences of determinism, let alone to leave out everything but moral responsibility and perhaps punishment, as has been common until recently, is not only to fail to treat of all of a subject-matter but also to fail to treat of what seems to be its most pressing part. Further, it is to fail to have all the help one can have in dealing with the question of the consequences of determinism. The fact of the matter is that certain general truths are clearer with some consequences than with others, partly because they are less obscured by theory—moral theory above all—and by controversy. Life-hopes are of particular importance in this connection. Having seen what is true there, it is easier to see what is true elsewhere, and in general.

It is my contention that reflection on the challenge of determinism in the seven areas—our outlooks on our own futures, non-moral feelings about other persons, knowledge, responsibility, the other two moral matters, and social institutions and the like—will bring into view or evoke two families of attitudes, attitudes in a fairly ordinary sense, and, in the first instance, two general responses to determinism, which responses are further evidence of the attitudes. For example, to think of determinism in connection with our own futures brings into view two attitudes, which in fact are two sorts of hope. Thinking of determinism in connection with moral disapproval brings into view two attitudes which are two sorts of moral disapproval. Thinking of the likely truth of determinism in each of the seven connections does or at any rate can issue in two attitudes—and initially the two general responses.

It is not that some of us take one of the attitudes and make one of these responses, and others of us take the other attitude and make the other response, but that *each* of us is, at the very least, capable of both pairs. Each of us has, or at the very least is capable of taking, both attitudes, and each of us makes, or is capable of making, both responses.

One of the responses we may call the response of dismay, the other the response of intransigence. Both, at least initially, are in a sense second-order responses. Whatever they may give rise to, they are not themselves outlooks on one's future life, feelings towards others, kinds of confidence about knowledge, moral judgements and feelings about responsibility or the standing of persons or kinds of actions, and commitments and the like to social institutions. Rather, the two responses are to determinism, and more particularly *to the challenge or other relation of determinism to the attitudes*—to the outlooks, feelings, claims, and so on.

It is best to speak of two attitudes in the case of *each* of life-hopes, personal feelings, and so on. Thus there are fourteen discriminable attitudes in all. It is *possible* to speak in the same way of responses—that is, to speak of two of them in connection with each of life-hopes, personal feelings, and so on. In the case of responses, however, it is perhaps best to speak generally, as I have and most often will, of two types.

Is it the case that there are further consequences of determinism? It is possible to think of an eighth: its consequence for our *sense of ourselves*. It is brought to mind by a uniquely strong inquiry into personal identity, one which raises the possibility of an alteration in our senses of ourselves. (Parfit, 1984, Pt. 3) This eighth consequence is perhaps also implied by thoughts that determinism diminishes us or makes us puppets. (Nozick, 1981, p. 291) Aided by a certain spirituality, F. H. Bradley may have regarded this consequence of determinism as somehow primary (p. 97), and philosophers of very different temperaments have given it distinctive consideration. (Dennett, 1984; Glover, 1987; G. Strawson, 1986) The concern in question, I think, is best expressed in terms of what turns up in what has already been distinguished—determinism's consequences for us as possessors of hopes; consequences for us in certain of our personal feelings which are reflexive or self-directed, and particularly pride (p. 35); consequences for our own moral responsibility and particularly our own moral credit; and consequences for things that enter into the other listed considerations. If one could succeed in distinguishing determinism's consequence for our *sense of ourselves* where this latter thing was otherwise—that is, not to be resolved into the given concerns—it would, I think, not be a consequential thing.

The seven questions with which we began—'Of what consequence is the likely truth of determinism to our thoughts and feelings about our futures?' and the others—can be expressed in several different more or less summary ways. *What is the consequence of determinism for families of attitudes which are integral to our lives?* Or *Is one or the other of the responses of dismay or intransigence, or a third instead, the somehow satisfactory one?* There is no short way to good answers to these questions. We begin on the way towards answers with the subject of our own attitudes to our own future lives.

1.2 LIFE-HOPES AND DISMAY

To contemplate one's own future in a general way, if one is ordinarily lucky or in an ordinarily tolerable state of life, is to feel a life-hope. Such a thing is reasonably so-called since it is, among one's hopes, the dominant one whose realization is taken at the time as what would make one's life or a coming part of it fulfilled, happy, satisfactory, or anyway of worth. It is the hope with which one is most persistently taken up. To lack such a thing absolutely is barely to have a life at all in what might be called a full human sense.

Like any hope, it is an attitude, which is to say a feeling in a wide sense. A typical attitude is open to different general characterizations, of which one is this: *an evaluative thought of something, feelingful and bound up with desire.* It involves feeling in a narrower and elusive but traditional sense, where feeling is somehow akin to sensation but unlocalized. It may involve desires of several kinds. It involves less of what can be called excitement or bodily commotion than typical emotions. A hope in particular is an attitude which has a single desire or want to the fore, so to speak, and involves a kind of uncertainty as to its satisfaction. A hope, in line with the general characterization of an attitude, is perhaps to be seen as *a desire for something, feelingful and incorporating evaluation, which desire is taken as not certain to be realized.* Hopes, evidently, are typically dispositions which recurrently issue into consciousness.

To contemplate one's own future in a general way, again, if one is ordinarily lucky, is to have one of the succession of life-hopes which mark so well the stages of an individual's life, and enter importantly into their definition. Perhaps a great majority of us are lucky in this way, since frustrations and defeats ordinarily do not destroy an individual's spirit, but are followed by new hopes. They need not be lesser ones. The fulfilment of hopes also gives rise to new ones. No one rests very long, let alone forever, in what is among the finest of states, the state of ambition realized or aspiration satisfied. One's name on a list, certificate, door, or book is not an enduring satisfaction, if there are any of those, but transient.

Often enough a life-hope has quite sharp definition: the achieving of some standing, position, or rank, the doing or the finishing of a thing, the possession of something, the securing of some state of mind, the making or altering of some relationship with another person, the development or succouring of someone, succeeding in a struggle, getting reparation, getting even or returning an injury, avoiding disaster, delaying death. Or, certainly, one's life-hope at any time may be a desire or want for some combination, somehow weighted, of such quite well-defined things. Despite the considerable fact of amoral self-interest alluded to above, of course, our life-hopes are sometimes properly described as having something other than an egoistic character. Often enough, they centre on the good of another person.

If life-hopes, whether or not combinations, and whether or not egoistic, are often well-defined, it is something like as common that they are not. What is hoped is that things will somehow turn out decently, that life if it changes will go on as well as it does now or no worse, that what is to come will be more or less all right. That is, the hopes have little more specificity than is suggested by those very descriptions—'life somehow turning out decently' and so on—and many like them. The descriptions are not replaceable by more precise ones.

The contents of all of these hopes, including the less well-defined ones, are at least in part states of affairs, where states of affairs do not include their own geneses, causes, or explanations. One may hope for the state of affairs in which enough food for oneself and one's family is assured, a patch of ground possessed, a job or a car got, a mortgage paid off, a shop opened, a political party or movement forwarded, children got on their way, a past lived down, a reconciliation achieved, a book written, a defeat put into the past, or a sickness survived. It barely needs adding that the depth or fervency of the hope does not have much to do with the relative worth of the possession, condition of life, judged from some external point of view. One can have a great hope for, say, something less than one's name on the door.

However, as most of their descriptions imply, life-hopes are at least typically for more than states of affairs. Our hopes in their contents are not only for the thing to be had, but for the *achievement* of it. They are not only hopes that some state of affairs should come into existence, persist, or change, by whatever means, say good fortune or someone else's action. My hopes are typically hopes that I will make something happen, bring something into existence, keep it, or change it—that I will succeed through my own actions in securing certain states of affairs. Most often what we aspire to do is to succeed in changing or maintaining our lives by way of our own strength, determination, judgement, wariness, guile, and by way of the various endeavours which flow from our own capabilities. In short, my hopes are typically *for* certain actions as well as states of affairs. It may be that such a feeling is more rooted or pervasive in some cultures as against others. It seems unlikely to be missing from any. It is persuasive to think of it as selected by evolution.

Even in so far as hopes are just for states of affairs as understood, as distinct from achievement, they are bound up with our future actions. They rest on and draw in beliefs about our own actions, what we will do in the future. We believe, for the most part, that we depend on ourselves. If what I hope for is the state of having the marks of success, and I am not greatly desirous of having earned them, I am none the less likely to believe that I will come to have them only through my own actions. Even the hope of meeting the right person, or dying in the right company, or the hope of surviving in the unpredictability of battle, is in this way taken to be in a way dependent on one's own actions. Certainly, despite some moods and moments, we are not fatalists in a certain traditional sense. That is, we do not believe the unbelievable thing that all or even much of what happens to us at future times will happen irrespective of what occurs between now and then, including our own behaviour.

In sum, then, our life-hopes of whatever kind have in them, or at least depend on, ideas or beliefs about our own actions to come. Actions figure as both ends and means. More particularly, our hopes have in them or depend on beliefs, ideas, or whatever somehow to the effect that in some significant way we do and will *initiate* our actions, much of the time or at least some of the time. They will not happen to us. Still more particularly, and fundamentally, we somehow believe or conjecture that *we stand to our actions in such an initiating way that we have at least some chance of fulfilling our hopes*. This initiation is integral to the idea of achievement, and as relevant, although in a different way, to actions as means. There are other expressions of the unspecific beliefs, ideas or whatever as to initiation, which initiation is as important to actions as ends as it is to actions as means. It is (I say) I who will act, and so may come to have what I want. It is I who will give rise to my actions, or bring them about, and so can have some optimism. It is I who in some way will conduct myself into my future.

There is no fatalism in this. We do not believe that our actions will come into existence irrespective of antecedents intrinsic to ourselves, such as desires, beliefs, and the like, and we do not believe either the vaguer and more ambiguous thing that these antecedents of our actions—our decisions, intentions and the like—come into existence irrespective of *us*. These fatalisms are unbelievable to all of us.

The large question must arise of whether the given beliefs and the like, somehow to the effect that we at least sometimes do and will initiate our actions and so have at least a chance of fulfilling our hopes, are out of place since or if the theory of determinism is true. An answer to the question is to be sought, evidently, by attempting to make our beliefs or whatever more clear, specific, and of course literal. They have been gestured at and labelled, rather than specified or clarified, by talk of initiation. What is important here, and wholly fundamental to the argument to come, is that there is more than one way of attempting to do so, more than one direction in which to go.

To follow one of these ways or directions, which we shall in this section (1.2), is to come upon certain distinctive thoughts about the initiation of our future actions and hence something bound up with those thoughts, a distinctive kind of life-hope. It is to come upon a kind of hope, perhaps to be an actress, which is one member of a certain family of attitudes. To follow the other line of reflection, which we shall later (1.3), is to come upon different thoughts about the initiation of our future actions, and a different kind of life-hope. This second kind of hope, in a sense, can have the same content—*to be an actress*. However, it is a member of a different family of attitudes. Neither of these lines of reflection is a matter of invention or advocacy. In each case we find out something about ourselves.

To proceed on the first line, let us bring to mind two related groups of natural and more contentful thoughts about the initiation of our future actions. The first group of these thoughts has to do with a particular conception of the future, and the second with the constraints of environment and our own natures.

We may think and say that our actions are such that our futures are in part *open*, *alterable*, or *unfixed*. Questions about them are not yet answered. More particularly, it is not that the questions have already got answers, stored up, although answers as yet unknown to us. There are no answers yet—they do not exist. Our futures are not laid out for us, waiting to be discovered, but in some crucial way or degree are to be made or formed by us. In part they will be our products. Our futures are not absolutely bound to the present and past, such that they can involve no break from the present and past. They do not merely *run on* from the present and past, containing no real opportunity.

There is really only one troublesome fatalist, the logical fatalist, who argues from the premiss that it is *true now* that the future consists in certain events, however unpredictable in practice most of them are, to the conclusion that *it is fixed and unalterable now* that the future consists in only those events. (van Inwagen, 1983; Sorabji, 1980) We resist the premiss, or the inference, since we take the conclusion to be false or are fundamentally disposed against it. That this fatalism is resisted by virtually all philosophers and others who consider it, that the problem of fatalism is very nearly *defined as* the problem of showing the conclusion of the inference to be false, is entirely indicative. The fact confirms the existence of the attitude to the future, and particularly to our future actions, which is our present subject. It amounts to a proof, not that one is needed, of the existence of the attitude.

A second and related group of thoughts about our initiation of future actions takes our futures to be not wholly the products of, specifically, our environments and our own characters, bents, desires, weaknesses, temptations—the corpus of our dispositions. Our past life-hopes, unless we are very lucky indeed, have often enough been frustrated or partly frustrated, in our view, because of our own dispositions rather than anything else. Often enough, and rightly, we put down our past failures to ourselves. We are sustained, however, by the idea that we have the possibility of overcoming ourselves in the future—by which we mean the possibility of overcoming our characters, fears, and the rest. I am not inevitably the creature of my dispositions, but rather I have the chance—even if only a small chance—of being their master. I will not forever succumb to certain fears or illusions. I will not forever be rattled and made inept by certain persons or in certain circumstances. Similar things are to be said about environmental constraints. In such ideas there is a further indication of what may be taken, when we think about ourselves in the first way, as that which our hopes contain and on which they are founded.

It is evident that in these two related groups of thoughts, about an unfixed future and about escape from environment and dispositions, we take our actions to be owed to some determinate centre of ourselves, somehow intrinsic and fundamental. Or rather, we have a certain elusive image of such a centre. All the thoughts noticed so far may be taken to indicate this, directly or indirectly. It is plainest when I say I will overcome myself, but not much less plain when I say I will make, form or produce my future. What is the determinate centre in question? It is no body, or machine, or system, or programme, or mental event, or succession of mental events. Above all, to take the most likely candidate, it is no disposition or sum of dispositions.

The old and familiar answer that is hard or impossible to resist is that it is *my self*. It stands in some wholly obscure relation to one of the two elements discernible in retrospect in each mental event, a subject as distinct from a content.[1] It is particularly important that I take my self to be something that has the chance of mastering my dispositions, and hence to be distinct from them. As it seems, this self has the chance of mastering any one of them, and so is distinct from any of them.

There is a temptation, into which philosophers have fallen before now in other contexts of inquiry, notably contexts within the philosophy of mind, to declare the centre in question to be just a *person*, with the implication that we are all clear about what a person is. In an ordinary notion of a person, however, a body or part of one is at least a constituent of a person. But clearly, or anyway arguably, neither my body nor a part of it is a constituent of the initiating centre of which I conceive. My body, in fact, is typically conceived as *subject to* the centre in question.

Our thinking and speaking with respect to our selves, further and fundamentally, does not imply that they are merely items in standard causal sequences, caused causes of actions. My thinking and speaking about my self does not imply that it is merely a *link*. Talk of initiating, making, giving rise to, bringing about, producing, and so on implies, rather, an activity that is not itself a product. Above all, such an activity is implied by the idea that it secures to us open futures. More than that, our various expressions do positively suggest that an action, in being owed to an initiating self, is not owed to a standard causal sequence, or rather, to one which has the initiating self within it as an effect. The expressions do positively assert the self, an active source of the action.

Finally, the self is not presented to us as superfluous or otiose with respect to the initiation of actions. That is, actions are not such that although they are owed to a self, they also have some other explanation sufficient in itself. What we have, in the conception of an unfixed future and also of an escape from environment and dispositions, includes a denial of an alternative explanation of action. The expressions, to speak differently, are informed by something other than, but related to, the conviction of the indispensability of the mental, which is to say of the falsehood of epiphenomenalism.[2] They are informed by an idea of the indispensability of the self.

Is there room for doubt about all this? Is there room for doubt that in our thinking and speaking of the initiation of our actions we may claim or presuppose the existence of an uncaused and unsuperfluous self? Can it be claimed that in fact we do not ever have such an idea? Something like this *has* been claimed of what is called the self in contexts other than our present one, having to do with life-hopes. It has been claimed, in particular, in the context of the philosophy of mind, as a result of our failure to introspect a self, and also, very differently, in connection with ideas of moral responsibility—as we shall see. (Ch. 2) When life-hopes are the subject, the claim that we do not have such an idea of self is wholly unpersuasive.

What else but an uncaused and unsuperfluous self *could* rescue us from the situation in which our actions are simple products of our environments and the manifold of our dispositions? Still more clearly, what else but an uncaused and unsuperfluous self *could* provide for us an open future? Such a future is not merely a future which is somehow in our control, our doing, which future is none the less one that is already settled and not open to change. What we propose to escape is fixity, not just this or that kind or character of fixity. No doubt a fixed future which in some sense will be our own doing is better than a fixed future not in that sense our own doing, but both of them run against our aspiration. (Cf. Dennett, 1984, Ch. 3)

Again, it seems clear enough that the aspiration in question is not merely for a future that is in practice unpredictable, with nothing said as to it being fixed or unfixed. We are not satisfied with the idea that all the events which constitute our coming lives are in a category with the event which occurred when the ball on the roulette wheel came to rest unpredictably but inevitably on red 7. What we want are futures that are not settled.

This claim is not properly a matter of argument, but of every person's experience. Still, is there some other argument against it, perhaps drawn from the present context, rather than the philosophy of mind or moral philosophy? Might it be argued that there is no reasonableness in resting our hopes on an unfixed future, and hence, by way of the sanguine premiss that we *are* in general reasonable, that in fact we do not desire unfixed futures? That is, since there is no good reason to rest our hopes on a certain thing, it is no part of the obscure ground of our hopes. More fully, it may be argued that there is little or nothing to choose between two conceivable situations now in contemplation, both of relevance to the subject of life-hopes. One is the situation where future things are already fixed but not yet known, are unpredictable in fact, and the other is the situation where future things are not known, also unpredictable and not fixed. There is no reasonableness, it will be said, in going for the second option. Our real state of knowledge makes no difference between them.

One reply must be that it all depends on a person's experience up to the present. If things have gone well for a person, there is more to hope for in what follows on the assumption that the entire run of his or her life is fixed. This involves a large but decent inductive inference, an extrapolation from past and present to future. If things have not gone well, or not so well as was hoped, it is at least not unreasonable to have greater hopes on the assumption that the whole of one's life is not fixed, but is connected with the activity of a self. The alternative assumption, that of fixity, when conjoined with disappointment or defeat up until now, issues by way of an inductive inference in the prospect of more of the same.

Are we generally of the view that our lives have gone well, or of the view that they have not gone well, at least not so well as was hoped? I take it, although a qualification or two might be added, that generally we are more of the second and sadder view than the first. In reply to the objection, then, it can be said there is better reason for hope in the denial of fixity than in any acceptance of it. Given the sanguine premiss of our reasonableness, there is reason to think that we do *not* tend to the idea of a fixed personal future.

The direction of the reflections in this section will have become clear before now. To characterize them again, we first took it that our life-hopes depend on pre-philosophical and pre-theoretical beliefs, ideas or whatever to the effect that somehow we will initiate our future actions. The question was whether these beliefs and the like are out of place if or since the theory of determinism is true. There is one clarification of them which finds them to be bound up with a conception of an open, unfixed, or alterable future, a future such that in it we escape environment and dispositions. This clarification of beliefs and the like as to initiation can also be said with some reason to be pre-philosophical and pre-theoretical. The same can be said of what follows, that we have the idea or whatever of a determinate centre, a self, which is uncaused in its activity and which is not superfluous. There is one final thing which needs to be made explicit, or more explicit. The self is not, so to speak, an agency or mechanism of chance. The futures owed to it, if unfixed, are not a matter of *chance*. True chance, at any rate on a large scale, would be about as damaging to hope as fixity. To take it that I, in or as my self, give rise to my actions, is not to make them a matter of randomness. Rather, they are things which are subject to the self.

Indeed the direction of all this will have been clear enough. What we arrive at is the conclusion that we share, when we think of our life-hopes in one way, a picture of ourselves related to what have certainly been common enough, *indeterminist theories of the mind*. In particular, the common idea of one's self is in a way akin to the idea of an originator, that which originates our intentions, decisions and the like, and our actions.[3]

The conclusion is not at all well expressed as being that the given beliefs and so on about initiation can be taken to include some indeterminist theory of the mind. It is rather the case that the given beliefs and ideas include what is best called an *image*, an image to which the indeterminist speculations stand as theories—attempted developments, improvements, or clarifications. There can be no doubt that what is included in our thoughts is not so explicit or developed as the indeterminist theories of the mind. It would be absurd to claim that in considering our futures we are all possessors of an articulated conception. What is not absurd, but seemingly undeniable, is that we have an image or idea that stands to the indeterminist theories as many of our ordinary ideas stand to more or less developed conceptions and theories in science, other parts of philosophy than the philosophy of mind, and also politics.

When we think in this first way of the initiation of our actions, then, we partly think of it as effectively indeterminist. To do so, as will perhaps already have been clear, is to have *a certain sort of life-hope*. This is partly so since, as we have seen, ideas of our actions—ideas of them either as ends or as means—give much of the content to life-hopes of whatever sort. To have the present sort of life-hope, whether about being an actress, surviving in battle, or whatever, is to have a hope best characterized in ways of which we know: a hope for an unfixed future, a hope for a future in which we are not creatures of our environments and our dispositional natures. A life-hope of this sort, as anticipated earlier, is a member of one of two families of attitudes. The other members have to do with the other parts of our existence which are affected by determinism.

It has not been argued that our initiation-ideas with respect to life-hopes of this kind amount *only* to a kind of antecedent image of indeterminist theories of the mind. Our ideas, when we think in this way, do not have to do only with *origination* of actions. My hopes of this kind also depend, to be brief, on such beliefs as that I will not be in jail, or under persistent threat, or greatly ignorant of what can be done. They also have to do, that is, with what is underdescribed as the absence of obstacles or external forces. They have to do with willingness or self-directedness, what will be called *voluntariness*. (p. 29) To speak only of this part of our beliefs or ideas, however, the part having to do with *origination*, there is no doubt that it is out of place since or if the determinist theory is true. It is out of place in the plain sense that it is logically inconsistent with the determinist theory.

No question whatever arises about the fact of this inconsistency. It would be perfectly pointless to set out to give a proof of the logical inconsistency of this part of our beliefs or ideas and the determinist theory. This is so since *no sense* can possibly be attached to the idea of an unfixed future, or a future which somehow escapes or is released from environment and dispositions, other than that of a future not subject to the nomic connections asserted in a determinist theory, but somehow subject to the person. That is the clear and inescapable *definition* of an unfixed or released future, or, at worst, an ineliminable part of the definition. Similar remarks are to be made of the image of the self, as distinct from its activity. Here too there is palpable inconsistency with determinism. There is no more need or place for proof of the given inconsistencies than in the case of the inconsistency between the assertion, say, that Napoleon was for a time married and that he was at that time a bachelor. There is no question of whether or not we are in a situation which must be resolved partly by way of the proposition that not both *p* and *not-p* are true. We are in precisely such a situation.

What we come to, then, is that the likely truth of the theory of determinism forces us to abandon certain images or ideas which indubitably are part of our life-hopes of a certain kind. The given ideas or images, it seems, must go. Thus, it may seem, we are deprived of the hopes. These desires must collapse. What is important to us, in our contemplations of our future lives, is denied to us. Nothing significant remains of these hopes. This is *the response of dismay*, the response of dismay as it pertains to our life-hopes. We shall also encounter it in other connections. Here it is a dismay which is owed to coming to believe of life-hopes we have that they *depend on a necessary condition which cannot be satisfied since or if determinism is true*. Further, there is no adequate replacement for these hopes.

It is worth remarking in passing that it is of course essential, here and in all of what follows, to have in mind a firm and strong conception of determinism, or of near-determinism. A vague or uncertain one, or indeed one unattended to in the course of reflection, is near to useless in considering the consequences of determinism. Although what will be said of consequences of determinism does *not* depend on a particular determinism, but has a considerably more general application, it will come as no surprise that I have in mind my own determinism, expounded in the companion volume to this one. To have it in mind is to have in mind more—something like William James's understandably coloured account of a more general determinism.

It professes that those parts of the universe already laid down appoint and decree what other parts shall be. The future has no ambiguous possibilities hidden in its womb: the part we call the present is compatible with only one totality. Any other future complement than the one fixed from eternity is impossible. The whole is in each and every part, and welds it with the rest into an absolute unity, an iron block, in which there can be no equivocation or shadow of turning. (1909, p. 150)

The existence of dismay in connection with life-hopes will be of importance in itself to the argument to come. What is yet more important is the existence of the particular attitude to the future, a kind of desire or want, whose foreclosure by determinism issues in the dismay. This attitude, whose existence is indubitable and which contains a part inconsistent with determinism, is certainly no transient phenomenon which arises in thinking about determinism. It is *natural*. That is to say, at least, that we do have it, and have it spontaneously, and that it involves no internal incoherence or any such thing.

On the first of these three points, I shall not struggle to establish propositions that are not needed, that every human being without exception feels the desire—we may call it just the desire for an unfixed future—or of course that having it is some kind of condition of being human. That the desire, or at the very least the capability of it, is a general fact about us, in an ordinary if not wholly strict sense, is indubitable. That the desire is spontaneous in the sense of not being put upon us or evoked in us by philosophers, priests, or other such personnel is as clear. As for the third point of naturalness, it seems as clear that the desire, whatever else is to be said of it, and whatever has been manufactured out of it by speculative philosophers, is unconfused and cannot be said to contain anything that could be called an internal mistake.

A word or two more can usefully be said of these points, given one recent account, distinctive and admirable, of the human consequences of one particular theory near to a determinism, in fact called 'naturalism'. (Dennett, 1984) The account does not contemplate life-hopes, or advance or consider the general line of argument on which we are engaged. (Cf. p. 103) The account, none the less, may give rise to a suggestion which is certainly false, that the only desire in the neighbourhood we are now considering is one which is had by some few persons adversely affected by certain benighted philosophers— philosophers who conceive of determinism or argue about it in terms of one or another too simple or too extravagent idea or metaphor. They may conceive of or argue about determinism in terms of an exceedingly simple causal model of persons, a 'Sphexish' model suitable to the seemingly mindless digger wasp *Sphex ichneumoneus*, but wholly unsuitable to our own causal complexity. Or, they operate by way of such extravagant metaphors as those of the Invisible Jailer, the Nefarious Neurosurgeon, the Cosmic Child Whose Dolls We Are, or the Malevolent Mind-Reader.

On the contrary, to repeat, the attitude with which we have been concerned is not something owed to philosophers, and it is not, to speak quickly, a no doubt rare desire to be other than a *simple* causal mechanism, or a desire to be free from the grip of the Invisible Jailer or whatever. These desires *can* indeed be satisfied despite determinism. It is rather a kind of desire, which is clear and distinct and has nothing to do with simplicity or some other agent, for an unfixed future.

The response of dismay, incidentally, is also natural, in at least the sense that it too is a general and spontaneous fact and is unconfused and without internal mistake. More remains to be said of it (p. 349, Ch. 9), but not anything that will conflict with that judgement.

1.3 LIFE-HOPES AND INTRANSIGENCE

It is certainly possible, and not necessarily on another day or in another mood, to accept the theory of determinism as true, and come to feel differently about its bearing on life-hopes. This different response in fact involves life-hopes different in character or kind from those we have been considering. This is not a matter of a different starting-point of inquiry, although I shall say a word more about that starting-point in a moment. That is, we can begin again from thoughts to the effect that our life-hopes do indeed rest on our *initiating* our actions, at least sometimes, on our being related to our actions in such an initiating way that we have an opportunity of fulfilling our hopes.

To begin with, let us look not at a case of good hopes for the future, but at the case of someone whose hopes are small and declining. A man without a job, for the first time in his life, may hope in this weak way that he will be able to get one, to have again the existence he has always had before. His life-hope for the future centres on a picture which has in it a number of elements—say his independence of others and of society, his satisfaction in having his children perceive him as their able supporter, purposeful activity in place of empty hours and unsustaining activity, the enjoyment of things now denied to him, an escape from condescension. Certainly it is a hope involving both a state of affairs and achievement. If he does have such a hope, however, it is small and declining, indeed a dying hope. Now, as these words are written, such hopes for many men are just that.

Why is his hope as it is? To enter into his situation is very easily and naturally to come to a particular answer. It is that his hope has declined because he believes or is near to believing that the world of his life will not change, but will continue to frustrate his hope. It is that belief or near-belief of his, that the world of his life will continue to deny him what above all he wants, that is the explanation of his near hopelessness. More particularly, it is his perception that his future activity in simply passing time—the drudgery of watching television and of whatever else goes in place of work—will flow from certain desires and intentions of his, but certain reluctant or entirely second-best desires and intentions, as distinct from desires and intentions into which he enters fully, desires and intentions which he embraces.

Reluctant desires and intentions, we can say, are those which operate in situations to which the agent is somehow opposed. *Embraced* desires and intentions satisfy the condition that they operate in situations which the agent at least accepts. These two types of situations—there is more than one sub-type of each—can also be called *frustrating or obstructing* situations and *satisfying or enabling* situations.

We can then take it that the beliefs or ideas which enter into and on which we ground hopes may consist in something so far unconsidered. To say that life-hopes falter when a man lacks the thought that he will initiate his actions is to say, in part, that his hopes falter when he lacks the thought that his actions will flow from certain desires and intentions which he embraces—no doubt both antecedent and active intentions.[4] His actions will flow instead from reluctant desires and intentions. In explaining full hopes by saying that a man believes that he can initiate the actions which will shape his life, we can take it that he believes just that his actions will flow from his embraced desires and intentions.

One may feel a resistance to the idea just proposed. The formulation of our grounding thought with respect to life-hopes, that we can initiate our actions, does in a direct way convey or suggest an unfixed future, escape from environment and dispositions, and a self. That we can initiate our actions does not in so direct a way convey the present idea, that a person's actions may flow from his own embraced desires and intentions. It may be said rightly that the present idea, that hopes are fully supported by way of the idea of embraced desires and intentions, conflicts with the previous idea, that they are supported by the idea of what can somehow override the corpus of one's desires and intentions—and it may be maintained that it is only the latter supporting idea that can be found in our thought and talk about initiation.

It would in fact be something like rash to attempt to rule out the proposal that our thoughts about the initiation of action can be taken as having to do fundamentally with embraced desires and intentions. That would be to depend on a particular formulation of those thoughts in too confident or exclusive a way. It is reasonable to think that we should not be wedded to one formulation. There are others. Here is one: We shall often or sometimes be in such a position that actions which will secure our life-hopes will be within our doing. Or: We shall often or sometimes be in such a position that we will not be defeated in the desire which is our life-hope.

Evidently there is no single canonical pre-theoretical expression of our grounding thoughts with respect to our hopes. There can be no doubt that philosophy, in so far as it advances, advances through precision, clear distinctions, a resistance to loose talk. That truth needs to be brought into compromise with another. It is the truth that in attempting to deal with our experience, it is necessary to resist the temptation of thinking that it is to be indubitably captured in just these words or just those, by exactly this perception rather than any other. In the beginning, at any rate, a certain looseness is necessary. It is worth adding, in recollection of Aristotle, that different subject-matters allow of different degrees of precision. This part of any inquiry into determinism will allow of less precision than other parts— clarification and confirmation.

We have so far seen one sort of satisfying or enabling situation which may be expected to turn up in one's future and so give a basis for a life-hope. The *world of a man's coming life*, as it was said, may be one which allows him hope. The *way of a woman's world*, in her anticipation, may constitute a situation which allows her hope. By contrast, her hopes may falter or die when the way of her future world is not one to which she is disposed, but rather the related frustrating or obstructing situation. 'The world of a man's coming life', and 'the way of a woman's world'—certainly these are descriptions of a general and relatively vague kind. They are none the less at least useful, if not essential. In speaking of the world of a person's coming life, we speak of such things as the customary or ordinary responses and activities of other people, the state of a society and its economy, the availability of things, a person's corpus of feelings, and a good deal more.

The world of a person's coming life, or the way of his or her coming world, is surely the *principal* kind of satisfying or frustrating situation with respect to very many of our desires. It is such situations that are often most pertinent to our life-hopes. It has been an oversight of philosophers, in inquiries distantly related to our own, to have paid them no attention. Their large importance can be gauged from the large extent to which we are social beings, involved in and dependent on societies. That is not to say there are no other sorts of satisfying and frustrating situations, no other sorts of determinants of embraced or reluctant desires. Let us glance at them in something like a descending order of pervasiveness, beginning with those most likely to enter our lives.

Suppose it is central to a man's life-hope that he direct his capabilities and energies effectively at a single goal. He seeks to arrange his obligations, various endeavours, his time, to some extent his personal relations, perhaps his expenditures, and no doubt his self-indulgences and distractions, so as to further his life-hope. He may want and need, differently, to have a realistic view of himself, or to escape the grip of what can illusorily present itself to him as truth, rationality, principle, decorum, or taste. The state of affairs which enters into his hope can be something of the sort mentioned earlier. He wants above all to own a little land, to become a salesman or a craftsman, to bring to fruition a line of research, to finish a novel, to become a judge, or to have an acceptance in his family or among acquaintances.

It may be that the way of his world, in the sense we know, has not been against him in his ambition, and will not be, or at any rate nothing so much as the state of the economy and so on is against the man with no job. However, something else may be against him. He may, looking to the future, not have anything like a decently confident anticipation that he will be able to direct his energies effectively towards his goal. This will be a matter, evidently, of desires which delay him in his progress, or take him off his track. There is certainly nothing incoherent in supposing that the desire which is a life-hope may be frustrated by other desires. Lesser desires, indeed desires for what is also disdained, can be stronger desires. One can do what is typical of many lives—and part of the lives of all people—which is to succumb to the temptation of immediate satisfaction.

It is evident, then, that a second kind of enabling or obstructing circumstance with respect to one's life-hope is the circumstance in which the hoped-for state of affairs is or is not achieved as a result of the effective dominance or want of effective dominance of the desire which is one's life-hope. If our hopes require the idea that our world will not frustrate us, they also require the idea that we will not frustrate ourselves. The desires and intentions that move us will be those that are constitutive of or essential to our fundamental hopes.

There are related cases of self-frustration which are stark and extreme, but of less relevance to the general run of persons. The alcoholic or the heroin addict may be deprived of the expectation that he will be able to act on the desire, which itself may be a life-hope, to give up drink or heroin. He faces a future in which desires which he has for drink, or heroin, are desires he wants not to have. (Cf. Frankfurt, 1969, 1971.) He will do what in a fundamental way he wants not to do. Others of what are sometimes called behaviour-disorders are similarly stark and extreme: sexual abnormalities, kleptomania and the like, and compulsions generally.

A third sub-type of enabling or frustrating circumstance has to do with independence of other particular individuals, or of the ascendancy of other particular individuals over us. My hopes may depend on my belief that the desires on which I shall act will not in some way be formed for me by someone who has a dominance over me. I shall not be as a child to another person. Relatedly, and more starkly, there are threats and what have been called coercive offers. It is possible to take too narrow a view of threats in particular. Not all of them, by any means, are close to the philosopher's staple example, that of a man who has a gun held to his head. A person's prospects may be greater or lesser, in ordinary life, and seen to be such by him or her, as a result of respectable threats, threats without guns.

Fourthly and finally, there is the kind of frustrating circumstance which amounts to personal bodily constraint. A bodily disability, want of health, an injury, prison or other confinement—these too must touch or drag down or destroy a person's hopes. As before, there is the contrasting situation, where a person can have the belief that his desires will not be impeded in such a way.

A richer and more precise account might be attempted of beliefs and ideas as to these four kinds of satisfying and frustrating circumstances. It is not needed. What seems evidently true of each of the four reasons for hope and contents of it—anticipations of satisfying or enabling circumstances of the four kinds—whatever fuller account is given, is that each is logically consistent with determinism. The truth, if it is one, that my actions and activities will not be owed to serious constraints of my social world, that I will not in this respect act out of reluctant desires, is evidently not in conflict with the truth of determinism. So with truths about actions and activities not issuing from such things as my own weakness, but from my dominant desire, the desire which is my life-hope. So with truths about independence of others and freedom from threat, and truths about personal bodily constraint.

To speak generally, there is no logical inconsistency between a determinism and the summary proposition of *voluntariness* or *willingness* that *a man's or a woman's actions can issue from his or her own embraced desires, be done in satisfactory or enabling rather than frustrating or obstructing circumstances.* Nor would there be inconsistency if we enlarged the account by adding one or two other satisfying or enabling circumstances of somewhat lesser importance to life-hopes—say a circumstance having to do with anticipated knowledge rather than ignorance.

As in the case of the logical *inconsistency* between determinism and the earlier foundation and content of life-hopes, having to do with one's self, there is no room for doubt about the fact of logic—in the present case, the fact of logical *consistency* between determinism and the ground and content having to do with embraced desires. To speak of our own theory of determinism, nothing whatever in the specified nomic connections and in particular the specified causal sequences is in conflict with the proposition about embraced desires. In order to have inconsistency, we should need to have some primitive conception of causation, one involving a kind of animism. That is, we should have to suppose that a caused desire, in virtue of being caused, was an unembraced or reluctant desire. It is entirely possible, despite difficulties of one kind and another, and various controversies, to arrive at a clear and at least defensible account of causation.[5] It settles the matter. The characterization of causation in terms of certain conditional statements leaves no room for doubt, having to do with causation itself, as to the consistency between the theory of determinism and the given grounds for life-hopes.

As with the earlier ground and content of life-hopes, having to do with one's self, there is no call for anything that could reasonably be called a proof of the fact of logic. It may well be possible, with our fact of consistency, as in the case of many indubitable consistencies, to give a further analysis of the conceptions involved, and so to provide a further account of the consistency. To do so would not be to settle what was until then unsettled. Indeed, an analysis of plain consistencies which purported to put their consistency into doubt would in fact be self-defeating, such as to unseat the analysis.

To come to the end of these reflections, what we have is that it is entirely possible to rest a life-hope on the sufficient belief, a quite clear belief, that one will in the future be acting out of embraced desires, acting in satisfactory rather than frustrating situations. Or rather, to remember again that one's future actions are likely to be ends as well as means, it is possible to have as both content and basis of a life-hope the prospect of acting out of embraced desires. Evidently this is an attitude fundamentally different from and in conflict with the one considered in the last section, involving the idea of a self. It is a life-hope different in kind from the life-hopes involving a self.

This attitude, whatever else is to be said of it, is a natural one in the same sense as the other. (p. 24) It is as good as universal. It is certainly not factitious, the work of philosophers or the like. It involves no internal conceptual shortcoming. Further, there is the evident reasonableness of the desire. That is, it is for and based upon a clear, large fact, that for the most part we do and shall act out of embraced desires.

Given the naturalness and reasonableness, it is hard to resist the idea, at least for a time, that in so far as the initiation of actions is concerned, our life-hopes need involve and rest on nothing more than embraced desires, satisfactory situations.

That we have or can have such substantial life-hopes is the principal source of a certain response, different from dismay, which we may make in the matter of determinism and life-hopes. It is *the response of intransigence*. It also has a lesser but significant source of a different kind. It is in part a response to the response of dismay and its associated desire, involving a self, an unfixed future, escape from environment and dispositions. Intransigence and perhaps its associated desire are in part a *dismissal* or *rejection* of dismay and its associated desire.

That latter desire, if certainly we feel it, and if it is natural, is crucially a kind of image—of one's self. An image, we may feel, is unsatisfactory, something that falls well short of giving us the reassurance of an explicit idea or argument. Its unsatisfactoriness is something for all of us, certainly, and not just for philosophers or other conceptually demanding persons. No one, in serious matters, is likely to remain content with the insubstantial. Further, although this is of much less importance with respect to the wide fact—the fact that the given desire and the response of dismay are as good as universal—the image is not much improved on in indeterminist theories of the mind, which are near to chimerical. As for dismay itself, it is by definition no satisfactory thing, but a thing which gives rise to resistance or opposition.

The response of intransigence, at its strongest, is that a determinism is no threat whatever to our hopes of the kind that matter. A determinism leaves our important hopes as they were. Nothing changes. We have no need whatever to succumb to the response of dismay in connection with our hopes. The truth of determinism is indeed inconsistent with something. But it is inconsistent with what does not matter. There is that which *does* matter with respect to our hopes, which is action out of embraced desires, and determinism is fully consistent with that. The response of intransigence, when it is not at its strongest, is that determinism does not much touch our hopes. Things remain fundamentally as they are. Here and elsewhere, as will be clear, brevity excludes the giving of a full and non-schematic account of a phenomenon in its diversity. To speak of the response of dismay, or of intransigence, is to speak of what has variations, degrees, colourings—all of which must be passed by. It may indeed be that really to convey the diverse reality of the phenomena we should have to attempt to use something close to the methods of imaginative literature. (Cf. p. 35)

The desire we have been considering, a second kind of life-hope, is like the first in being a member of a family of attitudes. We have attempted no full or general picture of the character of either family, but it was remarked in passing (p. 22) that the first family of attitudes has to do fundamentally with *origination*. To use again a second label, it also has to do with *voluntariness*. The second family has to do *only* with *voluntariness*. Attitudes of the first family issue in dismay, and attitudes of the second family do or may issue in intransigence. We now proceed with the other members of both families, and with further instances of dismay and intransigence.

1.4 PERSONAL FEELINGS

Few parts of our experience are as satisfactory as our experience of the love of others for us, and their affection, loyalty, trust, goodwill, and support. Much the same is true of what is somewhat different, our experience of certain more judgemental attitudes of others to us: their admiration, their approval, their inclinations to commendation, compliment, and the like. To speak a bit less lamely than one does in calling the experiences merely satisfactory, it can be said that love and the like and admiration and the like enrich our lives, give delight to them, and sustain them.

What is in question, to describe it more generally, is our having the good feelings and the good judgement of others, as evidenced in their particular actions on our behalf, or in their continued endeavours, or perhaps in their conduct of the whole of their lives. To have nothing of the love of others, their acceptance of us and their sustenance in adversity, and to get no honour, esteem, or marks from them, is to have merely a grey time in this world. To have a life from which one's reciprocally warm feelings were removed, and one's pride or satisfaction in having the good opinion of others, would be to exist in less than a full human way.

What we want, of course, is not properly described as our feelings of reciprocal warmth, pride, and so on, if those are somehow understood as separate from our *true* beliefs about others' actions and lives. That is, we do not value the conceivable situation where we have certain feelings, but for no good reason. What we want and value is not merely something internal to ourselves, but something which essentially includes the relevant doings and manifestations of feeling by others.

The worth of it is more than indicated by the fact that we are not at all inactive in connection with the good feelings and good judgements of others. We do in fact seek out their good feelings and judgements. It is not too much to say that we pursue them, and that sometimes we pursue them indefatigably. Life-hopes, certainly, are importantly hopes for the good feelings and good judgements of others with respect to us. If argument were needed for the importance to us of these attitudes of others to us, our behaviour would provide it.

As for the character of our reactions to those actions of others which evidence good feelings or judgements with respect to us, it is clear that they are not rightly conceived as moral reactions, although it is obvious that the two kinds of reaction shade into one another, and that we are quick in all circumstances to find moral support for ourselves. It is possible enough to be grateful to someone for a good turn which one feels—in so far as one can manage impartiality on the subject—to be something he ought not to have done. I may not feel less warmly to the good reviewer of my book as a consequence of the thought that the review was not a work of monumental impartiality. No doubt I shall be inclined to avert my eyes from the partiality or whatever. It would no doubt be difficult or impossible to have a recognizable feeling of gratitude as a result of having been benefited, with the agent's intention, by an act that was monstrous or on the way to it. Part of the reason may be that one would feel not only benefited but also injured—the latter by being a kind of accomplice. I shall leave unconsidered this question of the relation between morality and our personal responses to the good feelings and judgements of others, although more will be said of relevance to it. It is plain enough that the personal reactions or attitudes in question are discriminable from moral reactions and can persist in a kind of opposition to many moral responses.

So much, in introduction, for the place in our lives of experience of the good feelings and good judgements of others—in sum, the place of our *appreciative feelings* towards others for their good feelings and judgements. As will be clear, no close or taxonomic account has been attempted, and at least one side of the subject-matter has been left untouched—our appreciation of others for actions which benefit those close to us, notably our children.

There is a counterpart of the appreciative feelings. It is that part of our experience which can be put under the heading of the *resentful feelings*. The heading covers a good deal. The feelings in question are personal responses to others on account of actions which evidence dislike and so on of us or bad judgements on us. The spectrum of our responding feelings can be taken to run across hatred, vengefulness, grievance, reproach, umbrage, hurt and pique. Perhaps more so than the appreciative feelings, they are desirous. They may have in them desires to return the hurt.

The resentful or accusatory feelings with respect to others are not a satisfaction in life. They are sometimes nurtured, and sometimes fed on, but it is impossible to think that anyone who was spared them would sensibly choose to bring them into his or her life. That is to say, importantly, that no one would choose to bring into his or her life that which gives rise to his or her resentful feelings: judgements and feelings of others against oneself. Also, the feelings themselves, considered intrinsically, are at the very least a burden. Still, there is something else. In our lives as they are, some others will in fact reject us, go back on their loyalties, disdain our works, or withhold their approval. Do we wish, in this circumstance, not to have the resentful feelings?

It is possible, in some moment of high rationality, to wish oneself free of the resentful feelings, where that is a wish not about the actions and attitudes of others, but a wish about oneself. It is to wish oneself free of the feelings despite the existence of grounds for them. Still, there presumably is some sense in the idea of a proper indignation, or indeed the idea of a decent rage. If keeping a feeling of affront alive or feeding on resentment may be transparently a bad thing, for the person engaged in the activity, it strikes one as unsatisfactory that a woman betrayed or ill-used should be short of feelings in response. One may feel this too of classes of people, indeed nations, who have been victimized or viciously treated. This has to do, not with a recognizable moral judgement against betrayal, ill-use, victimization, or vicious-ness, but some less clear impulse having to do with the propriety and humanity of resentful feelings, or at least ways, degrees, and durations of them.

To move to a more tractable matter, there can be no doubt of the *rootedness* as distinct from the desirability or defensibility of the resentful feelings in our lives. Despite what has just been wondered about their desirability or defensibility, we have in fact often had urged upon us the policy of escaping them. Never, it may seem, was a policy less likely of settled or general success. Far from escaping them, we must struggle even to make a start. They seem to be part of the stuff of our lives, and, despite some small victories, it may indeed be difficult to imagine ourselves free of them. No doubt good men resolve to have good cause for their resentful feelings, but few good men resolve with any confidence not to have them at all. Given this, any proposal about the ending of them which has something effective behind it, say an arguable claim of fact or logic, as distinct from religious or conven-tional moral exhortations, which have lost any force they may once have had, is unsettling. One may feel asked to subtract a part of one's nature.

Both the appreciative personal feelings and the resentful personal feelings are feelings directed towards others. There are related groups of feelings which are directed by ourselves towards ourselves. When these reflexive feelings are related to the resentful feelings towards others, they have to do with our acts of self-hurt, and perhaps self-disdain. In the other case, they have to do with self-help and the like. I can certainly reproach myself for an act by which I damaged my own prospects, and feel something uncommonly like self-commendation on other occasions—certainly there does occur self-praise, and it has something like the basis of our sincere praise of others. None the less, it seems that self-directed feelings of the two kinds play a lesser part in our experience than the two kinds of feelings about others. (Cf. p. 13) What is in question in connection with the self-directed feelings, as with the feelings about others, is not morality. When I reproach myself for the self-hurting act, I do not think in a moral way that I have wronged myself.

What are our grounds of belief and the like, or presumed grounds, for our appreciative and resentful feelings? Suppose I have in the past wounded a friend and patron by my unkind talk of him. Since then I have made good recompense, and taken care not to cause hurt again. He is now in a position to help me again. A third party, a past adversary and competitor of mine, with a score or two to settle, and aware of my hope, contrives to have my friend and patron understand that I have persisted in my wounding ways. There is some truth in his report.

Why, despite that, when I come to know of my adversary's activity, am I vengeful or bitter? That is, on what beliefs or ideas—no doubt ready assumptions on my part—does my vengefulness rest? Or, as it may be as correct to ask, what beliefs or ideas enter into my attitude? One thing is not in doubt. It is that they are beliefs or ideas which can be expressed by saying that my competitor *could have done otherwise* than damage me as he did. Even given our opposed interests, and our past history of competition and strong feelings, he could have refrained from doing what he did. But what precisely are the beliefs or ideas in question? As with life-hopes, there are two possibilities.

The first set has in it, first, the assumption that my adversary's act of reporting my talk was not something done without a realization of the nature and likely effect of the act. He knew what he was doing, and hence the effective distinction between that and what he might have done instead. The act was certainly not done in ignorance, or merely thoughtlessly, or inadvertently. His report, I am sure, was far from being the activity of someone who in fact makes trouble because he lacks a sense of the uncertainty of human relationships, or the susceptibilities of a hearer. In general, I assume that the act was done out of clear knowledge, not as a result of any relevant kind of ignorance, and hence in an awareness of the alternative.

Secondly, I assume that my competitor was not unwilling in his action—in the sense that he was driven or compelled to act, by some despised or unsupported part of himself, against another more significant or even fundamental part of himself, perhaps an impulse to truth, fair dealing, or considerateness. Nor was the action the somehow uncertain upshot of a conflict within him. The action, then, was not subject to constraint in one of its several internal forms. His desire in doing what he did was not in that way a reluctant one.

Thirdly, I assume that the act in question was not, so to speak, unnatural to the agent. Such an act as he performed, although done in knowledge and not internally forced upon its doer, is sometimes an act out of character, or at odds with the doer's personality, or clearly not within his ordinary way of carrying on. I do not suppose, in the present situation, that *this* act was such. It was far from being true, I suppose, that my adversary in his malicious report was not his usual self. He was, in my view, exactly his usual self—a person who also in the past has not been restrained by honourableness or whatever.

Fourthly, I do of course assume that he is, despite what I see as his shortcomings, as normal as the next man. He is a man, no more immature in any radical sense than the rest of us, and not of a personality that is radically out of kilter. He is a long way from being a deranged character who sees the world as consisting in a plot against him, or a person who quite fails to have any empathetic comprehension of the feelings of others. Nor is he so extraordinary as to be the victim of all of his passing desires, a leaf in their breeze.

Fifthly, although the question of the influence of others on him may arise, I of course take it that his action cannot be described as owed to someone else. His judgement was not distorted by someone able to manipulate him. He was certainly not the puppet of another person, or acting under threat, or in another way not his own man.

Taken together, these five considerations, to which some others might be added, unquestionably enable me to say things which fortify or indeed increase my feeling. The vicious action, I say, was wholly his. It was no accident or misfortune, not something which befell or happened to him. It came from his nature, his established and persisting nature. He was in no way external to it, a bystander or a victim of it.

This account of ordinary assumptions we may make, assumptions which very certainly can underpin our resentful personal feelings, or be incorporated in them as the only assumptions about the initiation of action, has been derived in good part from the unprecedented essay which first widened the consideration of consequences of determinism, and which will be further considered below. (P. F. Strawson, 1962) As will be apparent enough, the assumptions are of the same character as, and in good part overlap with, one of the two sets of grounding beliefs for life-hopes considered earlier. (pp. 25 ff.) Those were beliefs having to do with a man's actions flowing from his own embraced desires, and hence beliefs about actions not frustrated by the way of his world, certain desires of his own, the dominance of others, or bodily constraints. The first and last of these possible considerations is not so germane to personal feelings as to life-hopes. Also, when we think of our life-hopes, we are not likely to have in mind, in connection with our life-hopes, that we ourselves are relatively normal individuals. More generally and more importantly, what is fundamentally a very similar set of considerations making for what has been called voluntariness or willingness (p. 29) differs significantly and takes on different casts of feeling in different contexts. There is a good deal to be gained by reflecting these differences in our inquiry, rather than relying on a general and uniform account for all contexts. For one thing, we defeat, in ourselves as well as others, a resistance to the general which derives from no more than forgetting that the general proposition can be replaced by a set of particular and persuasive propositions.

The five assumptions I make in the imagined case of my patron and my competitor, which are quite sufficient to support my feeling, do not exclude a determinism. They can be and are properly understood in such a way that they do not. In particular, nothing in them fights with the three hypotheses of the determinism that has been expounded. It does not at all follow from the three hypotheses that all actions are done out of any kind of ignorance, that they are somehow forced upon somehow unwilling agents by themselves, that they are acts unnatural to the agent, or done by abnormal agents, or that they are somehow owed to someone other than the agent. The three hypotheses do not deprive our resentful feelings of the given assumptions.

Evidently we can transfer these conclusions to counterpart beliefs which underpin our appreciative personal feelings. It follows in no way about a generous act of giving, or a piece of shrewd support, from the fact that the desires and intentions behind it were items in certain causal sequences, that the act was done obliviously or out of internal compulsion, was an act out of character, or was owed to abnormality or external constraint. If there are some differences between the grounds or elements of resentful and appreciative feelings, as indeed there are, they are fundamentally alike and both are consistent with determinism.

What we may do, then, when we bring together the likely truth of determinism with the fact of personal feeling, some of it entrenched and enriching, some at least entrenched, is to see that we evidently do have the possibility of persisting in this feeling. We can maintain that certain considerations are quite sufficient for this feeling, and that these considerations are in no way threatened by determinism. To speak differently, and more precisely, appreciative and resentful feeling of a certain fundamental type can persist. It is feeling for or against another person, bound up with a set of facts about another person, a set which has certain good or bad desires and intentions to the fore. Such feeling is a member of the family of attitudes having to do with only voluntariness or willingness (p. 29), the family whose other member of which we know is an attitude to the future, an attitude of hope, resting on or having in it only an idea of embraced desires.

This is the response of intransigence. It comes roughly to this: we *do*, in considerations having to do with the absence of ignorance, overmastering desire, unnaturalness, and so on, have real and effective grounds for personal feeling; they *are* consistent with a determinism; any other grounds are as nothing beside them; if these other imagistic and insubstantial grounds are inconsistent with determinism, the fact need not unsettle us, need not disturb us in our human ways—things can remain as they are.

In this intransigence, whatever else is to be said of it, we have the natural idea that the five grounds of personal feeling that have been noticed are the worthwhile sum of what is conveyed by saying that the persons who do us good or ill generally *could have done otherwise*. As remarked before, that those words catch hold of whatever beliefs or assumptions support our feelings is not in question—no more in question than that the grounds of our life-hopes are somehow caught by the words that we do in some significant way *initiate* our actions. The natural idea, to speak a bit differently, is that what is conveyed by saying someone could have done otherwise than he did is properly to be taken as this: he could have done otherwise in so far as considerations of ignorance, his own desires, his not being himself, abnormality, and dominance by others were concerned. That is, none of those possible limiting facts was a fact about his action.

In this intransigence we have one way, but not the only way, of responding in the matter of determinism and the personal feelings. We can respond differently, as a result of taking or recalling another attitude. We can be dislodged from the position we have taken up. We can again begin with the plain thought, that personal feeling is based on a proposition somehow to the effect that others generally *could have done otherwise*, and come to rest in another place.

We can be taken by the perception that persons who could have done otherwise have true of them *more* than that they acted with knowledge, without internal constraint, naturally or in character, in a normal maturity, and without being subject to threat or the like. It is wholly possible to take the five considerations to be a part but not always all of what is rightly expressed by saying that they could have done otherwise. More important, it is possible to think that the rest is what is fundamental.

Consider again the example of my adversary and the harm he does me. He reports my unkind talk, in my view, out of desires to pay back old scores and to try to deprive me of the support of my patron and friend. My vengeful feeling, we have so far supposed, can rest on the fact that these specific desires did not involve certain things—ignorance and the others. Hence his action was his own. My vengefulness, as we have said, is directed at a certain considerable corpus of dispositions, with the mentioned pair of desires having a prominent place in the corpus.

It is all too possible to raise, and to be captured by, certain questions. Should my vengefulness be directed at only the corpus of dispositions? Can it properly be? It is natural to reply that despite what has been said so far, my feeling is rightly directed against precisely *a person*. If I have strong feelings about what I take to be a pair of vicious desires, within a certain corpus of dispositions, I also have strong feelings about *my adversary*. I indubitably have feelings about *him*. It is not that I have feelings of which it can be said only that they are directed at a human being. Can we contemplate the idea that the person in question is to be taken as just identical with the corpus of desires and other dispositions? Well, to speak in a quick but defensible way, this is but a *collection* of things. It is, to me, a collection of things that is disagreeable or worse, but that is not the point at issue. A collection of dispositions must seem to lack just the *unity* which is the mark or essence of a person.

There is another stronger if related line of thought. My vengefulness may be objected to, perhaps objected to as unreasonable. What will be offered against me, above all, is *explanation* of my adversary's action. It was the consequence of those desires, which desires themselves have a certain history. It was owed, as well, to other things, which things also have their explanation. I shall naturally say, in reply to this sort of objection, that my adversary could have restrained himself. He could have overcome those things, his dispositions. That, as it seems, distinguishes him from the corpus of dispositions. I shall need to say, in order to defend my vengefulness, that *he could have done otherwise*

where that means something other than we supposed a little way back.
(p. 35)

Saying he could have restrained his passions does not seem to carry
only the thought, for what it is worth, that no single desire of his was
so strong as to overbear all his other desires and inclinations. It seems
to carry the thought that he, as distinct from any one of his
dispositions, might have overborne the desires which issued in his
action. My adversary, in my vengeful view of him, was not just a set of
directed pressures, so to speak, in this case pressures not opposed to
one another, and all of them directed towards the act. Something else
was on hand, different from a pressure, but capable of resisting
pressures. If the metaphor is baffling, it is not therefore misleading.

The general idea to which we have come is one encountered earlier,
in connection with grounds for life-hopes—the idea of a self. We can
also get to the idea by other routes related to those we have. If I suppose
that my vengeful feeling is owed to my perception of a certain corpus
of dispositions, the question will indeed arise of their explanation. I
cannot take it, in answer, that they have *no* explanation. Nor, it must
seem, if they do have an explanation, can I resist transferring my
vengeful feeling to *it*, to whatever has given rise to them, shaped them,
or released them. Furthermore, to be secure in my vengeful feeling, it
must be that *this* source or whatever is not itself the product or
whatever of something else. I must find a proper object of feeling
which does not allow for further regress. I come again to what we
gesture at in speaking of a self.

Two or three related lines of reflection, then, issue in the image of an
uncaused and unsuperfluous entity, the image which gives rise to the
originator and its activity of origination in indeterminist theories of
the mind. In the image we have what must seem to be a necessary
condition or indeed element of personal feelings of appreciation and
resentment. It is a necessary condition of personal feelings of a certain
type or character. It does not need remarking at this point, except out
of pique, that there remains an occasional philosopher who can
succeed wonderfully in mistaking it for just a requirement of
randomness. It is not that. (Watson, 1982, p. 13; cf. Honderich, 1973a,
p. 208)

There is a general way of distinguishing between the ground we now
have for appreciative and resentful feelings, involving origination, and
the conflicting one considered before, involving only voluntariness,
which ground gave rise to the response of intransigence. The earlier
ground, it was said, can be expressed in this way: typically when a
person acts, in so far as ignorance, internal constraint, his not being
himself, abnormality, and dominance by others are concerned, he

could have acted otherwise. None of these possible limiting facts was a fact about his action. The ground we have lately been considering for our appreciative and resentful feelings can be expressed in this way: typically when a person acts, in so far as the possible limiting facts just mentioned are concerned, *and also* in so far as his dispositions and indeed all his properties are concerned, he could have acted otherwise. *He*—he who is not a property of himself—could have risen above all his desires, temptations, weaknesses, and so on. Given his entire state just as it was, he could have acted otherwise.

When we have in mind this ground for our personal feelings, a ground involving both voluntariness and origination, we have in mind what is inconsistent with necessitated intentions and actions— inconsistent with the theory of determinism. It is not true, if determinism is the case, that a person could ever have acted otherwise in the given sense. No doubt can exist about the logical relation between the theory of determinism and the given ground for personal feelings. The two are indeed inconsistent, since the theory of determinism is to the effect that given a man's dispositions and other properties at the time of his forming of an intention, the latter thing was necessitated, and, further, that the subsequent action was also necessitated.

As dismay was a natural response for each of us with respect to determinism and our life-hopes, so too is it a natural response to determinism and personal feelings. Appreciative and resentful feelings, the first kind entrenched and of great value to us, and the second kind at any rate entrenched, are out of place given the truth of determinism. Or rather, a determinate category of both appreciative and resentful feelings are out of place, and, to speak of the appreciative feelings, no other category can be satisfying—there can be no satisfaction in feelings involving only voluntariness, which by comparison are of little worth. The feelings that are out of place depend essentially on or involve a proposition or propositional image which is false. That it is unclear exactly how the feelings depend on or involve the proposition —that question has been left untouched—does not affect the issue. (p. 110)

In sum, with respect to personal feelings, we have two inconsistent possibilities. We can take them to be attitudes having to do with only the voluntariness of actions, and respond intransigently to determinism, and we can also take them to be attitudes having to do not only with voluntariness but also origination, and we may then fall into dismay with respect to determinism. It is better to say, simply, that we *have* the two conflicting attitudes, and make the two responses. We can in fact move from either attitude and its associated response to the other attitude and its associated response.

1.5 KNOWLEDGE

Our life-hopes and our feelings towards others are fundamental parts of our existence. They are parts of an existence which also has something different in it, wholly pervasive attributes, notably the attribute of being informed by knowledge. A danger to our knowledge is therefore a wide or encompassing danger. Further, since our knowledge is directive not only of our hopes and personal feelings, but of all our desires and intentions, anything that puts into question our knowledge also puts into question the rationality of what is also pervasive, which is desire and intention. It makes suspect for us what we take to be the truths on which our desire and intention depend. It is not too much to say that what threatens our knowledge threatens our existence as we conceive it.

What can be called the Epicurean tradition of objection to determinism, does not often make clear its own strength.[6] Those in the tradition have most often been concerned somehow to trace knowledge to the laws of logic or the like, or to claim the inconsistency of such suppositions as that reasons could be causes. What lies under such objections, or is uncertainly conveyed by them, is the proposition that mental acts and ordinary bodily actions are prerequisites of knowledge, or, more precisely, that a certain freedom in these acts and actions is such a prerequisite. The Epicurean tradition, then, if it can rightly be seen as offering a direct objection to determinism, perhaps by way of the argument that determinism applies to and undermines itself, is fundamentally an answer to one of a specifiable class of questions about the consequences of determinism, with which we are now concerned.

The questions of this class, although they have not until now been described in this way, are those which arise from the seeming conflict between determinism and *our freedom in mental acts and bodily actions*. They include the questions at which we have just looked about life-hopes and personal feelings. What is the consequence of determinism for assumptions of our own freedom made in connection with life-hopes? What is the consequence of determinism for assumptions of others' freedom made in connection with personal feelings? That the issue of determinism and knowledge comes here, as we saw, cannot be denied by way of the truth that belief is involuntary. As might have been remarked in our earlier discussion, it is an ordinary fact that questions of *responsibility* arise about belief and knowledge. The maxim that ignorance of the law is no excuse points directly to the further truth that belief and knowledge do involve more than what is involuntary. So too does the ordinary fact that we blame people for being careless about finding things out.

Our knowledge is with reason divided into three sorts, firstly knowledge of propositions or that such-and-such is the case, secondly the kind of knowledge which consists most importantly in sense-experience, and thirdly what can be called practical knowledge or simply ability, such as knowing how to tie one's shoelaces. (Pears, 1972) It is the first sort that must be most important here.

It is plain, as argued already, that our propositional knowledge is in essential ways owed to our ordinary actions. This is no elusive claim to the effect that believing or knowing in themselves have an 'active' character, that they themselves are somehow intrinsically active, or the more arguable claim that we construct 'theories' which guide our sense perception. Nor is it any philosophical speculation about connections between the meaning of concepts and our activities or operations. It is a claim which is trivially but clearly exemplified by the simple truth, to take but one example, that my knowledge that Colin McGinn is next door is owed in part to my having gone there to see. Many of my pieces of ordinary knowledge do have as necessary conditions intended movements of mine which I can easily specify. More generally, the vast corpus of my particular knowledge about the world is evidently the result, in part, of my past actions—actions, again, in the most ordinary sense. This truth is not affected by further ones, that no particular piece of my knowledge has but a single action as necessary condition in its background, and that I cannot begin to specify all of my actions which were necessary conditions of any particular piece of knowledge. Evidently an individual's ordinary actions will have to have a role in any model or theory of the accumulation of his knowledge.

Also, as anticipated above, there is a like proposition that is more important, having to do with mental acts. It clearly depends on there being a distinction of a satisfactory kind between active mental events—mental acts—and passive mental events. Some have doubted that the distinction can be made. We can go some way to making it by supposing that mental acts are purposive or goal-directed, which is at least in part the fact that they are subject to an ongoing desire. They can be characterized further by way of such ideas as those of interim goals and plans. Despite the existence of this proposal as to a difference between mental acts and other mental events, the attempt has sometimes been made, occasionally by determinists, to deny any distinction. Also, it has happened that *all* of what goes on in our minds has been taken to consist in mental acts somehow conceived. (Geach,

1957) These contentions, passed by earlier without notice, need consideration. Let us pause to give it.

That there is a prima-facie difference between active and passive mental events is evident enough. We do ordinarily speak in many ways of our beliefs and also our desires as not being a matter of activity but of passivity. We cannot but think or feel such-and-such, or escape this or that sensation. However, as is apparent, we also speak of what we evidently take to be somehow active: attending, questioning, inquiring, speculating, judging, trying to prove, making up our minds and so on. We make a difference between deliberating and vacillating, and also make like contrasts in other cases, for example between (i) the claim that someone solved a problem and (ii) the claim that the solution came to him. It is not difficult to be inclined to the argument that the latter difference is evident in the fact that the two claims can indeed be so understood that the second does not entail the first. (Taylor, 1966)

Perhaps the denial of a difference between mental acts and other mental events has been partly owed to the fact that the difference does not involve a sharp boundary, that mental acts do shade into other mental events. This is no good reason for the denial. For what it is worth, there is a somewhat related difference between ordinary actions and other bodily events. Some bodily events are *in a way* or *in part* actions—falling down can be an example. Sometimes the denial has not been owed to direct reflection on the matter but has been a consequence, correctly or incorrectly drawn, of a general theory of the mind.

Perhaps the main source of a denial of a difference between mental acts and other mental events has been the absence of an account of mental acts which makes them one with or sufficiently like bodily actions. It is clear that we cannot give an account of them much like clear and standard accounts that have been given of ordinary actions.[7] One difficulty has to do with intention. It does seem that *some* mental acts are preceded or accompanied by active intentions, or things very like them. This may be so of the acts which enter into considering a proof or carrying forward an inquiry, or indeed remembering an address or simply deciding on something or choosing between alternatives. However, there also appear to be mental acts which are *not* preceded or accompanied by active intentions—it seems this can be true of those mental acts which *are* the active intentions involved in ordinary actions, or the like things that sometimes precede or accompany other mental acts.

The absence of or even the impossibility of a unitary general analysis of both mental acts and bodily actions is perhaps no better reason than the others for a denial of the difference that has been made between them and other mental events, in terms of purposiveness or goal-directedness. Furthermore, more can be added to that account. It brings mental acts and bodily actions more closely together. Mental acts do in fact share discernible attributes with actions. They may involve trying or struggling. They may be deliberate or careless. We may indulge in them or refrain from them. We may take credit for them or feel remorse about them. As already implied by saying that questions of responsibility arise in connection with knowledge and belief, others may blame us or hold us responsible for mental acts, or for not having performed them. Any attempt to argue that there are the same or very like facts about *all* mental events—say seeing something, being subject to a desire, or having a thought—must necessarily be a lame attempt.

Therefore, in addition to the fact that our propositional knowledge is owed in essential ways to our ordinary actions, there *is* also the more extensive fact that it is owed to what can properly be distinguished as our mental acts. Pieces of knowledge owed to discriminable ordinary actions are necessarily also owed to the discriminable mental events involved in those actions. Other pieces of knowledge are not owed to discriminable bodily actions but are owed to discriminable mental acts. To find the solution to a puzzle, or to get the answer to a question, often enough involves mental acts whose existence is clear to us, but does not involve ordinary actions which we can specify.

If ordinary actions and also mental acts are necessary conditions of our pieces of particular knowledge, it is also true that they are necessary to what can be distinguished from such pieces of knowledge, and also from our general knowledge in a certain ordinary sense. Acts and actions are conditions of what can be called our *general conceptual scheme*. A first part of this is made up of the arrays of categories upon which we depend to organize our existence. A second consists in what can be inadequately described as logical conceptions and generalizations. It includes the conceptions of truth and probability, the laws of logic, and the canons of empirical or scientific inquiry. It also includes informal counterparts and ramifications of these, which govern our ordinary way of carrying on as believers and knowers. In a third part our general conceptual scheme can be taken to include several evaluational systems, one of them having to do with morality. A good deal of our evaluational systems cannot be given the name of knowledge, but evidently much can. It involves descriptive categories. Further, by way of a single example, morality involves a principle of transitivity: if a is worse than b, and b worse than c, then a is worse than c.

Our general conceptual scheme may appear to us to have the character of a great datum, something different in kind from a product, and far from a contrivance. Particular parts of that scheme, say the laws of logic and arithmetical truths, have a yet more independent standing. Be that as it may, we cannot suppose that our conceptual scheme is the work of anything other than ourselves. Most of us, despite occasional defences of what is called the independent reality of propositions, numbers, and so on, cannot suppose that our conceptual scheme has any reality apart from us, that it could outlive consciousness. Our conceptual scheme was in fact the slow creation of our species. To think of that process, inevitably, is in part to think of the ordinary actions and the mental acts of our predecessors and ourselves.

So much for introduction. Suppose now (i) I am the returning officer for an election, obliged to determine and declare the winner, and lack returns as to the voting in one crucial constituency, or (ii) that my aim is to complete a calculation, but I lack a value for one variable, or (iii) that I am faced with a moral problem and cannot satisfactorily conceive the effect of a possible action on a lover, or (iv) that I am trying to decide on the acceptability of a philosophical theory, and cannot persuade myself of the coherence or incoherence of some transition of argument in it. In each case there is a specifiable bodily action or mental act, or a number of them, that I cannot perform. In each case, then, there is evidence which I lack. The result is a want of belief and knowledge. What reasons I have for a concluding proposition cannot count as good ones.

Suppose now that I get the final piece of evidence in each case. But suppose also that I come to accept or at any rate contemplate that my resulting belief, and what I would ordinarily take to be my knowledge, is an effect of a certain causal sequence, as specified by the theory of determinism. Suppose, above all, that I accept or contemplate that each act and action of mine and of others which contributed to that result was an event of which the theory of determinism is true. These will include, further back, myriad acts and actions which entered into the development of our conceptual scheme, and so contributed indirectly to the result. In each case, what occurred was a necessary event: an effect of certain causal sequences. To say the same thing differently about each act and action, no other event could have occurred in its place.

Consider in particular my fourth enterprise, to decide on the acceptability of a particular philosophical theory. I may now feel that my final situation, including a view of the coherence of a part of it, and also including my contemplation of determinism, is in a way like my situation *before* I became clear about the coherence question. That is, I can suppose that there may exist facts such that different acts and actions, logically possible acts and actions never performed, would have issued indirectly or directly in their discovery, and that these facts would have provided further reasons for or against my conclusion about the theory. In particular I can suppose that these facts would provide reasons such that the reasons I actually have for my conclusion are not good ones, or are not sufficient.

For some of us, it may require an effort of will even to contemplate the truth of a determinism, or a near-determinism. Perhaps it may be an impediment, too, that the present contemplation of it, in connection with the given example, must have to do not with a particular act or action, but with an indeterminate number of them, of which we have no specific conceptions. Be that as it may, to succeed in contemplating or to accept the truth of a determinism as applied to our knowledge-claims is to do something which can evoke the response of dismay. To have a picture of ourselves and of all the makers of our maps of belief, so to speak, as having been fixed to following only certain of the logically possible paths of inquiry, is to have a picture which can very naturally raise doubt in us as to the terrain. They and we have not *explored* reality, but have been guided, however voluntarily, on one tour. By way of this thought and like ones we may succumb, at least for a time, and indeed recurrently, to an agnosticism or scepticism. Or, at any rate, we can feel that such an agnosticism or scepticism should be the consequence of an actual acceptance of determinism. Our knowledge-claims should be abandoned. Or, at least, we should lose confidence. What we took to be a ground for them is illusory.

What contributes essentially to this dismay, evidently, is the attitude that a wider and in some sense a complete spectrum of actually possible acts and actions in the past would have been *necessary* to present knowledge: a spectrum wider or richer than the one fixed by the nomic connections of a determinism. The idea of such a spectrum of possibilities is tightly attached to a certain image of the initiation of acts and actions. It is again the image of origination, the germ of indeterminist pictures of the mind. Like the image of movement across all of the spectrum, it is an image which cannot coexist with a determinism.

In short, we have or can have the attitude that what is needed for knowledge, true knowledge, is not only voluntariness—centrally, here, the absence of certain impediments, of which more below—but also origination. That this is inconsistent with determinism issues in the response of dismay. To speak differently, we have an attitude to propositions, beliefs, and the like, an attitude of confidence, which is vulnerable to an acceptance of determinism, and issues in dismay. Similar remarks are to be made about a related attitude to ourselves and others as *inquirers* and *knowers*.

This response in connection with knowledge is undoubtedly most natural in connection with certain things. These include claims to knowledge with respect to philosophical, scientific, or other theories, and also our resolutions of moral problems. This is so since both, as we ordinarily suppose, issue in the end from exercises of judgement. Dismay is most natural here for the reason that it is mental acts that have our attention. It is much the same fact, evidently, that verdicts on philosophical or scientific theories, and the outcomes of our moral deliberation, have neither the necessity of syllogistic conclusions nor the necessity of the deliverances of sense-experience.

Is it the case that the given attitude having to do with origination, and the response of dismay, are not only most natural here, but that they are possible only here? Elsewhere, as in thinking of (i) the example of the election or (ii) the calculation, involving a variable, we may give less attention to mental acts. They have less prominence. So with other cases, including the fundamental case of perceptual knowledge. Ordinarily I do not *judge* that I see a tree or a colour. None the less, it would surely be odd if our claims to knowledge, of all kinds, did not share a common vulnerability, to one or another extent. This would be odd if knowledge of all kinds is owed in part, as surely is true, to our own acts and actions and those of others, however antecedent these are to our concluding beliefs.

In fact it is possible to take a determinism to raise doubt about *all* of what we ordinarily take ourselves to know. This can come about by way of its relevance to what was called our general conceptual scheme. Sense-experience is categorized by us. As for syllogistic conclusions and the like, impregnable as they seem to be, it is not impossible to feel that we might have had an alternative and in some sense a superior system of necessary truths. We can and do overcome psychological barriers to doubt in this connection, or at any rate we can perceive reason for the attempt.

The response of dismay, then, with respect to knowledge, is that a determinism undermines it. Given a determinism, the whole growth of human knowledge, including the development of our conceptual scheme, and what each of us claims to know now, is a matter of one vast fixed sequence, one system of nomic connections. Questions which might have risen in the growth of our knowledge in fact could not arise. Possibilities could not be considered. Ways of regarding reality were barred. Our good reasons therefore cease to be such, and all belief is or should be subject to doubt. They do not much matter, but there are also further consequences regularly claimed in the Epicurean tradition. The determinist's defence of his own doctrine as a piece of knowledge is undermined, and we accept that any affirmation of the possibility of knowledge would entail that determinism is in fact false.

If it is possible to make this response owed to a certain attitude, or at least to contemplate it, it is perhaps impossible to persist in it. Hume's famous remark, about what it was possible for him to believe in his study—in the course of his philosophical reflections—and what was the case outside, in practical life, is of relevance. Dismay with respect to knowledge, further, is rightly seen by us as in a way more consequential, because more general, than dismay about either life-hopes or personal feelings. At any rate, each of us is capable of moving to a different attitude to the acts and actions which are conditions of what we ordinarily take to be our knowledge, and thus each of us is capable of a different response.

I must allow, certainly, that some kind of freedom in act and action is necessary to knowledge. More particularly, I accept that in order to know something, I must have a certain confidence that requisite questions have been asked. I must have a confidence, perhaps, that requisite sense-experience has been had, or requisite theoretical possibilities considered. To lack this freedom, whatever it is, to acquire good reasons, is to be barred from belief. As to what this freedom is, an answer different from the one we have is pressed upon me by my empiricism, a common and untheoretical empiricism, and my attention to our ordinary existence as knowers. The answer is that the requisite freedom is voluntariness. We can resist our own demand for more.

To recall life-hopes and personal feelings, we can take them to be fully secured by voluntariness—by my actions being done out of embraced desires, by the actions of others not being subject to certain constraints and disabilities. Or, to speak more carefully, certain types of life-hopes and personal feelings, satisfying to us, can be secured by voluntariness. We can take the same position with respect to knowledge. We can take the attitude that knowledge requires the satisfaction of certain *desires for information*, desires involving the proposition that certain acts or actions will issue in belief and knowledge. My wanting to have the return of votes from the crucial constituency, or to know the value for the variable, or the fact about the effect of a possible action on a lover, or the fact with respect to the coherence of the transition in the philosophical theory—each of these desires is informed by the proposition that the answer to a certain question will rightly settle an issue, give me what I want, which is one or the other of the two possibily true beliefs.

It is an uncontested fact that when I cannot act on my desires for information in certain ways—when I am constrained in certain ways—I cannot have the knowledge which is my goal. Is it not reasonable to think that knowledge, in so far as acts and actions are concerned, is no more than a matter of being able to act on existing desires for information? Is it not reasonable to think that when I can act on my existing information-desires, and they themselves have arisen out of previous acts and actions owed to information-desires, I have *all* of what is with reason required for knowledge, in so far as acts and actions are concerned? No doubt there is no discerning, now, the beginning or all of the growth of the knowledge which informs my present information-desires, including the beginning and growth of our conceptual scheme. More than that, there is a kind of problem. There were, presumably, early acts not so informed, or not informed at all. But facts about our present state—that we do act out of a great history of information-desires—are not to be abused on the ground that we cannot see back to the beginning of the history.

Is there not a pointlessness in the other view, the one requiring origination? Our knowledge rests, assuredly, on truth and good reasons. To have knowledge is necessarily to have a conception of truth, and to have good reasons. Let us again suppose that the truth of propositions is correspondence with fact, or, as we can say, with reality. Good reasons, we can say, are a matter of that reality, and also of logical connections: in general, that propositions entail or provide evidence for other propositions. The reflection that gives rise to the response of dismay depends on the conception and supposition of a reality *other than or in addition to* the one we know, the known subject-matter of the growth of our knowledge. Dismay can also be taken to depend on a supposition as to *other reasons or further reasons* than good reasons of the kind we know. This is a supposition pertaining to the further reality and also to something other than the logical connections we have.

No doubt it must remain unpersuasive to declare, as philosophers have, that such conceptions are in fact no conceptions at all, that they want content, significance, or sense. We *can* properly be said to speculate intelligibly about the existence of facts that have been and will forever be beyond our experience and definition, facts associated with logically possible acts and actions which have never and will never be performed, logically possible paths of inquiry forever closed to us. We can give *some* sense to talk of unknown and in fact unknowable logical connections. To do this is not to do the impossible, actually to get outside of the only conceptual scheme we have, but to make some use of ultimately general conceptions in it, notably the conception of a fact or circumstance. The philosophies which have made such endeavours are not unintelligible. Kant does not elude all sense when he maintains that there does exist that of which we cannot have experience, the noumenal world which lies behind the phenomenal world. Nor does Spinoza in maintaining that God or Nature has an infinite number of attributes, of which we know but two, Thought and Extension.

Still, to repeat, there is surely a pointlessness in any doctrine of a reality beyond. This is so in part since it involves so thin a conception of that reality. To whatever extent that it is put beyond our reach, it is indeed to that extent beyond our reach. The reality from which we are excluded by a determinism is as greatly beyond our reach as Kant's noumena or Spinoza's unknown attributes. What is the value of this faint picture? What are we to do with it? Certainly it is pointless in the sense of being useless to us, not only in any practical way but also theoretically, as a basis or criterion, or as stimulation to further knowledge. As for the satisfaction of knowledge-in-itself, as it may be called, and the dissatisfaction of ignorance-in-itself, these might be taken to depend on concreteness and particularity. There can surely be no great sense of loss with respect to what is near to I-know-not-what.

If we must allow the conceivability of other ideas than the one we have of reality, there is not only the pointfulness but the necessity of persisting with our own. We cannot, by the very hypotheses of our determinism, escape it. Furthermore, if it is possible to conceive of comparing or assessing alternative global knowledges—ours as it is against what logically might have been—it cannot be that our knowledge is anything like useless as an approximation of reality. We depend upon *it*, after all, for the thin conception we have of what might have been. We cannot conceivably take it to be insignificant. If we do this, we must discard what it allows us by way of intimation of a better.

These reflections could be added to—for example, by way of ideas which have become popular having to do with a dependency of knowledge on causation, but let us go no further. What we have can indeed enable us to avoid dismay, at least for a time, about determinism and knowledge. We can come to rest, although uncertainly and without guarantee, in a conflicting and arguable view. We may take the attitude that what is required for the only knowledge that we can possess, the only knowledge that can matter to us, is a voluntariness. This confidence consists in the large fact that we are not wholly frustrated, and often not frustrated at all, in our desires for information. In large part we are not subject to a set of constraints which it is fairly easy to describe, and which are akin to those of which we know, pertaining to life-hopes and personal feelings. They do have a character peculiar to the matter of knowledge. Further, we can continue to attempt to reduce the clear constraints under which we do find ourselves: ignorances, apprehensions, restricting orthodoxies, self-frustration, practical obstacles to inquiry, barriers and coercion and manipulation by those not concerned with truth or desirous of concealing it. A determinism is consistent with the voluntariness we have and which we can struggle to increase.

Our second response with respect to determinism and knowledge, then, may be a certain intransigence, to the effect that knowledge is untouched by determinism. It is not affected, let alone near to being undermined. Our existence as knowers is untroubled by determinism. We can rest easy. The main burden of the Epicurean tradition is quite mistaken, as are its related propositions to the effect that the determinist's defence of his own doctrine as a piece of knowledge is undermined, and that since we do have knowledge, determinism is false.

1.6 MORALITY

I may regard a particular action, say that of the Member of Parliament for Hampstead and Highgate in voting for a bill to reduce the resources of the National Health Service and to give advantages to those who have private medical insurance, as *right or wrong*. I may have the more or less reflective attitude, at least when doing moral philosophy, that right actions generally are those that fall into a certain category or categories. There are various possibilities. I may take it that right actions are all those not proscribed by the criminal law, or perhaps by my sense of some customary morality. I may take it, very differently, that they are those in accord with the Principle of Equality, that we are to take effective steps to try to make well off those who are badly off, with effective steps and the conditions of being well off and badly off defined in certain ways. I may take it that right actions are those in accord with some version of the Principle of Utility, or those somehow called for by some collection of duties—perhaps with duties of loyalty to one's family and certain others to the fore. I may take it, again differently, that right actions are those which are done out of a sense of principle, or benevolent intention, or truth to oneself, or some other fact having to do with the initiation of action, some fact about the agent in his action as distinct from concomitants and consequences of his action. (MacIntyre, 1967)

The particular judgement or conviction about the action of the

Member of Parliament, if I am consistent, will of course be consistent with my general view about the rightness of actions. The particular judgement and others like it may be consequences, or sources, of my general view—or in some other relation of mutual dependency. (Rawls, 1972)

I may also have a view of the MP himself, most importantly of his character, a view perhaps but not necessarily based in part on his particular action. I have an attitude to him *as a person*, as having a certain *moral standing*. He is a man whose actions generally are, or generally are not, in line with the correct principle for right actions according to my lights. Partly because of this, if not only, he may be for me a man of honour, or of moral tenacity, as his action may help to show, or an opportunist, or someone with a very selective eye for injustice or need, as again his action may help to show. I am likely to have, as well, some attitude or view about the general question of what all men and women ought to be like. All of us, I suppose, should strive to have certain dispositions rather than others. Again, if I am consistent, the particular judgement about the MP and the general view of what people ought to be like will be related.

It is to be noticed that to have a view of the MP himself, as what we can call in a traditional way a good or bad moral agent, is not the same as *morally to approve or disapprove of him for the given action*. We may think well of him in general as, say, a person of humanity or decency, perhaps to be revered, and yet disapprove of him for his vote, taking it to be out of character, or a lapse, or owed to misjudgement. We may have a generally low view of his character, moral perception, or sensitivity, but feel what might be called moral admiration for him in so far as this particular and uncharacteristic action is concerned.

In speaking of this third matter, moral approval and disapproval, I have in mind our feelings or attitudes, and not any resulting acts of commendation or condemnation, praise or blame, which will be considered later. (Ch. 4) They are feelings having to do with responsibility. As already indicated (p. 11), in speaking of our *holding* a person responsible for something, I have in mind exactly our feeling of moral disapproval, and in speaking of *crediting* someone with responsibility for something, I have in mind our feeling of moral approval. To hold a woman responsible for an act, or to credit her with responsibility for it, is not to perform a purely intellectual operation, but to have a feeling about her with respect to the act. It is not barely to ascribe moral responsibility to her, where that is to have beliefs or whatever about the initiation of the act, perhaps to judge truly or falsely that she is morally responsible. Such beliefs, images or judgements, which are of the ordinary factual kind, enter into or support our feelings, in a way analagous to the way in which such things enter into or support life-hopes and personal feelings. (pp. 16 ff., 35, 41) Something more will be said of the matter in due course. (pp. 131 ff.)

So—we have moral feelings and make moral judgements about the rightness or wrongness of particular actions, and also about types or classes of actions. Secondly, we have feelings and make judgements about people with respect to their characters and personalities, to which their actions over periods of time, perhaps their whole lives, are of primary importance. Here too we are concerned with individuals and types. Thirdly, we have feelings about particular people with respect to particular actions. That is, we hold an individual morally responsible for a particular action or group of actions, or credit him or her with responsibility for it. (Cf. Parfit, 1984, pp. 98 ff.)

The three parts of morality now roughly and perhaps too firmly distinguished, having to do with right actions, general moral standing, and moral responsibility, evidently stand in certain relationships. These, to my mind, have not traditionally, if ever, been made clear. A clearer understanding of the relationships is fundamental to an economical and effective consideration of the consequences of determinism for morality. To be clearer about them is to see that the challenge of determinism to morality is wider and more fundamental than has been supposed, and also more easily specified. It will not be possible, however, or necessary, to arrive at much more than a schematic understanding of morality. Questions will be passed by.

To put aside for a time the approving and disapproving of persons for particular actions, and to persist with the subjects of feelings and judgements about the rightness of actions themselves, and about what men and women ought in general to be like, it is a fact that a good deal of moral philosophy is addressed to the general question of what actions are right. In answer, argument is given for a general moral principle, one of those mentioned above or another, some specification of the class of right actions. The question of what it is to be in good moral standing, the question of what men and women ought to be like, is dealt with, if at all, very much on the side. One may get the impression that the question is somehow peripheral to morality. So with the moral philosophy of Mill, and Utilitarianism generally.

In some other moral philosophy, perhaps quite as much, the concentration is the other way on. The question addressed is that of what sort of persons we should be. The good man gets all the attention, along with the bad man. We are told what sort of character or what virtues are had by good men and women. There may be the implication that the question of what actions are right is somehow peripheral in morality. So with the ethics of Aristotle and successors of several kinds.

As already implied in connection with the example of the MP, it is possible—it certainly need not be self-contradictory—to say that a man did the right thing, and that in the doing of it he gave an indication of being a morally questionable or indeed morally appalling character. (The point is different, of course, from the point that one can morally approve of a bad man for an act, or disapprove of a good one.) The MP voted as I feel he ought to have, but did so, perhaps, out of a disposition to self-serving careerism or to toadying. He does not actually have the principle which in my view made his action right, and perhaps has no respect for it. As evidently, a man may be taken to do the wrong thing, and in doing it give some evidence that he is morally admirable. The standard case here is one where the agent acts out of feelings or commitments of which I wholly approve, and judges the nature of the effects of his action to the best of his ability, but in fact misjudges them. Good intentions, but an innocent or condonable mistake as to the situation.

This fact, that right actions and good moral standing of agents do not always go together, or wrong actions and bad characters, is one of three facts which may consort to produce a certain upshot of mistake, very common indeed. The second fact is one noticed a moment ago, the concentration for whatever reason of much moral philosophy on either the question about right actions or the question about the good man. The third is the fact of our ordinary way of carrying on, illustrated so far in this discussion, in which feelings and judgements about actions, and feelings and judgements about men and women, are certainly discriminable parts. We do ordinarily separate the two matters.

The mistake is the idea that if one puts aside the issue of morally approving or disapproving agents for their actions—crediting them with responsibility or holding them responsible—and of course commending or condemning them, there remain *two* fundamental moral questions rather than one, two logically distinct questions. There is the question of the rightness of actions and the question of the goodness of agents. In fact it is true, or nearer the truth, despite our proceedings so far, to say that there is but one question where two are perceived. This one question is certainly open to different expressions.

It can be expressed in this way: (i) *How ought the world to be?* Or, better, since in morality we are concerned with the world in so far as it is in our control, there is this expression: (ii) *How ought the world to be, in so far as we can affect it?* What that comes to can also be put in this way: (iii) *What actions are right?*—so long as the words are not taken in a certain narrow way, of which more in a moment. It can also be put as (iv) *What sort of people ought we to be?*—so long as those words are not taken in a certain narrow way.

It is possible to answer this fundamental question in a way which directs attention to actions and their concomitants and consequences. The Principle of Equality, other answers having to do with fairness or justice, and versions of the Principle of Utility, are evidently of this kind—consequentialist answers, as we shall call them. (Cf. Parfit, 1984, Pt. 1) In these cases, we are given instructions which have to do with the satisfaction of desires in acting, and also, more important, such satisfaction as a consequence of acting. We are to secure certain totals or distributions of satisfaction, or certain totals *and* distributions.

However, it is possible to attempt to answer the fundamental question in ways which concentrate on the agent. Agent-related answers, as we can call them, to a greater or lesser degree identify right actions as those which have a certain initiation, often an initiation in and true to a certain kind of person. Do the act, we may be told, which flows from a pure good will, from being a certain sort of person. Do the act which is true to a universal principle about how men in themselves ought ideally to be. Certainly there is nothing inapposite or irrelevant about saying, in answer to the fundamental question, that right actions are those which come from the Kantian pure good will, or are in accord with some other universal principle about the genesis of actions in sympathy or love, or are actions which issue from or preserve the integrity of the agent. Nor, however, is there anything inapposite or irrelevant about saying, in answer to the fundamental question, that we ought to be the sort of people whose actions are in accordance with the egalitarian principle or some other consequentialist principle.

In the two sorts of moral philosophy noted above, consequentialist and agent-related, the relevant subject-matter must in fact be taken as specified by something close to our single question, best expressed as that of how the world ought to be, in so far as we can affect it. However, the question actually addressed in each of the two sorts of moral philosophy is typically so formed as to presuppose, or by custom to suggest, a certain range of answers to the single question. In the first kind there is addressed the question 'What actions are right?' taken in a certain narrow way. That is, what is presupposed or suggested is that all the arguable answers to the single question are answers having to do with certain concomitants and consequences of actions. Answers in terms of the nature of agents are in effect put on one side. In the other sort of moral philosophy there is posed the question 'What sort of persons ought we to be?', again taken in a narrow way. As that is usually understood, it presupposes or suggests a range of answers that has to do only with agents, with their initiation of actions. As will have been noticed, this range of answers has to do not wholly with what we have called the general moral standing of agents, but also with moral approval and disapproval or the initiation of actions, but let us leave that complication alone.

Both ranges of answers are in fact about how the world should be in so far as we can affect it. No doubt the selection of a question carrying a presupposition is natural enough, given someone's conviction that the answer to the question of how the world ought to be falls into a certain range. There is the unhappy result, however, that the subject-matter is characterized in such a way as to close off relevant moral issues. A range of answers is excluded from consideration without argument. Argument *is* needed. To exclude the other range of answers is to make a fundamental moral claim. It is to make the claim that either consequentialist or agent-related moralities are mistaken.

There is a related point. It sometimes seems to be supposed, curiously, by those who give agent-related answers to the fundamental question, that those who give consequentialist answers are making some *philosophical* mistake, or, more precisely, that they are failing to perceive the somehow necessary nature of morality. (B. Williams, 1973) That is, something is supposed other than the fact that the dispute between agent-related and consequentialist doctrines is a ground-level moral dispute. That is exactly what it is, a dispute as to the right answer to the question of how the world ought to be in so far as we can affect it.

That there is a single question rather than two logically independent ones is best indicated and perhaps proved by the fact that each sort of moral philosophy, despite appearances, gives and must give a recommendation both as to actions and as to what sort of persons we ought to be. (Cf. B. Williams, 1981, p. 53) At any rate, both go a good way towards dealing with both matters. If a kind of Utilitarianism is pressed upon us in connection with actions, there is a certain upshot with respect to persons. The good man or woman is at bottom this kind of Utilitarian. If being true to oneself, or preserving one's integrity—whatever that may finally mean—were given as the whole recommendation with respect to being a person of good moral standing, then the matter of actions must be resolved in a certain way. Right actions are those in which the agent is true to himself or herself.

More generally, and whatever the form of question which is chosen, it evidently is impossible to give an adequate and tolerably complete view of the good agent without giving a view as to what actions are right. It is similarly impossible to give a view of right actions without giving a view of the good agent. This is fundamentally what makes it true, or more true, to speak of one rather than two questions.

None of this gives us the conclusion, however, that we cannot do either of the different things of concentrating on persons or concentrating on actions. The questions at the start of this section and at the start of the chapter can stand, and we shall persist with them. I can, in considering a certain episode involving a person and what he or she did, direct myself either to the person or to the act—both matters being sufficiently distinct from that of moral responsibility. Given my moral outlook, one of these things will be more natural or apposite. That is certainly not to say, to repeat, that there are *logically independent* questions. The analogy is a weak one, and in some ways misleading, but there *is* an analogy with concentrating on the effects with respect to a sequence of physical events, or concentrating on the causal circumstances. I can ask 'What are the effects?' or 'What are the causal circumstances?' It is clear that to do so is to direct attention to a part of what is a single subject-matter. It is reasonable to say that the fundamental question is what causal relations exist with respect to the sequence which is the subject-matter.

So much for a single fundamental question of morality, its various expressions, and two possible concentrations. The other large question, not less fundamental, has to do with moral approval and disapproval of persons for particular actions, crediting them with responsibility and holding them responsible. Images, ideas, beliefs, and judgements as to initiation of action enter into these feelings, and the feelings may result in acts of commending or condemning others for particular acts. To approve of a man for an action, to have such a moral feeling, is not to do something which is to be identified either with judging him to be in general a good man, as already noted, or with judging an action to be right. It is in fact something different from both, although there are relations between the three things. Let us consider what in a way are the most fundamental of the relations.

Suppose I have the view that right actions are those which are in accord with some principle of fair distribution of satisfactions and dissatisfactions, perhaps the Principle of Equality. (pp. 52, 223) I judge a particular action, say a politician's, which is in accord with the Principle of Equality, to have been right. I take it, secondly, that the politician acted out of a settled disposition to act on just the principle in question, and, of course, since he does have that settled disposition, that he does generally act on the principle. I thus take him as a man to be morally all right. Thirdly, I may of course approve of him for the particular action in question, this approval involving a cerain belief about the initiation of the action, a belief to the effect, as we can loosely say, that he was responsible for it.

Does my judgement as to the first matter, the rightness of the particular action, involve only the fact that it was in accord with my favoured principle of fairness? Does it also somehow involve the possibility of *assigning responsibility* to the agent—holding him or her responsible, or crediting him or her with responsibility? Certainly judging the particular action to be right does not presuppose that the agent *is* in fact assigned responsibility for it. The matter of assigning responsibility need not arise. Nor, of course, is an action by definition something for which an agent is in fact assigned responsibility. We need not so define actions. An action, not to be precise, is a movement or stillness somehow owed to the mental. To say an action is owed to the mental is not to say that it is something for which the agent is to be assigned responsibility. Nor would we get that upshot if we were to define an action, as is reasonable, as something owed to intention. That an action is intentional is not the same fact as the one about responsibility. Indeed there are many perfectly intentional actions for which the agent is not held responsible, and not such that he or she is credited with responsibility.

Is it true none the less, by way of some argument, that to judge an action to be right or wrong is to presuppose that the agent *could* be assigned responsibility for it? The principle that 'ought' implies 'can' is first of all a principle about responsibility, and about acts of praise and blame. There, what it comes to is that to blame a man, to say that he ought to have done otherwise than he did, requires that he could have done otherwise. (Cf. Frankfurt, 1969; van Inwagen, 1983, pp. 162 f.) What of the rightness of actions? Suppose, to repeat, that I am committed to the Principle of Equality. An action is done, and it serves the end specified by that principle. It contributes effectively to making well off those who are badly off. However, it was an action for which the agent cannot be assigned responsibility. He was, perhaps, absolutely compelled to perform it. Is the action right?

Difficulties attend answering the question, and more so to answering it briefly, but the answer is surely no. The action is neither right nor wrong. One can come to this answer by keeping in mind that the fundamental question in morality, other than that of responsibility and praise and blame is properly expressed as this: How ought the world to be *in so far as we can affect it*? Morality is concerned with the world in so far as it is in our control. An action for which the agent cannot be assigned responsibility, and which he therefore cannot be taken to control, is an event which falls outside of morality's concern or province. Certainly if such an action by a man was one he was compelled to perform by the action of another man, that prior action may be within the province of morality, but that is nothing to the point.

To speak more generally, the very existence of the question of right actions depends on the existence of actions for which responsibility can be assigned. If there were no responsible actions, there would be no judgements, as we have them, as to the rightness of actions. The subject-matter as we know it would not exist. In brief, the rightness of actions depends on the possibility of holding people responsible and crediting them with responsibility.

To return to the action mentioned a moment ago, in accord with the Principle of Equality, but a compelled action and hence not one for which the agent can be assigned responsibility, I may certainly take it that it was a good thing that it happened. It was a good thing in just the sense that it was a good thing for Ghana that the first rainy season in 1986 was as it was, and so ensured a full harvest. I may say that it was an action which would have been right, rather than neither right nor wrong, if it had been an action for which the agent could be assigned responsibility. None of this affects the conclusion that the principle that 'ought' implies 'can' has to do with judgements of actions as right or wrong as well as moral approval and disapproval of agents.

We are examining the relations between right actions, good men, and moral responsibility for actions. One such relation, we have it, is that the possibility of assigning responsibility to someone for an action is presupposed by taking an action to be right. We have it that right actions involve a certain initiation. The rightness of an action presupposes something about the agent.

To revert for a time to a separate matter, one may be tempted to think at this point that *any* answer to the question of what actions are right—at bottom the question of how the world ought to be—must bring in something about the goodness or badness of the intention and dispositions from which it derives. That is, to recall the two sorts of moral philosophy, any answer must bring in something from agent-related as distinct from consequentialist moral philosophy. Very roughly indeed, an action cannot be right unless it comes from a morally acceptable intention. There is no need to succumb to the temptation. We must not run together the fact that a right action is one which presupposes that the agent can be assigned responsibility, and the disputable and disputed proposition that to be right it must come from a morally acceptable intention or a certain kind of agent. Also, the proposition that an action's being right does entail that men ought to have certain intentions is not the proposition that to be right an action must come from a certain intention.

Some illustration of the main point will be useful. For Kant, right actions are those done out of the a priori command of reason, expressed in the moral law somehow conceived. They are done, that is to say, out of the pure good will, which is distinct from feeling for oneself or others. Are we to understand that an action's rightness does not merely presuppose but *is* in part its being an action for which the agent can be assigned responsibility? (Cf. Nozick, 1981, pp. 310 f.) There are notorious obscurities and difficulties in Kant's moral philosophy, and in particular at this very point, but it may be that an action's rightness is so conceived. That is, the requirement that a right action is such a responsible one is a moral requirement. Part of what makes it right, as distinct from what is presupposed in taking it to be right or wrong, is that it was an action for which the agent can be assigned responsibility. One may wish to resist the judgement that such a fact is itself to be valued, as one may wish to resist the idea that the colour mauve could itself be valued in a moral way, putting aside any connection it is taken to have with other things. Perhaps there is no conceptual obstacle, however, to what may be the Kantian idea. It will hardly need adding, however, and this is the main point, that when right actions are conceived differently, responsibility-assignments are not in the given way internal to judgements about actions.

To turn now to the relation between responsibility-assignments and the matter of the general moral standing of persons, it will rightly be expected that we have the same situation. The question of what men and women ought to be like, what dispositions they ought to have, involves the matter of responsibility-assignments as much as the connected question of right actions. This is so, in part, since the question of what dispositions we ought to strive to have is itself a question of the rightness or wrongness of certain actions: those that contribute to the formation of dispositions. The actions need to be responsible ones in the given sense. That is, if there were no actions for which agents could be assigned responsibility, there could be no exhortations as to what we ought to be like.

Will it be said against this that in judging someone to be of an exemplary moral character, we appraise his dispositions, as distinct from any of his actions which formed or contributed to his dispositions? There is some inclination to agree. To praise a man for his honourableness may be to praise him for his character itself. It is likely we should not do so if we supposed he had not contributed at all to the formation of his character, but none the less we do direct our admiration to his character. However, this fact does not disconnect judgements as to good men and women from responsibility-assignments. At the very least, *something* of the connection mentioned above persists. To favour someone for his character would be a very different enterprise if we took it that his previous actions had *nothing* to do with it.

In any case, there is another point. Suppose that such character-judgements had absolutely nothing to do with the actions which issue in a man's character. They would none the less be judgements about a man's dispositions *to responsible action*. Dispositions being such, that is the very nature of judgements about them. In line with the fact that morality's fundamental concern is with how the world ought to be, in so far as we can affect it, our judgements about dispositions necessarily have to do with the controllable. That is, they would have to do with judgements as to dispositions to perform actions over which we have control, actions for which we are held responsible or for which we are credited with responsibility. The subject of good, humane or estimable men and women thus presupposes the subject of responsibility in this second way.

The account of the structure of morality now completed is indeed schematic, and hence in several ways unsatisfactory. There are perhaps yet closer connections between the three matters than have been indicated. What we have gives a certain fundamentality to moral approval and disapproval or responsibility, a fundamentality which is hardly disputable. What we have also suggests, although the subject has been left untouched, that our attitudes to actions, and our attitudes with respect to the standing of persons, owe their characters in part to our attitudes in connection with responsibility. There is more to be said than that our attitudes with respect to actions and standing *presuppose* the possibility of attitudes with respect to responsibility. The latter attitudes contribute to the nature of the former. If, as will be anticipated, and to look forward, we have a *pair* of attitudes with respect to responsibility, so too we have a pair of attitudes with respect to each of right actions and general personal standing.

1.7 MORAL APPROVAL AND DISAPPROVAL

Suppose a man foresees the divorce which will end his embittered marriage, and, out of certain desires, forms a certain intention and acts on it. One desire, as we believe, is to try to capture the affection and loyalty of his son, and in so doing to deprive his wife of them. He desires too, we believe, to reduce the money that will go to his wife in the division of their assets. He forms the intention to give a large gift of money to his son, which he does. The situation might be an extraordinary one, such that it would be possible to condone or excuse his action, but, if the situation is at all ordinary, we shall certainly disapprove of him morally, hold him morally responsible for the action and effects of it. We shall have disapproving feelings about him, which feelings may have expression in blame or condemnation, spoken judgements to the effect that he has behaved badly or appallingly. Such feelings or attitudes, as we have just seen, although their nature has not been much explored, stand in certain relations to and shape or at least colour our views of the rightness of actions and the moral worth of persons.

Such feelings or attitudes of disapproval, and also feelings of approval, are disapproval and approval of a person for or in relation to a particular action. The action of the husband, given that disapproval is in question, must be a wrongful one. Thus, while morally disapproving or approving of persons for particular actions is connected with the rightness of actions in the general way we have seen—in part, the existence of right and wrong actions presupposes the possibility of assigning responsibility to persons—the two things are also connected in the simple way that moral approval and disapproval depend on or are otherwise related to a view of what actions are wrong and what right. This remains true despite the fact that few of us, if any, operate in our lives by way of an explicit, general principle of right actions such as that of Equality or Utility. Something related might be said—it would not be simple—about the connection of approval and disapproval with our conceptions of good men and women.

In the example, to repeat, we take the husband's action to be wrong. The large remainder of what is involved in our disapproval of him importantly includes beliefs, ideas, or whatever about the initiation of his action. What do these come to? There can be no doubt, as in the case of the personal feelings of appreciation and accusation, that they can be expressed this way: *he could have done otherwise than he did*. However, the words do not in themselves reveal what is behind them. As readers will expect, given what has been found with life-hopes, personal feelings, and knowledge, the words can give expression to two different sets of thoughts as to the initiation of action, and enter into two attitudes we have—which attitudes issue in two responses to determinism.

It was remarked at the beginning of this part of our inquiry that a typical attitude may be regarded as an evaluative thought of something, feelingful and bound up with desire, the mentioned feeling being feeling in a narrow sense, somehow similar to or perhaps involving sensation. (p. 14) Although our fundamental concern has been with the thought within an attitude, and will continue to be so, it will be enlightening to attend particularly to the *nature* of the feeling and desire involved in moral disapproval, partly because all attitudes are in some way fusions of their elements. We might have done so with life-hopes, personal feelings, and, to a lesser extent, our confidence of knowledge.

Certainly, when we disapprove of the husband, we do have feelings about precisely his initiation of his action. It is not that we take his action to have been wrong, and thus have feelings about just it, no doubt pertaining mainly to the effects on his wife, and that for the rest we merely have bare beliefs or ideas about the initiation of the action. Certainly we have feelings about the initiation itself. Again, it is not as if moral disapproval were a matter of taking an action to be wrong, and, for the rest, only wanting to affect the future—wanting to prevent more such actions, or, perhaps more likely, wanting to bring about an act of restitution. Disapproval, to whatever extent it is forward-looking in this way, is not only this.

Consider first certain immediate feelings—*feelings of repugnance*—which perhaps are always involved in moral disapproval, of whatever kind. They need to be clearly distinguished from something else. With respect to the example, these feelings of repugnance have to do with the man's pair of desires, to capture his son's loyalties and affections away from his wife, and to deprive her of a fair share of the monies of the marriage. We have such feelings, too, about his forming of the intention, or deciding, to make the large gift to his son. We are likely to characterize the desires and the decision as shameful, low, or terrible. They have such a character for us, presumably, mainly because of the repugnant state of affairs to which they pertain: the man's wife being in the several ways injured. To regard the desires and intention as shameful, low, or terrible is also to have a feeling about the man. In fact, the two things run together. Whatever his general standing as a moral agent may be, he is now repugnant in having the desires and intention. He is in this episode such a man as does not reject them, knowing their import. The desires and intention are consonant with the whole of a corpus of dispositions.

The feelings of repugnance in question, if connected with intention and action, are not connected in the way of certain feelings to which we are coming. The feelings of repugnance are distantly related to those we have about things or instruments which have a grim or terrible purpose. These feelings are thus not passive, in the way of some aesthetic feelings, but have in them tendencies to action by which, perhaps, they are best identified. They have in them tendencies to withdrawal from, or avoidance of, the husband, or indeed tendencies to more positive action, that of trying to bring an end to, or to change, his persisting desires.

These, to repeat, are not our only feelings in disapproving of him, and they may not be the feelings which are to the fore. The feelings which may be to the fore, and can seem of greater importance, are conveyed to us by the most common expressions of disapproval. To say, if I do, that he has behaved terribly or abominably, that he should not get away with it, is at bottom not to be repelled by his desires or his decision, although I am that, but to be in another way of feeling. To say his wife's subsequent sad state is to be put down to him, or laid at his door, or to say that he is to be held responsible for it, in the most common sense of these expressions as well, is not to be repelled or appalled by his desires or decisions, but to be engaged in more aggressive feeling likely to issue in blame or condemnation. This feeling is other than repugnance.

What is most important for our concerns is the character of this feeling that may be directed at the agent in his act. It is not a tendency of the kind mentioned above, to withdraw from him or avoid him, perhaps to try to reform him, but a tendency to *act against* him. It is, further, a tendency in which we feel ourselves to have justification, the justification of moral principle. This gives to it, clearly, a certain strength and character. We are in fact allowed to be more overt and less restrained here than with the personal feelings (p. 33) where we lack moral sanction.

There can be little doubt that Mill states or overstates a fact when he writes, although not explicitly about moral disapproval, that 'we do not call anything wrong unless we mean to imply that a person ought to be punished in some way or other for doing it'. (1972b (1863), p. 45) Moreover, despite others of his views, having to do with the preventive or deterrent value of punishment, it is clear that he has in mind that in calling something wrong what we mean to imply is not only a need for preventive punishment, but something quite different, what we can call retribution for the act.

It is true, certainly, with respect to moral disapproval, that typically we stop short of the deed, because we take it that punishing a man for an action is not our business, or, say, because we take it that it would not be prudent, or we have some residual doubt about the situation. It is as true that a feeling of disapproval can coexist with a readiness to excuse or half-justify an action, with feelings of pity and with empathetic understanding, and, as already remarked, with the view that the agent in question is in general of decent or good moral standing. All of that qualifies the idea that disapproval may involve retributive feelings, but it does not at all refute it.

There can be no doubt that these feelings which we may have do consist in *retributive desires*. Our feelings consist in desires, which we take to be justified, that the person of whom we disapprove should suffer at least some discomfiture. He should in some degree have distress for the wrong he has done, if perhaps only the distress of knowing that he has the disapproval of others, a disapproval which is not self-concerned or idiosyncratic but is based on moral convictions or principles. What we want is at least that what he has done should be brought home to him. In other cases, perhaps such a case as has been imagined, our desires in disapproving of a man are stronger, and do issue in resolutions to act and of course in actions itself. The spectrum of retributive feelings of disapproval is thus a wide one, but all the feelings are essentially desires that the disapproved person should suffer at least some discomfiture, tendencies to act against him.

More will be said of the exacting of retribution in another context. (Ch. 4) Enough has been said here to raise the question of what beliefs, ideas, or the like are involved in moral approval and disapproval when it includes, as certainly it often does, not only feelings of repugnance and desires to affect future behaviour, but also retributive desires. Put differently, what is our particular attitude of moral disapproval? We shall approach an answer by way of a route different from before. With life-hopes, personal feelings, and knowledge, our procedure was in part to elicit and characterize an attitude, which attitude could then be seen to be inconsistent with determinism. Here let us proceed by first assuming determinism, and asking what can be concluded by way of that assumption with respect to the question of the existence of an attitude.

Suppose then that we do the unusual thing of contemplating that the theory of determinism was true of the vicious husband's action. We contemplate that his relevant thoughts and feelings, and his decision and action, were necessitated events, in the ways specified by the three hypotheses. Suppose we were to move on from merely contemplating this, and came to *believe* it. What effect would this settled acceptance of determinism have on our retributive desire that in some way he be subjected to some distress? There seems little need to linger about the answer. Is it not impossible to avoid the judgement that if we came to *believe* that his action, decision, and all things related to them were necessitated events, our retributive desire for his distress—to say nothing of anything else—would falter, weaken, and collapse? Surely our desire would not survive our coming to have the belief about necessitation.

It is proper to say, despite some misleading suggestions, that our state of feeling would be related to our states of feeling towards machines. If we do in fact manage vindictive personalizing feelings about machines, something close to retributive desires, we cannot persist in them. If we engage in kinds of fantasy or spuriously accusatory rages about things that do not work—a car or a corkscrew—these are but transitory and unsustainable passages of experience.

Will a sceptic say that we cannot judge now that settled belief in determinism would issue in the collapse of our retributive desires? There is a relevant fact here, which will also be of importance at a later stage. (Ch. 3) It gives strength to such scepticism, but not rational support. It is the fact that we, or at any rate very nearly all of us, do not believe any determinism, any determinism that deserves the name. Or, almost all of us within one great tradition of culture do not believe such a thing. More than that, we share a resistance to believing it. This certainly stands in the way of speculation, but it is a difficulty that can be overcome, and needs to be overcome in the interests of truth. In fact we *can* see from present evidence that the retributive desires which may and very often do enter into moral disapproval would in fact not persist if we came really to accept a determinism. It is not that the fact that disbelief in determinism is rooted in nearly all of us, and is one thing fundamental to our view of the human world, actually makes any effects of actually coming to believe it unpredictable. We can have evidence as to those effects in the lesser but clear effects on our feelings which attend the lesser thing—just contemplating that a determinism is true. This can be shown.

To return to the example, and to add something very relevant, suppose that one is at the pitch of one's moral feeling of the given kind about the vicious husband. The facts of the matter have just now become clear, and one's reaction to them is new and strong. Why is it that one is irritated, or more than irritated, by someone who introduces, however tentatively or commonsensically, the idea of a determinism? If we do not imagine this person as an irritating or Olympian figure pleased to bring truth to us from above, a philosophical determinist given to tutorial ways, and do not in any other respect introduce irrelevancies, it may seem that the answer is clear enough.

It can hardly be that we take him to be introducing a falsehood. If we do not take determinism to be true, we do not take it to be false either. It can hardly be, either, that our irritation has to do only with being faced by a relevant proposition of whose truth-value we are uncertain. No doubt our irritation *would* have to do with the intrusion of theory into our lives at an unsuitable moment, but the thought is unavoidable that we are mainly irritated by the possibility of *an obstacle to our own retributive desire*. We are irritated by being faced with an unwelcome excuse, in a way a total excuse, for the man against whom we have retributive feelings.

To accept that such desires would in fact not survive one's coming to believe a determinism is to accept that there exists a kind of our moral disapproval—that we now enter into a kind of moral disapproval—which is inconsistent with determinism. Further, if certain of our desires would falter, weaken, and collapse with the acceptance of a determinism, the reason can only be that one conception of the initiation of actions, whatever it comes to and however it enters into moral approval and disapproval, is inconsistent with determinism. The safely predictable effect on our desires provides us with an indirect argument to those related conclusions.

There can be no doubt as to the sort of conception of action-initiation that is suggested by this indirect argument. It can be indicated by saying, for example, that in taking a man to be morally responsible for an action in the given way, an essential part of what we take to be true is that the action had *an individual explanation*. (Honderich, 1976) It was in a particular sense his doing. That means, in part, that it is not to be explained by his dispositions. It is not explained in such a way that it would follow that another person of like dispositions would in the same situation perform a like action. The explanation, then, is not of a general kind. So to conceive the initiation of his action, certainly, is to have but a vague conception. Its clearest content, in the given respect, is the image of a self, which in fact is not greatly more than a kind of denial of a nomic explanation of action. If we struggle to clarify the idea, we come again to indeterminist pictures of the mind, and above all what is said of an originator and origination.

What we have so far is that an argument beginning from determinism shows that we engage in a certain kind of moral disapproval. That disapproval, involving an image of the self, is inconsistent with determinism. The response of dismay, in connection with moral responsibility, is that since or if a determinism is true, moral responsibility is an illusion. It is such since the truth of the propositional image of the self enters into and is a necessary condition of it. Since or if a determinism is true, our feelings of disapproval and approval for ourselves and others are indefensible.

This dismay, at bottom, has to do with both an apprehension and also a moral uncertainty related to guilt. Is this moral approval and disapproval now not deep-rooted in our lives—on the way to being as deep-rooted as the personal feelings themselves? *Can* it be given up? We must have the apprehension that it cannot. The thought that others cannot in this way be held responsible for their actions also carries the implication that we, in our ongoing feelings, are involved in a falsehood which has certain consequences. Certain of our dispositions to action which cause distress to others rest on falsehood. Here there is cause for moral uncertainty if not guilt.

There is, too, a third and perhaps more direct way in which we may be affected by the idea that moral responsibility of a fundamental kind is illusory. If it is such, *I* am not in this way morally responsible for my actions, and hence not a subject for approval or disapproval. I get no credit of a certain kind, and I am diminished by not being open to judgement. The occasional moral pride I feel rests on illusion, as does what is more common, the lesser feeling that by my life, at least for the most part, I have not earned moral disdain. It must seem, too, that certain feelings of regret, remorse, and guilt are without sense. To think these things is to feel deprived of standing.

Furthermore, to recall what was shown earlier, there is the fact that what is false can be taken as a presupposition of the rest of morality. Only those actions are right or wrong which are actions for which an agent can be held responsible or credited with responsibility. Men and women can be of this or that moral worth only if they can be assigned responsibility for their actions. Is this presupposition not the presupposition of a moral responsibility involving the retributive feelings? In short, to respond with dismay to the issue of determinism and moral responsibility is to be dismayed about the possibility of all of morality. To answer in a certain way the fourth question with which we began, that of the relevance of determinism to moral responsibility, is to be committed to a related answer to the fifth and sixth questions, about the worth of persons and the rightness of actions. (p. 11)

If this moral responsibility is an illusion, there is also another kind of consequence for the connected matters of the worth of persons and the rightness of actions. It was implied earlier that it is at least arguable to take right actions to be those which have certain concomitants and consequences. This consequentialism carries the corollary that good men are of a certain kind. However, as was said, it is also possible to take right actions to be those which have a certain inception in the agent, and again to take good men to be of a related kind. One agent-relative principle of right actions is the Kantian one that we are to do the action which flows from a pure good will. As was asked (p. 61), can it be that this principle in part *defines* right actions as responsible ones, as distinct from presupposing that right actions, somehow defined, are responsible ones? If so, doubt about moral responsibility will have a direct effect on the principle.

Whatever is to be said of the Kantian principle, there is another principle of right actions which definitely *does* bring in responsibility in something other than the presupposing way. It is the principle that we are always to act so that each man gets what he *deserves* for what he has done. For a man to deserve something for an action *is* in part for him to have been responsible for the action. The idea of desert, as distinct from the idea of right action, is itself in part the idea of responsibility. What follows, it seems, is that what we can call the

Principle of Desert must be given up if moral responsibility is an illusion. There is that consequence, and it is a further possible source of dismay. We shall consider it further in connection with the seventh of the questions mentioned at the beginning, that one having to do with the relation of a determinism to large social institutions and practices. (Ch. 4) A main one of these is punishment.

It is clear, then, that our moral disapproval and approval can take the form of an attitude which involves thoughts as to the initiation of action which do not have to do only with voluntariness or willingness —centrally a matter of unconstrained and unconflicting desires on the part of the agent—but also and fundamentally with origination. To have this attitude is inevitably to be dismayed by determinism, and dismayed as well with respect to the matters of right actions and the general moral standing of persons.

However, it can also be made clear that we are the possessors of another attitude, and thus have the possibility of the response of intransigence with respect to moral responsibility and the other matters. The attitude and the response can be brought into view, or rather a part of it can, by seeing more of the size of a certain fact than we did when passing by it earlier. Here too, incidentally, we shall proceed by way of a kind of argument or reflection different from the one employed in connection with life-hopes, personal feelings, and knowledge—and also different from that one just employed in connection with the first of our two attitudes having to do with moral responsibility. To some extent, as already implied, arguments of all these types could be advanced in the case of each of life-hopes and the other six things affected by determinism.

The fact passed by earlier is that our moral feelings, judgements, and activity—our lives in so far as they have to do with the three parts of morality that have been distinguished—are not only reactive but may also be purposive. It is not just that we react in feeling and behaviour to actions and people, but also that we may do so to a certain end. This fact was in sight when it was allowed that moral disapproval does involve wanting to affect the future—to prevent more actions of a certain kind, or to bring about acts of restitution. (p. 64) Also, it was allowed that feelings of repugnance may include tendencies to change or end a person's repugnant desires. (p. 64) It might have been allowed, too, in connection with Mill's claim that our calling things wrong implies a need for punishment, that the punishment in question is not to be conceived entirely in a retributive way but also in a preventive way. (p. 65)

Nothing said so far about moral approval and disapproval, right acts or moral standing provides anything that could be called *an explan-*

ation of the content of ordinary morality. That is, no attempt has been made to specify what purpose we have in morality, considered in terms of its content. To try to give at least a sketch of such a thing is another way, different from the way of reflection on examples, or the assumption of determinism, to bring into view attitudes we have, or to succeed in not overlooking them. The enterprise is peculiarly in place with morality, as against life-hopes, personal feelings, and knowledge, since ordinary morality is a construction of ours in a way that they are not.

In trying to sketch such an explanation of ordinary morality, it is preferable not to fall into speculation about purposes other than our ordinary purposes now, purposes which are open to being discerned without the aid of imagination. (There is something to be said in some contexts for at least a variant of Francis Bacon's alarming opinion that in doing science the imagination is to be hung with weights.) It is therefore preferable to eschew speculation about the original rise of morality, its primitive emergence, or such speculation about all of us as turns up in psychoanalytic theory. The latter theory, whatever insights it includes, is in the view of a great majority of philosophers not such as to satisfy general criteria of conceptual adequacy, evidence, and explanatoriness. What is to be considered, then, is the plain question of why we now have morality, or better, why we give the support we do to it. However, there are presupposed questions which need some prior attention. What, in terms of its content, *is* ordinary morality? *Can* we be said to support it?

As implied a moment ago, the characterization of ordinary morality so far given has for the most part not been concerned with its content. What has been sketched is its several structural parts—responsibility, right acts, moral standing—and their relations, and certain of our moral feelings. That is, not a great deal has been said of the claims in which ordinary morality consists—claims as to what obligations we have, what our ideals should be, and so on. It was noted that different and opposed principles of right action are advocated in moral philosophy. It can be said of almost all of these—including the Principles of Equality and Utility and opposed principles which locate the rightness of actions in intentions or other sources—that they do not give us much of the content of ordinary morality. As remarked above, few of us run our lives by such general principles, and those institutions of society which are in part shaped by morality can hardly be said to be shaped by the general principles. As for several less well-specified general moralities—perhaps the outlook of an established church—their want of specification stands in the way of there being a clear question of what adherents they have, and what institutions they shape.

However, almost all of the philosophical and like moralities can be regarded as having things in common. What they share, unsurprisingly, is also what can also be discerned as the content of ordinary morality. Ordinary morality has been effectively characterized as consisting in four requirements, those of non-maleficence, positive beneficence in some degree, fairness, and non-deception, the latter including a requirement about the keeping of promises and agreements. (Warnock, 1971; cf. Foot, 1978) These are specifications of what actions are right and what men and women are good. We are required, first, to restrain our passions in the pursuit of our own interests, and so not do positive harm to others. We are, secondly, to help others or to seek their good, in certain ways and to certain extents. Thirdly, we are in a sense not to discriminate, but to extend our concern to all the members of relevant classes of individuals rather than only to those who are somehow closer to us. Fourthly, we are for the most part to be truthful. What needs to be added to this, and complicates the matter considerably, is that ordinary morality allows or indeed requires a considerable qualification of all these requirements—in the direction of benefiting those who are close to us or to whom we are in other special relationships, above all our families. To them we are taken to have special obligations. (Cf. Parfit, 1984, pp. 95 ff.)

If the philosophical moralities can be said to have these requirements in common, they do of course give them different shapes and weights. They conceive them differently, and fit them differently into some system. In the case of moralities of justice, of which the morality of the Principle of Equality is one, dominance is given to the third requirement, fairness. Each of the first and second requirements has also been given dominance in philosophical moralities, and truth has also been given at least a precedence in some systems.

Given that these four features provide us with a tolerable characterization of the content of ordinary morality, can we in fact be said to support it? This large question can be given only a fragment of an answer. Certainly our support for morality is in fundamental ways self-interested and thus inconsistent. It is also uncertain. With respect to self-interest and inconsistency, there can be no doubt that ascendant classes within societies construe and manipulate this morality to their advantage, sometimes managing remarkably well to conceal the fact from both others and themselves. Certainly they go beyond what is allowed for by special obligations. It cannot conceivably be said that morality is followed consistently. Marx's importance, it can be supposed, properly rests largely on his determination to record this large fact—the use of morality, law, and a good deal else by ascendant classes—more so than on his philosophical elaboration of the fact in a theory of history which makes morality a part of a society's superstructure, somehow determined by a supporting structure of what are called economic relations and forces. (G. A. Cohen, 1971; cf. Honderich, 1982d) To move quickly from social classes to individuals, it is clear that almost all of us fall into *akrasia*, seeing the better course and following the worse. We are in general not resolute about following the better course as we see it, but uncertain.

Despite these several considerations, however, and others tending in the same direction, we do give *a* support to morality. We are persistently inclined in our lives to kinds of defence of non-maleficence, beneficence, fairness, and truth. Social institutions support these requirements in theory, and to some degree in fact. To be self-interestedly and uncertainly in their support is not to give them no support at all.

To come on to the main question, of why we support morality, it would be strange to suppose that we do not see something to be gained by our support, that our support for it has no advantage to us, that it does not serve an ongoing purpose we have. It would be almost as strange to suppose that all that can be said for our support, or even what can mainly be said for our support, is that it serves the end of satisfying what what have lately been considered, our retributive desires.

Our purpose emerges from our awareness that for several reasons, a principal one being the limited sympathies of individuals as agents, *things are likely to go badly.* (Warnock, 1971) Things are likely to go badly, more precisely, for those other individuals whom agents affect and who are beyond the ranges of sympathy of the agents. As a consequence of the limited sympathy or worse of the husband in the example, things go badly for his wife. We ourselves, in some degree detached from the struggle, have his wife within the range of our sympathy. More generally, our general sympathy with those others whose interests do not directly affect our own, which sympathy is as much a fact about us as our retributive feelings, issues in an attempt to constrain the conduct of agents with respect to their competitors, opponents, and adversaries. The constraints we attempt to place on their conduct are of course constraints having to do with maleficence, non-beneficence, unfairness, and deception. It is not to be forgotten, of course, that each of us, in different circumstances, is agent, victim, and sympathizer. If our third role goes a considerable way to explaining morality, our second must be as important. The purpose of avoiding or limiting the distress of individuals—including ourselves—is the principal explanation of morality.

If we now reconsider moral disapproval, with these general facts in mind, it is possible to come to something different from before. We can very reasonably think and feel that we may disapprove of others in order to serve the purpose of morality, whatever else may be true of our feelings. Better, we can *recall* that we do so. Our disapproving, at least to an important extent, may be a matter of desires pertaining to the future. Those people we select for disapproval, or of course approval, and perhaps for blame or praise, are those whose selection serves our purpose.

Clearly we do not disapprove of all persons who have performed acts which have given rise to unfortunate states of affairs. Some of those who fail to help others, in ways that are generally required, are excused disapproval. So with some of those whose acts go against fairness and truth, and perhaps, depending on how it is conceived, non-maleficence. We disapprove, roughly speaking, of those whose behaviour can be altered by condemnation or blame, and, unless it is altered, will continue to conflict with the requirements of morality and hence our moral purpose. We may have in mind the altering of likely future behaviour somehow related to the act that has been done—perhaps the behaviour of not putting right what has been done, not making restitution for it. We may have in mind altering or preventing likely future behaviour of the same kind as the wrongful action that has been done.

A fuller picture of moral disapproval, in so far as it involves our purpose in morality, can be had by reflecting on groups of persons of whom we do not disapprove, despite the states of affairs to which they give rise or contribute. As might be expected, what turns up in this context is fundamentally like what turned up in connection with one way of thinking and feeling about determinism and life-hopes, and determinism and personal feelings. As might also be expected, and was mentioned earlier, there are certain differences, at least differences of emphasis. The simplest difference is that certain considerations are naturally to the fore with personal feelings and morality, and less so with life-hopes.

We do not morally disapprove of, hold morally responsible, a man who performed an action which we take to have gone against, say, the requirement of fairness, if we believe the action was owed in an essential part to his *want of knowledge* of its effects. He predicted them badly, but to the best of his ability. That is, his desires and intention in the action were perhaps in conformity with fairness, but his possible judgement that his action would conform to fairness was mistaken in some non-culpable way. No doubt we will seek to improve his information or his judgement—our endeavours of this kind are also determined by our purpose in morality—but we take it that his desires and intention, as evidenced in his judgement about the action, were themselves not such as to make it likely that he will again frustrate the purpose of morality. Moral disapproval, which has to do precisely with desires and intentions, is out of place.

We shall not hold responsible, for the same general reason, a man whose action was subject to *external constraint*. We do not think the worse of the Pennines rock-climber who sits where he is, and so fails to get help for his injured companion, if a rock-slide has trapped both of them. His desires and intentions are very likely also acceptable to us, both in themselves and in their relevance to future conduct. We suppose that he does have a disposition to beneficence, such that he would get help but for being trapped.

The point is not the simple one that what he actually does is in part the effect of something external to him, the rock-slide. All of our actions are affected by external facts. What is fundamental to our not disapproving of the climber is not that he was affected in his intentions and action by the rock-slide, but that his desires, intention, and action do not in any way repel us or put us off, and do not suggest any future frustration of the purpose of morality. To say we do not think the worse of him because his action was subject to physical constraint is to say we do not think the worse of him because a fact of the world stood in the way of his acting on his own acceptable disposition to give help. The external fact is not what makes disapproval out of the question, but is consistent with our supposition as to dispositions he has, which dispositions make disapproval out of the question.

Thirdly, we do not disapprove of a man whose action of failing to give help, say, was owed to an effective threat by someone else. My sitting where I am, and not telephoning the police gets me no disapprobation if a man with a gun is sitting across from me. My desires and intentions in so doing do not bode ill for the future, regarded in terms of the aims of morality. The point again is not simply that I am affected by another person's possible action, but that the fact defeats any presumption that my dispositions are not in accord with the purpose of morality. As for the instrinsic nature of my desires and intentions, two things can be said, of which the first is that they are reasonable. The second, which will get more emphasis in the case to which we now go on, is that I may be reluctant to do what in fact I do, which is to sit still.

Suppose, fourthly, that a man desires both to go on drinking as much wine as he does, and also to stop, since his drinking is dragging down his life and thus affecting others. Moreover, with respect to this conflict of desires, he has a third strong desire, which is that his desire to reduce his drinking should be the effective one. It, rather than the desire to go on as he has been, should actually govern his behaviour. Perhaps he has no desire even to have the desire to drink so much. Or, perhaps more likely, he greatly prefers the desire to reduce his drinking to be the one that issues in action. Or, he unequivocally judges that it is morally right, given the effect on his family, that the desire to reduce his drinking have sway over the other. The judgement is sincere, in no way suspect. Suppose, however, despite his feelings to the contrary, that what actually happens is that he goes on drinking as before. (Cf. Frankfurt, 1971; Slote, 1980)

Our attitude to him will be one governed by the firmness of our belief about his second-order desire, preference, or judgement. If we have a settled belief that his second-order desire is strong, and unopposed by a second-order desire going the other way, or that his second-order preference is indeed great, or that his moral judgement is an unequivocal and committed one, we shall at least be impeded in any disapproval of him. We may be puzzled about what it is that explains his going on drinking excessively, but we shall have to suppose that there *is* something more, perhaps a bodily fact, a bodily cause of alcoholism, which is of relevance to the situation. We shall not be fully disposed to hold his behaviour against him.

One reason will be that he will not respond to our doing so. That is, given that he already has a commitment to only moderate drinking, which commitment is unfortunately inefficacious, it must seem that blame would have no use. That is on the assumption, of course, that the facts are indeed as they have been described. If we suppose, differently, that some strengthening of his second-order desire, preference, or judgement would have the desirable effect of reducing his drinking, we shall be differently disposed. A second reason for our not being disposed to blame him is that certain of his desires and intentions are tolerable or indeed impressive. Conjoined with something else, the upshot is that he is running down his life, and hurting others. None the less, in virtue of his second-order disposition, and the struggle that his life involves, he himself is unlikely to have our revulsion. Certainly we shall try to inhibit any such tendencies we feel.

Fifthly, and briefly, we do not disapprove of the insane for their conduct. At any rate we do not do so if we have certain beliefs about their desires and intentions. Sixthly, we do not disapprove of the very young. It can be said that they are the victims of their desires, often desires which are owed in some direct way to their environments. They have not come to that maturity in which one actually has an awareness of an attitude towards one's desires, as distinct from their objects. They do not have second-order desires, preferences, or judgements.

Given this brisk survey, we can draw a certain conclusion, or better, perceive a certain fact. As must be expected from the discernible purpose of morality, we do have a certain attitude of moral disapproval, and of moral approval, different from the one previously considered. We do feel moral disapproval for or hold responsible those whose behaviour can be altered, and, unless it is altered, will continue to conflict with the requirements of morality and hence our moral purpose. We do feel moral approval for those whose behaviour can be confirmed, and so will continue to accord with the requirements of morality and hence our moral purpose.

We do have an attitude of moral approval and disapproval, which, in so far as the initiation of an action is concerned, is centred on a certain set of facts, those we have surveyed. To order them differently, they are the facts that the agent is mature and sane, acts out of a certain knowledge, does not act out of a certain conflict of desires, and is not subject to external constraint by either his situation or another person. If we return to the example of the vicious husband, it is certainly possible to take an attitude to him which is informed by just such ideas.

They could be elaborated in various ways. More could be said which would draw on a general inquiry into the nature of all actions. For example, more could be said of the relation between the antecedents of the action and the action itself—say the degree to which the action is represented by its intentions. More could be said, certainly, in enlargement of reflection on desires for desires. Here we could attempt richer accounts of personality, character, and mental life. In place of speaking of desired desires, we might speak instead of the unified, unconflicted, and directed person. We could consider the question, in developing such a picture of the person, of a higher order of desires than the second. None of this is essential the conclusion to which we have come—that we are possessors of attitudes of moral disapproval and approval which importantly have to do with our purpose in morality.

As at like points before now in our inquiry into the consequences of determinism, no question can arise over the logical consistency of a determinism and the given ideas as to the initiation of action. An action whose initiation has the given set of properties is perfectly consistent, in particular, with the three hypotheses. It can be said, incidentally, with the aid of certain definitions which themselves give expression to the attitude we are contemplating, that not only moral responsibility but also 'free will' is logically consistent with the three hypotheses. A man's will in an action is defined as the desire that actually moved him to act as he did. His will was free, it can be said, if

it was the desire which he himself desired to be effective, and so on.
(Frankfurt, 1971)

The response of intransigence with respect to a determinism and
moral responsibility rests in part on the reassuring fact of consistency.
It rests as well on the intrinsic recommendation of the given ideas as to
the initiation of action: they are the ideas that accord with the purpose
of morality. We can feel that the truth of a determinism is consistent
with what principally matters in connection with moral responsibility. A determinism is to be allowed to be inconsistent with
something else, a certain image, that of the self, and hence with
retributive feelings which are central to the definition of a different
attitude. We lose nothing of value, so far as our rational purpose in
morality is concerned, if we abandon the image, those feelings, and the
given attitude. They are irrelevant to our purpose. So we can feel—
while we persist in intransigence with respect to moral responsibility.

What remains to be said is something about a conceivable misconstruction of the attitude that we now have in view, an attitude which
has to do only with voluntariness, and not also with origination. The
misconstruction consists in mistakenly taking the given attitude for
something else, which can be called *the objective attitude*. It is an
attitude which we may take up to a mixed group of individuals whom
we believe to be wholly immature, perhaps permanently so, or to suffer
from a severe disorder of mind, personality, or feeling. They may be
deluded, deranged, or entirely untouched by the distress of others and
hence bereft of the usual restraint owed to sympathy and a moral
sense.

Such people are regarded by us as individuals to be managed, treated,
controlled, trained, guarded against, detained for their own protection,
or imprisoned for the safety of others. In general, our attitudes to such
individuals are attitudes of a detached and at least a manipulative or
managing kind. Our attitudes are informed by *no more than the desire
to take efficacious steps in dealing with problems, challenges, and
dangers*. In place of resentment at an insult or a piece of offensiveness,
we may be taken up instead with devising the most efficacious policy,
treatment, or the like.

The objective attitude, as specified, *does* share something with the
attitudes of moral approval and disapproval with which we have lately
been concerned. That similarity may perhaps lead to the idea that the
attitudes with which we have been concerned are not true moral
attitudes at all. It may be objected that to have what is in fact an
attitude of moral disapproval to someone is not merely to be concerned
to affect his behaviour, to take the most efficacious steps to avoiding
certain future possibilities. It may be objected that latterly in our

inquiry we set out to discriminate a certain attitude *of moral disapproval*, and come to something that is nothing of the sort, but no more than the objective attitude.

The proper reply is that while the attitudes that have lately been discriminated do indeed have a character that derives in part from our purpose in morality, that is not all that is to be said of them. The given attitude of moral disapproval is indeed one, as was said initially (p. 70), that *importantly* is a matter of desires pertaining to the future. *In part* it is that. The given attitude, none the less, if it shares something with the objective attitude, is evidently also different from it—as must be expected from the simple fact that the given attitude is specified as *not* having to do with those who are either insane or very immature. The line of thought we are considering depends on taking the objective attitude as specified: informed by no more than the desire to take efficacious steps in dealing with problems, challenges and dangers. That is *not* a full or proper characterization of the attitudes having to do with moral responsibility that we have been considering.

A full and proper characterization will include what has not much concerned us, but must be included: what were earlier called feelings of repugnance. (p. 64) These were noticed not in connection with the attitudes that have lately been discriminated, which have to do only with voluntariness, but in connection with the earlier attitudes considered, which have to do with both voluntariness and origination. However, feelings of repugnance are as much a part of the attitude of disapproval lately discussed. Their being such distinguishes what we have from the objective attitude as defined, and goes a good way to making evident that what we have is in fact a recognizable attitude of *moral disapproval*. If it is now supposed, differently, that these feelings are to be assumed to be part of the *objective attitude*, the argument we have been considering loses its force. It becomes uncertain that the objective attitude, as now defined, is not recognizably moral.

More can be said to distinguish the discriminated attitude of moral disapproval from the objective attitude as originally or lately defined. It is a part of the discriminated attitude, although there has been no need to mention the fact until now, to give a kind of consideration to the person in question, the person of whom we disapprove. That is, his or her views are to be considered. This part of the discriminated attitude, which cannot be clarified quickly, has no real counterpart in the objective attitude as defined. Further, it is part of the discriminated attitude, although unmentioned until now, to present *reasons* to others. It is not as if morally disapproving of someone, in the given way, were no more than doing whatever would get him to act in a certain way. It is, rather, a matter of *argument*.

The objective attitude was first characterized in the distinguished essay mentioned earlier (p. 36) which first widened consideration of the consequences of determinism. (P. F. Strawson, 1962; cf. 1985, Ch. 2) The central theme of that essay, which does not reflect the main contentions of our own inquiry, cannot easily be related to them, but it does suggest a further contention.

It is that the mistaken view of the attitude that has lately been discriminated—the mistaken view of it as being tantamount to the objective attitude—has a further consequence. The mistake, and only the mistake, causes us to think of and to move to the other attitude, the one that issues in dismay. To put the matter differently, it may be contended that it is only those who have a quite insufficient grasp of the attitude of moral approval and disapproval lately discriminated, and so take it not to be a recognizable moral attitude at all, who are moved in the direction of the attitude involving both voluntariness and origination, and issuing in dismay. The contention would therefore leave us with the proposition that those who have a full and proper understanding of the attitude lately discriminated will have no other inclination. They will not also be inclined to require both voluntariness and origination in connection with moral approval and disapproval.

The contention is mistaken. Our present concern is the attitude having to do only with voluntariness and issuing in intransigence. It is not the case, however, that when that attitude is rightly seen or recalled, we thereafter have no other inclination. We *can*, by considerations of the kind set out before (pp. 64 ff.), find ourselves thinking and feeling differently. We do not get to the attitude having to do with both voluntariness and origination by having a mistaken understanding of the attitude having to do only with voluntariness. Rather, we find good grounds in ourselves.

1.8 CONCLUSION

What has been said of the first four of the listed areas of consequence with respect to determinism—life-hopes, personal feelings, knowledge, and moral responsibility—suggests what we can take to be the case, without further inquiry, with respect to the fifth and sixth matters, right actions and the moral standing of persons. Because of the connection of these matters with moral responsibility, as already suggested in part, we here have two discriminable attitudes and may make two responses. Or, to say the very least, each of us is capable of two attitudes and the two responses. The attitudes and responses are not so definite, but the situation is not so different from what we have as to require us to pause over it.

In sum, then, we may focus on a conception of the initiation of action which has in it an image of origination in addition to ideas of voluntariness. In so doing we take it that origination is a necessary condition of what is in question—life-hopes, personal feelings, knowledge, or the parts of morality. On the other hand, we may focus on a different conception of the initiation of action, which has to do only with voluntariness, and have attitudes involving only it. If we give our attention to origination as well as voluntariness, we fall into dismay in all cases. If we attend only to the voluntariness of actions, and give it a certain regard, which we can, we may and are likely to make the response of intransigence.

We have not much delayed, in our survey, to reflect on the general nature of an attitude or feeling, or to enter into an ongoing philosophical discussion of attitudes and like things. It is, although attitudes are not exactly emotions, the discussion having to do with the analysis of emotion. (Leighton, 1985; Kraut, 1986; Solomon, 1986) We have, rather, proceeded on the basis of a quite standard view, roughly to the effect that an attitude is no relatively simple or unitary thing—not, say, a sensation-like feeling or a judgement—but rather is an evaluative and feelingful thought bound up with desires. So too is a response such a complex or fusion, although we have not looked into that at all.

If our concern had been the philosophical analysis of an attitude or feeling, we would have considered much more of the relations of the elements within them, or rather, their somewhat different relations in different attitudes. We would also have considered the several confusing ways we have of thinking and speaking of them. For example, as has been apparent, to be describable as 'having an attitude of moral disapproval', taken as *including* the thought of the voluntariness of an action, is also to be in a state which falls under the description of 'taking the attitude that the voluntariness of the action justifies disapproval'—which latter description makes the thought *external* to the disapproval in the given sense. Further, if our enterprise had been the analysis of attitudes, we should have given more attention to physiological states or changes. (Lyons, 1980; Alston, 1967; Budd, 1985)

None of this, of which something more will need to be said in another connection (pp. 110 ff.), has been necessary to the enterprise in hand. It has been, to repeat, the enterprise of establishing the broad fact that each of us has or tends to have each of two inconsistent attitudes with respect to consequences of determinism, and each of us in the first instance may make two inconsistent responses. Each of the families of attitudes is natural. In itself each attitude involves us in no incoherence or any like thing. It is certainly not something which is put upon us by theory—certainly not by philosophers—but something we find in ourselves. So with the responses.

Clearly this situation calls for further reflection. In particular, it is no satisfactory situation and appears to face us with a kind or kinds of choice. Despite what has been said of the defensibility of an attitude or a response in itself, there must be a question about attitudes, and, above all, the question of whether dismay or intransigence or some third response is, as we can say, our best course. There is also the further matter, so far left untouched, of determinism's seventh area of consequence—social institutions, practices, and habits.

Before coming to those further and culminating stages of our inquiry, there is one other issue to be considered. Indeed it is rather more than what is properly called an issue. It is *the traditional philosophical dispute as to the consequences of determinism*. If we have not yet resolved the problem of the consequences of determinism, we have quite enough on hand to deal with the traditional dispute. What is still to be said, in the further stages of our inquiry, will be of the order of what has been said already—it will have to do with attitudes and responses. If we have not yet seen all of the possibilities of our situation, we have seen that it is, so to speak, fundamentally a situation of attitudes and responses. That general fact is established, and is enough in order to deal with the traditional philosophical dispute as to the consequences of determinism.

2

Compatibilism and Incompatibilism

2.1 A LONG BATTLE

The claim that we have two attitudes in the case of each of the consequence-areas of determinism, and the claim that in the first instance we do or may make two responses, and a further claim to be advanced in due course about a choice to be made from these two responses and another—these three claims will be thrown into sharper definition and their distinctiveness clarified if we look at the long battle, the traditional dispute, about the consequences of determinism. It is this traditional dispute about consequences between two parties, rather than the subjects of the conceptual adequacy and the truth of determinism, that has most engaged philosophers, at any rate philosophers within the main current of philosophy in the English language. It is a dispute carried forward as zealously now as in the past.

There is also a second reason, other than the making of a clear distinction between doctrines, for looking at the long battle. The two parties to it, Compatibilists and Incompatibilists, or exponents of freedom as voluntariness and exponents of freedom as voluntariness plus origination, propound the principal alternatives to the contentions of Chapter 1 about the consequences of determinism, which contentions will be defended further and added to in what follows, centrally by way of an answer to the question of the choice among responses. Any adequate defence of these contentions depends in part on an argued rejection of their entrenched alternatives, alternatives which have always been thought and sometimes declared to exhaust the possibilities. (G. Strawson, 1986, p. 6) That very definitely they do not is a principal contention of this examination of the consequences of determinism.

Our clarificatory purpose in particular will be securely served by allowing Compatibilists and Incompatibilists to speak for themselves. They themselves, that is, will establish the distinction in question. Also, the quoting of considerable passages from their works will be as quick and effective a way of exposition as any other. In fact we shall do little more than glance at the long battle. In the seventeenth century it was already a controversy of which Hobbes could say that it had given rise to 'vast and involuble volumes . . . which fill not only our libraries but the world with their noise and disturbance.' (1839–45, (c. 1650), Vol. iv, p. 234) It has since persisted, if a bit more quietly. By one reckoning it is something like four centuries old. (Kenny, 1975, p. 123) It may well be older. By another reckoning it began, along with the dispute about the truth of determinism, with the Stoic philosophers of the several centuries before and after Christ. (Sorabji, 1980, Ch. 4, Ch. 14; Huby, 1967) The fact of its longevity need not be dispiriting. It need not make one abandon hope of a solution. As we shall also see, to claim to have the solution, as I do, may not be entirely vainglorious.

The materials of the dispute were certainly in existence before the dispute—or before its clear beginning. Among the many distinctions made by Aristotle between causes, disposition, origins, originating principles and the like, one is of importance to us. The following passage is from the *Eudemian Ethics*.

. . . if anything existent may have the opposite to its actual qualities, so of necessity may its principles. For what results from the necessary is necessary; but the results of the contingent might be the opposite of what they are; what depends on men themselves forms a great portion of contingent matters, and men themselves are the sources of such contingent results. (1915 (c.350 BC), 1222^b)

There is obscurity in this, and more in the surrounding passages, and certainly ground for objection, all of which may be owed in part to the historical transmission of the original text and by difficulties of translation. Aristotle's thought, or one of his thoughts, appears to run as follows. Each existent thing has a character which is in some way shared by whatever it is from which the thing comes. A thing which *necessarily* happens must have a like source—it too must occur necessarily. A thing which does not necessarily happen, and thus which might have been otherwise, or might not have happened, must also have a like source, such that this source might have been otherwise or might not have existed. At least some of a man's actions are such that they might not have occurred. They must depend on something of a certain kind in him. Perhaps it can be speculated that this thing, for Aristotle, is *a somehow sufficient cause that may or may not operate*. (Cf. Kenny, 1979, Ch. 7)

In the *Metaphysics* (1048^{a}3 f.), at any rate, according to one translation, we have the enlargement that

. . . it is necessary in the case of non-rational powers that when an agent and a patient are brought together the action and effect take place, whereas in the case of rational powers this is not necessary; for every one of the non-rational powers can have but a single effect, whereas the rational can have contrary effects, so that if they were under the same necessity as are the irrational they would have contrary effects at the same time. But this is impossible. It is necessary, accordingly, that something else be decisive in rational action; I mean wanting or deliberate choice. (Kenny, 1975, p. 124)

What we have added here is roughly that a man has a *rational power*, which power can give rise to contrary effects, his doing of one thing or another—say his voting for or against Pericles. A rational power is therefore different in kind from a non-rational power or ordinary disposition, which issues in just a single effect. If we ask how a rational power gives rise to what it actually does give rise to, say voting for Pericles, we cannot suppose this is a matter of necessitation, since, by some sort of parity of reasoning, we should have to conclude that it also necessitates voting against Pericles. But voting for and against Pericles is impossible. Hence rational powers not only can give rise to contrary actions, but these actions are not necessitated. Such a power consists in deliberative choice.

In Book Six of the *Nicomachean Ethics* (1139^{a}30 f.) more is said of rational power or deliberative choice.

The origin of conduct—its efficient, not its final, cause—is choice; and the origin of choice is appetition plus means–end reasoning. So without understanding and reasoning on the one hand, and moral character on the other, there is no such thing as choice; for without reasoning and character there is neither well-doing nor its opposite. Reasoning, in itself, moves nothing; only means–end reasoning concerned with conduct. . . . for good conduct is the end in view, and that is the object of the appetition. Therefore choice is either appetitive intelligence or ratiocinative appetite. (Kenny, 1975, p. 16)

Something of what is intended here, again roughly, is that the efficient cause of a man's action, which efficient cause is choice, has essentially to do with desire or the like and also with reasoning about means to an end, the end being the goal or final cause of the action. The reasoning in itself would not issue in action. Desire or the like for the end is also necessary. Choice is thus desirous means–end reasoning. (Cf. Kenny, 1979, Ch. 2)

In the ideas of these three passages—ideas of a somehow sufficient but non-necessitating source or principle of action, of a rational power which can give rise to either of two upshots, and of choice as desirous reasoning—we clearly have an antecedent, perhaps the prime antecedent, of indeterminist pictures of the mind, and in particular the idea of an originator. In certain essential respects it is about as contentful as those pictures, which is not to say very contentful.

Earlier in the *Nicomachean Ethics*, in Book Three (1109^{b}30 f.),

Aristotle is directly concerned with morality, and in this connection offers his well-known account of what can be called voluntary action.

> ... moral excellence or virtue has to do with feelings and actions. These may be voluntary or involuntary. It is only to the former that we assign praise or blame, though when the involuntary are concerned we may find ourselves ready to condone and on occasion to pity. It is clearly, then, incumbent on the student of moral philosophy to determine the limits of the voluntary and involuntary. ... Actions are commonly regarded as involuntary when they are performed (a) under compulsion, (b) as the result of ignorance. An act, it is thought, is done under compulsion when it originates in some external cause of such a nature that the agent or person subject to the compulsion contributes nothing to it. Such a situation is created, for example, when a sea captain is carried out of his course by a contrary wind or by men who have got him in their power. But the case is not always so clear. ... An involuntary act being one performed under compulsion or as the result of ignorance, a voluntary act would seem to be one of which the origin or efficient cause lies in the agent, he knowing the particular circumstances in which he is acting. (1953 (c.350 BC), p. 77, p. 81)

Again there are problems of interpretation, some of them having to do with the fact that the relevant Greek terms are only inadequately rendered into the English terms 'voluntary' and 'involuntary', or indeed into any other English terms. What we can take away from Aristotle's discussion, of which the given passage preserves no more than the main theme, is that there are certain things, having to do with ignorance and compulsion, which are commonly regarded as standing in the way of a man's action being voluntary, and hence his having praise or blame for it. Certain conditions which must be satisfied if a man's action is to be voluntary—in one understanding they are necessary conditions but do not comprise a sufficient condition—are that the cause of his action lay within him, and he acted in a knowledge of what he was doing.

Aristotle in another place in the *Nicomachean Ethics* appears to bring together the first three passages, having to do with origination, with the fourth, having to do with voluntariness, into something like a logically necessary and sufficient condition, in so far as the initiation of action is concerned, for moral approval and disapproval, for crediting a person with responsibility for something or holding a person responsible for something.

> It is when the act is voluntary that the moral issue presents itself. We blame the doer and, with that, his deed becomes an unjust act. ... By a voluntary action, let me repeat, I mean one which (a) it was in the agent's power to do or not to do, (b) he performs not in ignorance but with full knowledge of the person affected by his action, the instrument he is using, the object he seeks to

attain, (c) in no particular is determined by accident or *force majeure*. (1953 (c.350 BC), p. 159)

There are, it is to be admitted, some difficulties in taking this fifth passage as an amalgamation of the first three and the fourth. Here we clearly have 'voluntary' used in a wider sense than in the fourth passage, and as we have been using it in our own inquiry. But it seems a secure assumption that Aristotle takes us to have it that moral responsibility for an action to depend both on its deriving from rational power or desirous means–end reasoning, and its being voluntary in the narrow sense, where voluntariness is only a matter of the absence of compulsion and ignorance.

Aristotle can hardly be said to consider seriously any clarified thesis of determinism (Sorabji, 1980; Huby, 1967), although in one passage in the *Nicomachean Ethics* he reports on a deterministic argument which he then quickly and carelessly rejects. (1953 (c.350 BC), p. 92) Clearly, however, he has an idea of determinism.

My principal interest in him has to do with two matters, two speculations, connected with what is plainly true, that he took rational power to be an indubitable fact. The first and most important speculation is in part that he claims or would have claimed that all men or all clear-headed men have a certain conception of the initiation of action, which conception has to do with rational power as well as voluntariness. Further, all men see that it is rational power as well as voluntariness that is a necessary condition of moral approval and disapproval. All men agree, as a matter of a single, settled conception having to do with the initiation of action, that this approval and disapproval would be impossible if men lacked choice or rational power as conceived. They would agree that the mere voluntariness of an action, voluntariness in the narrow sense, having to do with ignorance and compulsion, would not be sufficient to preserve the agent's moral responsibility for it. They have some sort of settled belief to this effect. Further, their settled belief as to rational power is, and is taken by them as, a belief inconsistent with determinism.

Given this speculative understanding of Aristotle, what stands in the way of his being described as our first Incompatibilist is not greatly more than the implication that the dispute existed within the Greek philosophy of his time. As remarked earlier, it seems not to have. That is, there may have been no exponents of freedom as no more than voluntariness—a freedom consistent with determinism.

A second and certainly more secure speculation, well supported by the general tenor of Aristotle's work, is that he would take the fact of a man's rational power to be itself a fact which confers a status upon him. It separates him from the brute world of non-rational powers. The

our approval and disapproval. The question of moral responsibility is unaffected by an acceptance of determinism.

(v) Less precisely, as the second passage indicates and as other passages demonstrate (1839–45 (c.1659)b, pp. 274–5), Hobbes can be said to be *captured* by a determinism. It consists not merely in truth, but in truth of great sway, truth which must carry all before it. His commitment to a determinism is not unlike Aristotle's commitment to rational power or origination.

(vi) Finally, and importantly, Hobbes takes the claims of his philosophical opponents in the Aristotelian tradition to be the product of no more than confusion, a confusion produced by philosophical and theological custom. They have not done all that is necessary, which is to attend to their own thoughts and words.

His adversary, Bishop Bramhall, was taken to be opposed to him on all counts. In fact there is an agreement between them, and between them and others, which is fundamental to the argument now being pursued in this inquiry. However, Bramhall is absolutely persuaded that anyone worth attending to has a determinate conception of liberty not far from that of Aristotle—according to our speculation about Aristotle—and hence he is wholly disdainful of the definition of liberty as no more than voluntariness.

> . . . true Liberty consists in the elective power of the rational will. . . . Reason is the root, the fountain, the original of true Liberty which judgeth and representeth to the will, whether this or that be convenient, whether this or that be more convenient. Judge then what a pretty kind of liberty it is which is maintained by T.H., such a liberty as in little children before they have the use of reason, before they can consult or deliberate of anything. Is not this a Childish Liberty? and such a liberty as in brute beasts, as bees and spiders . . . ? Is not this a ridiculous liberty? Lastly (which is worse than all these) such a liberty as a river hath to descend down the channel. . . . Such is T.H.'s liberty. . . . T.H. appeals to every man's experience. I am contented. Let everyone reflect upon himself . . . . (1676, pp. 651–2)

Bramhall like Aristotle also takes man's rational power, the supposed fact of origination, as distinct from voluntariness, to be that which gives significance and dignity to human existence. In Bramhall's case, this is intimately connected with religious belief, and in particular doctrines of righteousness, sin, and a divinely ordered scheme of things.

Hume, although he is sometimes cited as the founder of the tradition of Compatibilism, of freedom as voluntariness, does not advance greatly beyond Hobbes in fundamental conceptions, as can be seen from the following famous passages. Still, they have shaped, indeed governed, the tradition of Compatibilism, and are as important as any to be considered.

It is true, if men attempt the discussion of questions which lie entirely beyond the reach of human capacity, such as those concerning the origin of worlds, or the economy of the intellectual system or region of spirits, they may long beat the air in their fruitless contests, and never arrive at any determinate conclusion. But if the question regard any subject of common life and experience, nothing, one would think, could preserve the dispute so long undecided but some ambiguous expressions, which keep the antagonists still at a distance, and hinder them from grappling with each other.

This has been the case in the long disputed question concerning liberty and necessity; and to so remarkable a degree that, if I am not much mistaken, we shall find, that all mankind, both learned and ignorant, have always been of the same opinion with regard to this subject, and that a few intelligible definitions would immediately have put an end to the whole controversy. . . .

I hope, therefore, to make it appear that all men have ever agreed in the doctrine both of necessity and of liberty, according to any reasonable sense, which can be put on these terms; and that the whole controversy has hitherto turned merely upon words. (1963 (1748), p. 81)

After making use of his definition of causation as constant conjunction in his argument for determinism, Hume comes on to his definition of freedom.

. . . to proceed in this reconciling project with regard to the question of liberty and necessity; the most contentious question of metaphysics, the most contentious science; it will not require many words to prove, that all mankind have ever agreed in the doctrine of liberty as well as in that of necessity, and that the whole dispute . . . has been hitherto merely verbal. For what is meant by liberty, when applied to voluntary actions? We cannot surely mean that actions have so little connexion with motives, inclinations, and circumstances, that one does not follow with a certain degree of uniformity from the other, and that one affords no inference by which we can conclude the existence of the other. For these are plain and acknowledged matters of fact. By liberty, then, we can only mean *a power of acting or not acting, according to the determinations of the will*: that is, if we choose to remain at rest, we may; if we choose to move, we also may. Now this hypothetical liberty is universally allowed to belong to every one who is not a prisoner and in chains. Here, then, is no subject of dispute. (1963 (1748), p. 95)

He then maintains that his liberty, voluntariness, which is wholly consistent with necessity, is in effect universally believed to be all that is essential to moral approval and disapproval, and to commendation and condemnation. Indeed, for us to add something else would be destructive. We see that necessity, the very denial of origination, *is* required for praise or blame.

. . . necessity . . . has universally, though tacitly, in the schools, in the pulpit, and in common life, been allowed to belong to the will of man, and no one has ever pretended to deny that we can draw inferences concerning human actions, and that those inferences are founded on the experienced union of like actions with like motives, inclinations and circumstances. . . . The only proper object of hatred or vengeance is a person or creature, endowed with thought and consciousness; and when any criminal or injurious actions excite that passion, it is only by their relation to the person, or connexion with him. Actions are, by their very nature, temporary and perishing; and where they proceed not from some cause in the character and disposition of the person who performed them, they can neither redound to his honour, if good; nor infamy, if evil. . . . as they proceeded from nothing in him that is durable and constant, and leave nothing of that nature behind them, it is impossible he can, upon their account, become the object of punishment or vengeance. According to the principle, therefore, which denies necessity, and consequently causes, a man is as pure and untainted, after having committed the most horrid crime, as at the first moment of his birth, nor is his character anywise concerned in his actions, since they are not derived from it, and the wickedness of the one can never be used as a proof of the depravity of the other. (1902 (1748), pp. 97–8)

For Hume as for Hobbes, (i) it is plain that we all share a single firm conception with respect to freedom which must be decisive in settling the problem of liberty and necessity. All men have ever agreed, and could not mean otherwise by their words. (ii) It is said or at the very least implied, further, that we have a belief to the effect that this freedom alone is the prerequisite of disapproval, hatred, blame, and vengeance. (iii) To add a denial of necessity to this freedom—to add origination to voluntariness—would in fact make moral disapproval and the like impossible. (iv) The acceptance of a determinism leaves moral responsibility precisely where it was, given the compatibility of determinism and voluntariness. That nothing changes can be no surprise for the additional reason just mentioned, that moral responsibility *presupposes* a determinism. (v) Importantly, the whole problem of liberty and necessity is an intellectual or theoretical one. It is to be settled by putting a few intelligible definitions in place of ambiguous expressions, by attending to what we mean.

Kant accepts that all that of which we have experience, including all the springs of our own actions, are subject to a determinism. It is, of course, a foundation of his philosophy that the very existence of our experience is in a way dependent on universal causality. Every aspect of my performance of an action, then, and all of what preceded it, considered in terms of ordinary reality, or in its 'empirical character', conforms to 'the laws of causal determination'. (1950 (1781), p. 468).

However, the existence of moral obligations is no less indubitable a fact, if a fact about another order, another realm. That I am sometimes culpable for an action, and to be blamed for it, is such a fact. It inescapably follows that I performed it freely. As for what this comes to,'. . . we must understand . . . by the term freedom . . . a faculty of the spontaneous origination of a state; the causality of which, therefore, is not subordinated to another cause determining it in time.' (1943 (1781), p. 300) This faculty is one of Reason.

The seeming contradiction is escaped, in Kant's view, by the idea that the faculty of origination can also be regarded as outside the realm of experience. It is not in its 'empirical character', but in its 'intelligible character', that 'the faculty of spontaneous origination' can be truly so described. (1950 (1781), p. 300) Very evidently this way of dealing with the unavoidable idea that 'the freedom ascribed to the will seems to stand in contradiction to natural necessity' (1959 (1785), p. 75) bears no relation whatever to the Compatibilism of Hobbes and Hume. The latter makes no use of an idea of two realms.

The doctrine is most plainly expressed by Kant in the following passage from the *Critique of Pure Reason*, which is free of his usual technicalities.

... let us take a voluntary action, for example, a malicious lie by which a certain confusion has been created in society. First of all, we endeavour to discover the motives to which it has been due and then, secondly, in the light of these, we proceed to determine how far the action and its consequences can be imputed to the offender. As regards the first question, we trace the empirical character of the action to its sources, finding these in defective education, bad company, in part also in the viciousness of a natural disposition insensitive to shame, in levity and thoughtlessness. .... We proceed in this inquiry just as we should in ascertaining for a given natural effect the series of its determining causes. But although we believe that the action is thus determined, we none the less blame the agent, not indeed on account of his unhappy disposition, nor on account of the circumstances that have influenced him, nor even on account of his previous way of life; for we presuppose that we can leave out of consideration what this way of life may have been, that we can regard the past series of conditions as not having occurred and the act as being completely unconditioned by any preceding state, just as if the agent in and by himself began in this action an entirely new series of consequences. Our blame is based on a law of reason whereby we regard reason as a cause that irrespective of all the above-mentioned empirical conditions could have determined, and ought to have determined, the agent to act otherwise. This causality of reason we do not regard as only a co-operating agency, but as complete in itself, even when the sensuous impulses do not favour but are directly opposed to it; the action is ascribed to the agent's intelligible character; in the moment when he utters the lie, the guilt is entirely his. Reason, irrespective of all empirical conditions of the act, is completely free, and the lie is entirely due to its default. (1950 (1781), p. 477)

As for the idea that the freedom required for morality might consist in voluntariness alone, it is dismissed by Kant in the following passage from the *Critique of Practical Reason*.

Suppose I say of a man who has committed a theft that this act by the natural law of causality is a necessary result of the determining ground existing in the preceding time and that it was therefore impossible that it could have not been done.... how can he be called free at this point of time with reference to this action, when in this moment and in this action he stands under inexorable natural necessity? It is a wretched subterfuge to seek an escape in the supposition that the kind of determining grounds of his causality according to natural law agrees with a comparative concept of freedom. According to this concept, what is sometimes called 'free effect' is that of which the determining natural cause is internal to the acting thing. For example, that which a projectile performs when it is in free motion is called by the name 'freedom' because it is not pushed by anything external while it is in flight.... So one might call the actions of a man free because they are actions caused by ideas we have produced by our own powers, whereby desires are evoked on occasion of circumstances and thus because they are actions brought about at our own pleasure; in this sense they are called free even though they are necessary because their determining grounds have preceded them in time. With this manner of argument many allow themselves to be put off and believe that with a little quibbling they have found the solution to the difficult problem which centuries have sought in vain and which could hardly be expected to be found so completely on the surface. (1949 (1788), p. 99)

These passages do not give greatly more of Kant's view than a general impression. They overlook distinctions and doctrines expounded elsewhere. Nor shall I give more than an impression of why it is hard to demur when the view is described as 'a hopeless failure'—a description put on it in a full account of Kant's philosophy. (R. Walker, 1978, p. 148; cf. Boyle, Grisez, Tollefsen, 1976, pp. 112–15) There is no possibility of thinking that the contradiction between a determinism and origination is in fact avoided by trying to put Reason, the faculty of the will, character or whatever into two realms. Further, if the contradiction *could* be argued to be avoided by this division, then the originating will is wholly subtracted from the world of choices, decisions, and moral responsibility. That which actually does originate is quite removed from our actual subject-matter, the one to which we must attend.

As for the argument that moral responsibility must be regarded as such a kind of fact as licenses an inference to the existence of what it is taken to presuppose, origination, and in some way a denial of determinism, it is an argument that has to some extent persisted. It has lately been refurbished in a considerable defence of Free Will. (van Inwagen, 1983) For reasons that may already be apparent, and will become clearer, having to do essentially with the presumed *fact* of moral responsibility, it seems to me an argument without force. In a sentence, it is an argument which moves from desires and the like as to the nature of reality to a factual conclusion about the nature of reality.

Our present concern, however, is neither the attempt to avoid the inconsistency of determinism and origination, nor the argument for origination, but the consequences of determinism. Kant's view is very relevant to this. My purpose has been to illustrate a number of things.

(i) Kant takes it that a determinism in itself, with no more said, would be wholly destructive of morality. If a determinism could not be supplemented, so to speak, by its denial, nothing of moral responsibility and what presupposes it could exist. (ii) This conclusion is the result, in part, of Kant's absolute conviction that there is a truth, indeed 'a law of reason', to the effect that the freedom that is fundamental to morality involves origination, and that the attempt to argue that only voluntariness is required by morality is wholly mistaken, a departure from truth and usage, indeed a 'wretched subterfuge'. (iii) We are to understand, obviously, that this conviction about the necessity of origination to morality is not peculiar to Kant, but rather that all men or at least all clear-thinking men have his beliefs. (iv) Kant's philosophical opponents—no doubt he had Hume in mind—in conceiving man to lack the power to begin an entirely new series of consequences, have deprived man of his splendour, his capability of truly being a moral agent.

It would be mistaken and indeed absurd to suggest that the traditions of Incompatibilism and Compatibilism are wholly uniform —wholly uniform in the respects in which we are interested. There is none the less a considerable uniformity, quite enough for conclusions to which we are coming. Mill, to come on to him, illustrates both facts. He is to some extent different from Hobbes and Hume, but is well within their tradition. In his *Examination of Sir William Hamilton's Philosophy* he attends to the question of the good man, as distinct from the related question of moral responsibility. His question is whether goodness depends on an assumption of Free Will.

My position is, that a human being who loves, disinterestedly and consistently, his fellow creatures and whatever tends to their good, who hates with a vigorous hatred what causes them evil, and whose actions correspond to in character with these feelings, is naturally, necessarily, and reasonably an object to be loved, admired, sympathized with, and in all ways cherished and encouraged by mankind; . . . and this whether the will be free or not, and even independently of any theory of the difference between right and wrong; whether right means productive of happiness, and wrong productive of misery, or right and wrong are intrinsic qualities of the actions themselves, provided only we recognize that there is a difference, and that the difference is highly important. What I maintain is, that this is a sufficient distinction between moral good and evil: sufficient for the ends of society and sufficient for the individual conscience:- that we need no other distinction; that if there be any other distinction, we can dispense with it; and that, supposing acts in themselves good or evil to be as unconditionally determined from the beginning of things as if they were phaenomena of dead matter, still, if the determination from the beginning of things has been that they shall take place through my love of good and hatred of evil, I am a proper object of esteem and affection. . . . (1979a (1865), pp. 456–7; cf. 1961 (1843), p. 547 f.)

Mill adds a note which sums up and rejects the response of one of his many critics, Patrick Alexander (1866), and further indicates his own view, to the effect that morality in general does not depend on Free Will.

Mr. Alexander draws a woeful picture of the pass which mankind would come to, if belief in so-called Necessity became general. All 'our current moralities' would come to be regarded 'as a form of superstition', all 'moral ideas as illusions', by which 'it is plain we get rid of them as motives': consequently the internal sanction of conscious would no longer exist. 'The external sanctions remain, but not quite as they were. That important section of them which rests on the moral approval or disapproval of our fellow-men has, of course, evaporated': and 'in virtue of a deadly moral indifference', the remaining external sanctions 'might come to be much more languidly enforced than as now they are', and the progressive degradation would in a sufficient time 'succeed·in reproducing the real original gorilla'. A formidable prospect: but Mr. Alexander must not suppose that other people's feelings, about the matters of highest importance to them, are bound up with a certain speculative dogma, and even a certain form of words, because, it seems, his are. (1979a (1865), p. 457)

Does Mill allow in the first passage that among ordinary men, as distinct from such servants of doctrine as Mr. Alexander, some are not of his own convictions—that human goodness depends wholly on certain human qualities, and does not require any denial of determinism, and, as is certainly implicit in the passage, that voluntariness is sufficient for moral approval and disapproval? Does he allow that some ordinary men *do* take the goodness and badness of their fellows to be bound up with origination, with the question of 'whether the will be free or not'? Perhaps Mill can be taken to allow that goodness and badness *are* taken by some to presuppose something in conflict with the idea that all actions are 'as unconditionally determined from the beginning of things as if they were phaenomena of dead matter'— despite his assertion that this presupposition is in fact not needed either in individual morality or for the ends of society. It is to be granted, at any rate, that Mill is not so definite as Hobbes or Hume in conveying that the generality of men have some sort of belief, as distinct from anything else, as to the sufficiency of voluntariness for moral standing and of course moral responsibility. He does indeed speak of feelings. It could be difficult to deny, however, that he somehow has in mind a kind of belief, or also has in mind a kind of belief.

F. H. Bradley, while claiming to disavow both the tradition of origination with voluntariness and the tradition of voluntariness by itself, is in fact within the first one. In 'The Vulgar Notion of Responsibility in Connection with the Theories of Freewill and Responsibility', he writes:

... if, at forty, our supposed plain man could be shown the calculation, made by another before his birth, of every event in his life, rationally deduced from the elements of his being, from his original natural endowment, and the complication of circumstances which in any way bore on him... then ... he would be most seriously perplexed, and in a manner outraged.... one sees directly the ground of our man's dislike for rational prediction; for such prediction is, in a word, the construction of himself out of what is not himself.... If, from given data and from universal rules, another man can work out the generation of him like a sum in arithmetic, where is his self gone to? It is invaded by another, broken up into selfless elements, put together again, mastered and handled, just as a poor dead thing is mastered by man. And this being so, our man feels dimly that, if another can thus unmake and remake him, he himself might just as well have been anybody else from the first, since nothing remains which is specifically his. The sanctum of his individuality is outraged and profaned; and with that profanation ends the existence that once seemed impenetrably sure. To explain the origin of a man is utterly to annihilate him. (1927, pp. 15, 20)

Bradley subsequently considers Mill's idea, shared with predecessors, that unphilosophical persons may for a time be unsettled by a determinism because they take causation to consist in 'necessity', where that is something more than the reality of causation, which reality is no more than constant conjunction. Bradley replies to Mill on behalf of the vulgar.

When you speak to us plainly, you have to say that you really understand a man to be free in no other sense than a falling stone, or than running water. In the one case there is as little necessity as in the other, and just as much freedom. And we believe that this is your meaning. But we know that, if these things are so, a man has no more of what we call freedom than a candle or a coprolite, and of that you will never succeed in convincing us. You must persuade us either that the coprolite is responsible, or that we are not responsible; and with all due respect to you, we are going to believe neither. (1927, p. 25)

Our single shared conception of freedom, then, if Bradley is right, involves a conception of a self, which conception cannot exist in conjunction with the predictability entailed by a determinism. His own developed view of the nature and distinctness of this self, and its relation to acts, is derived in good part from Hegel. Certainly it is a view different in kind from Aristotle's, and also Kant's, but not so different as to put it outside of the tradition of origination.

My intention is not to pursue these matters, but to illustrate another philosopher's certainty that we possess a single shared conception of freedom, one which is inconsistent with predictability and determinism. Further, Bradley takes it that we somehow believe this freedom to be necessary to responsibility. Also to be noticed is his particular fervency, if it is only that, in what can be called the humanist commitment of some philosophers opposed to determinism. Man, if a determinism is true, falls to the level of a coprolite.

Jean-Paul Sartre, with respect to our main interest, if not much else, seems to be of Bradley's mind.

It is strange that philosophers have been able to argue endlessly about determinism and free-will . . . without ever attempting first to make explicit the structures contained in the very idea of *action* . . . No factual state whatever . . . is capable by itself of motivating any act whatsoever. For an act is a projection of the for-itself towards what is not, and what is can in no way determine by itself what is not. . . . This implies for consciousness the permanent possibility of affecting a rupture with its own past, of wrenching itself away from its past so as to be able to consider it in the light of a non-being and so as to be able to confer on it the meaning which *it has* in terms of the project of a meaning which *does not have*. . . . I am condemned to exist forever beyond my essence, beyond the causes and motives of my act. I am condemned to be free . . . man being condemned to be free carries the weight of the whole world on his shoulders; he is responsible for the world and for himself as a way of being. We are taking the word 'responsibility' in its ordinary sense as 'consciousness (of) being the incontestable author of an event or of an object'. (Sartre, 1957 (1943), pp. 433 ff.)

For Sartre we have an idea of action—certainly the idea is not to be taken as something peculiar to him—as necessarily in a way free, as something owed to a kind of origination. Such action, as nothing less would, carries with it a lot of responsibility. That much seems clear, whatever else is to be said. (Cf. M. Warnock, 1965, 1973; Danto, 1975; Caws, 1979; Olafson, 1967)

G. E. Moore focused the attention of philosophers on what is meant by saying that a man could have done otherwise than he did, or can act otherwise than he does, as distinct from saying that he acted or is acting freely. In well-known passages in his *Ethics*, Moore takes it, rightly, although he does not spell out the connection, that the rightness or wrongness of an act depends on its being true that the agent could have done or can do otherwise.

We certainly have *not* got Free Will, in the ordinary sense of the word, if we never really *could*, in any sense at all, have done anything else than what we did do. . . . But, on the other hand, the mere fact (if it is a fact) that we sometimes can, in *some* sense, do what we don't do, does not necessarily entitle us to say that we *have* Free Will. . . . Whether we have or not will depend on the precise sense in which is true that we can. (1912, p. 203)

What, for instance, is the sense in which I could have walked a mile in twenty minutes this morning, though I did not? There is one suggestion, which is very obvious: namely, that what I mean is simply after all that I could, *if* I had chosen; or (to avoid a possible complication) perhaps we had better say 'that I *should, if* I had chosen'. In other words, the suggestion is that we often use the phrase 'I *could*' simply and solely as a short way of saying 'I *should*, if I had chosen'. (1912, p. 211)

There is, therefore, much reason to think that when we say that we *could* have done a thing which we did not do, we *often* mean merely that we *should* have done it, *if* we had chosen. And if so, then it is quite certain that, in *this* sense, we often really *could* have done what we did not do, and that this fact is in no way inconsistent with the principle that everything has a cause. And for my part I must confess that I cannot feel certain that this may not be *all* that we usually mean and understand by the assertion that we have Free Will. . . . (1912, p. 217)

Moore adds that many people will require for Free Will not only that we could have done otherwise than we did if we had so chosen, but also (a) that we could have chosen otherwise than we did. He then notes that by the latter requirement we may mean (b) we should have so chosen, if we had chosen to make the choice. (1912, pp. 218–9) The sentence (a), if it is analysed into (b), is of course taken to be consistent with determinism, since it is then taken to assert only that the given acts and choices could or should have been otherwise if their causal antecedents—certain choices—had been different.

Moore is inclined to think that the several sentences as analysed are what is meant by saying we have Free Will. However, he ends by saying that he can find no conclusive argument against, or for, the view that saying we have Free Will involves saying we can could have done otherwise in some other sense.

J. L. Austin in his paper 'Ifs and Cans' produced what has often been taken as a refutation of all or some of Moore's account of 'could' and 'can'. (1961) His refutation depends in part on noting that 'I can if I choose' does not involve the idea that the choosing is a cause of the action, since, if this were true, it would follow if I cannot act, I do not choose to. Effects are in a sense necessary conditions of their causes. Moreover, it does seem to follow from 'I can if I choose' that I can, whether or not I choose to, which sort of entailment would certainly not hold if my choosing were a cause. Causes, he supposes, are necessary conditions of effects. Austin also offers strong argument against the idea that 'I could have done otherwise' means, say, 'If I had the opportunity and the motive to do otherwise, I would have done otherwise'. (Nowell-Smith, 1954)

Austin says hardly anything of what he takes to be the proper understanding of such sentences as 'I could have done otherwise' where they are 'absolute'—indicative rather than conditional. That is, he says little of such claims as 'I could have ruined you this morning (although I didn't)' as against 'I could have ruined you this morning if I had had one more vote'. There is the implication that it is claims of the former indicative sort that are involved in what we think about our freedom, and that they are inconsistent with determinism. He ends by saying:

It has been alleged by very serious philosophers (not only the two I have mentioned) that the things we ordinarily say about what we do and could have done may actually be consistent with determinism. It is hard to evade all attempt to decide whether this allegation is true—hard even for those who, like myself, are inclined to think that determinism itself is still a name for nothing clear, that has been argued for only incoherently. At least I should like to claim that the arguments considered tonight fail to show that it is true, and indeed in failing go some way to show that it is not. Determinism, whatever it may be, may yet be the case, but at least it appears not consistent with what we ordinarily say and presumably think. (1961, p. 197)

Moore and Austin are in agreement about something, and thus in agreement, despite various differences, with all the philosophers we have noticed. This agreement of theirs is of more significance to the present inquiry than their disagreements.

Moore supposes that there is a single use of 'He could have done otherwise' and the like that settles the issue of the compatibility of freedom and determinism, whatever other uses there may be. That is, we have a single understanding, some understanding or other, of 'He could have done otherwise', which settles the issue of whether the freedom somehow required for moral responsibility and the rest of morality is consistent with a determinism. Moore takes it, evidently, that this is our ordinary or standard use. Further, he is inclined to think that he has specified this crucial use of 'He could have done otherwise', despite not having a conclusive argument for his inclination. If he has some doubt about his inclination, he has no doubt that there is a single thing we mean by 'He could have done otherwise', which thing settles the principal issue.

Austin, despite his still greater caution in all matters of language, shares the idea that we do have a single way of thinking and talking in connection with freedom, which way of thinking and talking is what can settle the issue. Certainly its analysis remains difficult, even after errors of analysis have been put aside. But to get the right analysis of our single common belief would be to settle the issue. It is notable that this inclination of his is not much affected by his feeling that determinism had not been made clear.

To come on to disagreement between Moore and Austin, it was noted above about Hobbes, Hume, and Mill that they suppose that the settled conception in question is a conception as to voluntariness by itself. Moore, although uncertainly, is of their mind. In the cases of Aristotle, Kant, Bramhall, and Bradley, our conception of free action is taken to involve origination as well as voluntariness. Austin, if he was no philosopher to enter into familiar sorts of philosophical specu- lation, must none the less be taken as going some way in the direction of Aristotle and his successors. It might be said, speculatively, that he is inclined to accept a certain end, the conclusion that we share a single conception inconsistent with determinism, and is unwilling to embrace the available means of attempting to explain it, ideas of the self, powers, faculties, and so on. Moore's reflections, via his concep- tion of freedom, also take him close enough to the conclusion that we have a belief as to what morality requires by way of freedom, and that this freedom would be unaffected by the truth of determinism. Of Austin, it would be rash to say that he would actually conclude, via his different conception of freedom, that morality would be affected by determinism. His innovation in philosophy was accompanied by a great caution.

To revert to my principal point, it is that Moore and Austin take us to have a single conception as to freedom, which conception issues in an ordinary usage, and which conception settles what has been the dominant philosophical question of freedom and determinism, that of the consequences of determinism. Their view is shared by very many 'analytic' philosophers who have subsequently carried on the con- troversy about 'He could have done otherwise' and the like. The proposition is to be confirmed by a look at a run of issues of most general philosophical journals, or at collections of essays on determin- ism and freedom. (Berofsky, 1966; Honderich, 1973; Watson, 1982)

As is made explicit in almost all of the views considered so far, they have had to do with the consequences of determinism for morality. Does determinism affect or not affect that particular freedom in mental acts and bodily actions which is a condition of morality? They are views, as just remarked, which enter into the third and dominant part of the philosophical controversy about our freedom.

Another and wrongly differentiated part of the controversy, as we have seen, has concerned the Epicurean objection to determinism,

having to do with determinism's alleged inconsistency with knowledge. It was our different conclusion that the objection, when
seen clearly, is essentially an objection which has to do with
determinism's consequences for that freedom in mental acts and
bodily actions, whatever it is, which is necessary to knowledge, or, as
might have been added, to knowledge and related things. Thus, it was
said, the Epicurean tradition *is* part and parcel of the dominant part of
the philosophical controversy about freedom. This, it was said, has not
been seen by the parties to the dominant dispute. There are very rare
exceptions to the generalization. That they are unusual in *this*, in their
greater awareness of the breadth of the consequences of determinism,
does not make them unusual in their Incompatibilism and
Compatibilism.

The neo-scholastic philosophers Boyle, Grisez and Tollefsen (1976)
maintain that it is an undeniable proposition that one must have a
certain freedom, and no less than it, if one is rationally to affirm
anything. They explicitly take this to be a proposition necessarily
agreed by all of us. The freedom is one tied to an indeterminist picture
of our existence, a freedom of origination. In their characterization, I
have such a freedom in making a choice in this actual world if it is the
case that there is a possible world such that in it I do not make the
choice but everything else is the same in that possible world except for
the consequences of my choice. (Cf. van Inwagen, 1974, 1983)

More fully, rational affirmation is narrowly understood as affirmation which is *not* the sure result of necessary truth or direct
experience. It is, rather, affirmation in a circumstance where there are
two inconsistent possibilities as to truth, and the best that can be done
is to determine which is the more reasonable. Rational affirmation is
subject to a certain norm, different from the norms which govern
affirmation in a circumstance of necessary truth or immediate
experience. If I am rationally to affirm anything, this norm must be
operative or in force in my case. That is a possibility only if I have the
given freedom of choice. Since this freedom of choice is inconsistent
with determinism, there is the conclusion that determinism has as a
consequence the impossibility of rational affirmation. In particular, it
has the consequence that it is impossible rationally to affirm
determinism.

Grunbaum (1953, 1971) also has the distinction of seeing the
Epicurean objection rightly as an objection having to do with freedom
of decision and action rather than, say, the relation of determinism to
truth or its consistency with a supposed conceptual connection of a
reason and a conclusion. His view, however, is entirely different. Of
the Epicurean tradition he writes:

... it is first pointed out rightly that determinism implies a causal determination of its own acceptance by its defenders. Then it is further maintained, however, that since the determinist could not, by his own theory, help accepting determinism under the given conditions, he can have no confidence in its truth. Thus it is asserted that the determinist's acceptance of his own doctrine was forced upon him. I submit that this inference involves a radical fallacy. The proponent of this argument is gratuitously invoking the view that if our beliefs have causes, these causes *force* the beliefs in question upon us, against our better judgement, as it were. Nothing could be further from the truth; this argument is another case of confusing *causation* with *compulsion*. (1971)

These two views explicitly or implicitly ascribe to us a certain conception of freedom, different in each case, and maintain or imply that if we are not confused, we shall see that it is just what we believe to be necessary to rational affirmation or confidence in truth. In the one case the freedom in question is inconsistent with determinism, in the other case consistent. These two views pertaining to knowledge or the like display an evident congruity with those pertaining to morality—those of Aristotle, Kant, Bramhall, Bradley, and Austin on the one hand, and Hobbes, Hume, Mill, and Moore on the other.

Finally, there is a recent Compatibilist doctrine already noticed (p. 24) in another connection. (Dennett, 1984) It takes a somewhat different wider view of the consequences of determinism. It also has the distinction of illustrating or being coloured by, if not perceiving or asserting, something of the broad fact considered in Chapter 1—the fact of the two families of attitudes and the two responses. Certainly there are references to the question of what *wants* of ours are, and what wants are not, affected by a determinism, and also other consonant remarks. (Dennett, 1984, pp. 18, 171) In this respect, if not others, it can perhaps be regarded as marking a kind of transition to the view to which we shall come. Still, what we are mainly offered, indeed more or less officially and explicitly offered, *is* a Compatibilism, although a more uncertain one than has been supposed by critics. (G. Strawson, 1985; D. Locke, 1986; Watson, 1986)

For example, as a successor to the Compatibilist claim that causation is not compulsion or constraint, we have it that what is necessary, in considering determinism, is to escape the confusion of taking causation to consist in *control*. 'What we must do . . . is perform a long overdue bit of "ordinary language" philosophy, to see what we actually have in mind when we yearn for control and fear its loss.' We must find 'our everyday notion'. (Dennett, 1984, pp. 59, 51) We then see that the fact that I am caused to act as I do is not the proposition that I do not control my action. There is the different point, secondly, that the proposition that I am caused to act as I do is not the proposition that my actions are the product of any simple or 'Sphexish' causation. (p. 392) There is the point, thirdly, that we must see what people are actually thinking when they say someone could have done otherwise in a particular situation. (1984, p. 136) Finally, as already implied, the problem of determinism is fundamentally a matter of confusions, and may be an artefact of the methods philosophers have typically used to study it. (1984, p. 17) These have importantly to do with the metaphors of the Invisible Jailer and the like. (p. 392)

2.2 COMPATIBILISM AND INCOMPATIBILISM DEFINED

As remarked and as we have seen, and as would in any case be expected, the Incompatibilist party of philosophers is certainly not monolithic. Still, it is evident that almost all or at least very many members of the party, including many contemporary members we have not considered, share certain fundamental propositions and a certain attitude—an enumeration of which things gives us a definition of Incompatibilism. We can set out the definition or enumeration of commitments in such a way as to serve the ends of our inquiry, and in particular to make clear not only what distinguishes Incompatibilists from Compatibilists, but also what *unites* the two parties. What unites them, from the point of view of our inquiry, is more fundamental. Incompatibilists maintain the following things.

(1) Virtually all men have a single, settled conception of the initiation of action, which conception is written into their language. It is a conception that pertains to moral approval and disapproval, and praise and blame, and perhaps all of morality.

(2) The conception in question is not only of the voluntariness or willingness of actions, in a sense conveyed in our survey of the controversy about the consequences of determinism, but also of their origination, in a sense conveyed in the survey and also evident in other philosophy. Each of voluntariness and origination enter into this conception of the initiation of actions.

(3) All men have a belief of some kind as to the connection between the initiation of action and moral approval and disapproval. This belief is not to be confused with another they may also have, as to what the facts actually are with respect to the initiation of action—importantly, whether we do in fact originate actions. Nor, of course, is the belief simply the conception of initiation which they have. Rather, precisely, it is a belief as to what the facts *must be* with respect to the initiation of action *if* moral disapproval and the like are in place. It is a belief that

only voluntariness plus origination constitute a sufficient condition, in so far as the initiation of action is concerned, of moral disapproval and the like.

(4) It follows that we must accept that there can be no moral responsibility if we never do originate our actions, which we never do if a determinism is true. Our belief in moral responsibility must in reason collapse if we become convinced of a determinism. This effect on moral responsibility, of course, is a matter of the logical incompatibility of origination and determinism.

(5) The principal problems faced by anyone concerned with determinism and freedom are of intellectual or theoretical kinds. They are problems of analysis, definition, clarity, consistency, other logical relations, truth, and the like. There is the problem, more generally, of seeing clearly the fundamental propositions: that we have a certain single conception pertaining to initiation, written into our language, and that we believe only actions which satisfy it are such as to allow for moral responsibility and what depends on it, and perhaps such other things as personal feelings. This requires that we become clear about origination, and clear about voluntariness. We need to reflect adequately on our own thinking, acquire a full perception of our shared conception and belief, examine the language which expresses them, and so on. The problem is importantly or even primarily a linguistic one. A clear awareness of the inconsistency of our conception with determinism is to be secured, perhaps by the provision of a proof—yet another proof. None of this has to do with attitude or feeling.

(6) It is in virtue of their power of origination, if they have it, that men have a certain adequate stature. An adequate stature depends on their not being subject to causation, or rather an effective determinism, and hence being distinct in kind from other existing things, including other living things. This, unlike its five predecessors, is an attitude rather than a proposition.

It is worth noting that the Incompatibilist party of philosophers is not defined as asserting the existence of origination or the falsehood of determinism. Most of them do so—and thus pass beyond items (1) to (6) to one of the many obscure indeterminist pictures of the mind. However, Incompatibilists also include philosophers who are uncertain of the truth of an indeterminist picture. Austin might be included here, however tentatively. Finally, as well as including those who embrace an indeterminist picture of the mind, and those who are agnostic on that point, the Incompatibilist party includes some very few determinists who have conceived of the ground of moral responsibility and so on as necessarily including origination. They are, in the description of William James (1909), the Hard Determinists.

The second party of philosophers, the Compatibilists as defined, share the following commitments.

(1') Like their opponents, they assume and almost always assert that virtually all men share one settled conception of the initiation of action, one conception pertaining to moral disapproval and perhaps a little more. The conception is entrenched in language.

(2') The conception is of an action that is no more than voluntary. It has in it nothing about origination.

(3') All men somehow believe voluntariness by itself is sufficient, in so far as the initiation of action is concerned, to moral disapproval and so on.

(4') It follows that a determinism, being compatible with voluntariness, carries no threat to moral responsibility. Our ascriptions of moral responsibility would be unchanged by our coming to believe a determinism.

(5') The problems of determinism and freedom are, as Incompatibilists also believe, intellectual problems. There is the problem for Compatibilists of leading the opposing party of philosophers to take a clear and unconfused view of ordinary belief and language as to the conditions of responsibility, and to see their consistency with determinism. Merely philosophical habit and doctrine is to be escaped, and the plain fact of consistency is to be insisted upon. There is also the enterprise, taken as very necessary, of leading Incompatibilists to take up higher standards of clarity and contentfulness with respect to conceptions. These higher standards exclude indeterminist theories of the mind.

(6') Causal connection is or may be what can be called the commanding fact of all that exists. It is or may be even more than, to use Hume's description of something else, 'the cement of the universe'. (1938 (1740), p. 32) Determinism is or may be a great fact, an imperative of inquiry, such that all else must be brought into line with it.

The Compatibilists as defined, as just implied, need not be committed to the truth of a determinism. Some of them, following Hobbes, Hume and Mill, are so committed, and hence fall into James's category of Soft Determinists. Moore is otherwise, a Compatibilist who is officially agnostic about determinism. He has very many companions among contemporary philosophers. If they do not accept determinism, they have not been persuaded either—to take one central point—that Quantum Mechanics falsifies it. Perhaps there are Compatibilists, thirdly, who add a denial of determinism to the above commitments. Their view is that an indeterminism, while true, is not needed for freedom. They would of course have to depart from Hume's idea that determinism is essential to moral responsibility. (Cf. G. Strawson, 1986)

2.3 COMPATIBILISM AND INCOMPATIBILISM: BOTH FALSE

This inquiry into the consequences of determinism was begun with a consideration of, in fact an eliciting of, two conflicting families of attitudes which we share, attitudes to the initiation of action. (Ch. 1) They do or may give rise to two conflicting responses to determinism, dismay and intransigence. Time enough was taken to establish the truth of the empirical claim about two families of attitudes between which we move, which is fundamental. There is only one effective way of doing so, the one which was adopted. It is to prompt someone's consideration of his or her own attitudes, at bottom by actually evoking them. Doing so must be as much a matter of a kind of philosophical persuasion as anything else, or, to speak differently, a matter of invitation and reminder rather than argument in a more circumscribed sense.

It would be close to futile, or at the very least unpromising, to try by a certain means to establish the proposition that we all have the two kinds of attitudes—the means of a kind of merely linguistic argument, one which does not in effect make an active appeal to the attitudes of interlocutors. This is so since all of the system of terms having to do with the initiation of action—starting with 'freedom', and including even terms which are more apt for the expression of one attitude than another—in fact has a character akin to systematic ambiguity. The entire system is ambiguous as between different attitudes. To *stick with the words*, in a certain sense, is to fail to get in touch with the reality, the reality of the consequences of determinism.

I allow that there are problems raised by this reflection, having to do with what might be called the adequacy and inadequacy of language, but not such problems as must detain us. It is notable that Incompatibilists and Compatibilists, in their different purpose of attempting to establish the existence of a single conception, have been most successful when they have in fact been engaging in something like the evocation of attitude, however differently they have conceived their endeavours. This is the case with the Compatibilist essay which first widened consideration of the consequences of determinism. (P. F. Strawson, 1962)

As remarked already, I have no need to embrace or defend what does in fact seem to me the exceptionless truth that each of us can enter into both families of attitudes, and is capable of both responses—in fact, that in such circumstances of reflection and feeling as those imagined earlier, having to do with the scheming husband and so on, each of us *does* move between the attitudes and responses. It may be true, on the contrary, that some individuals are *immured* in one family of attitudes and one response, very likely intransigence rather than dismay, perhaps as a result of the kind of philosophical commitment which can at least obscure feeling. Those who are immured in this way—I certainly do not speak of the general run of philosophers inclined either to Compatibilism or Incompatibilism—are very few in number indeed. There cannot be many of us whose situation is one that may perhaps be suggested by the declaration with which the Compatibilist philosopher Moritz Schlick opens his chapter, 'When Is a Man Responsible?'

With hesitation and reluctance I prepare to add this chapter . . . For in it I must speak of a matter which, even at present, is thought to be a fundamental ethical question, but which got into ethics and has become a much discussed problem only because of a misunderstanding. This is the so-called problem of the freedom of the will. Moreover, this pseudo-problem has long since been settled by the efforts of certain sensible persons; and, above all, the state of affairs just described has been often disclosed—with exceptional clarity by Hume. Hence it is really one of the greatest scandals of philosophy that again and again so much paper and printer's ink is devoted to this matter, to say nothing of the expenditure of thought, which could have been applied to more important problems (assuming that it would have sufficed for these). Thus I should truly be ashamed to write a chapter on 'freedom'. In the chapter heading the word 'responsible' indicates what concerns ethics, and designates the point at which misunderstanding arises. Therefore the concept of responsibility constitutes our theme, and if in the process of its clarification I also must speak of the concept of freedom I shall, of course, say only what others have already said better; consoling myself with the thought that in this way alone can anything be done to put an end at last to that scandal. (1956, pp. 143–4)

Perhaps Schlick's passion indicates that he would have been unmoved by any attempt whatever to have him disclose in himself any trace of a disposition to dismay or the attitude from which it springs. Perhaps, for example, he had no inclination whatever to an unfixed personal future, and no retributive attitudes of the kind described earlier. (pp. 62 ff.) I doubt it, but if so, no matter. There is no need for a universal truth, no more than there is a need for universal truths about experience in connection with other problems of philosophy that have to do with contingent matters.

If what has been maintained about our families of attitudes and the responses of dismay and intransigence is true, then all of the propositions espoused by Compatibilists and Incompatibilists are false. What has been maintained about the attitudes, and dismay and intransigence, to my mind, is indisputable. Each of the five propositions of each party then *is* false. As for the sixth commitment (pp. 105, 106) of each of the two parties, about human stature and the sway of causation, it may in a way depend on the false propositions. That is, to take the Incompatibilist inclination that origination is required if men and women are to be of a proper stature, it must at least be touched by accepting, if one has to, that we do not have a common belief that only the inclusion of origination can give a place to responsibility and the like.

Let us see all this in detail, and strengthen the fundamental argument in several ways, by working through the items in question, beginning with the first proposition shared by the two parties.

It is, to repeat, that virtually all men have a single conception of the initiation of action in so far as moral responsibility and the like are concerned. This conception provides the single definition of the word 'free', and the related single definition of many other terms and usages. This has, although rarely, been in a way questioned. (Ayer, 1964, p. 6) In fact it is demonstrably false. It has been demonstrated false by our reflections on our own shared attitudes. We do not have a single conception of initiation in so far as moral responsibility and the like are concerned. We do not have *any* definition of freedom in the relevant sense: where such a definition is the one correct specification of a single thing, fact, or phenomenon. What is true, rather, is that we attend to two different sets of actual or possible properties of the initiation of actions. The fact is reflected by dictionary definitions of 'free' and the like. They move between our two attitudes—all of the definitions do so, under defensible understandings. 'Free' and related terms, as remarked earlier, are thus in a way systematically ambiguous.

A fortiori, to turn to the second Incompatibilist contention (p. 104), it is not the case that we have, as a single conception of initiation in so far as responsibility and the like are concerned, a conception of voluntariness joined with origination. We do have such a conception but we also have another, which has nothing of origination in it. None of us is debarred from the feeling that malignant desires in an action, or want of principle or uncaring disdain in an action, when there is voluntariness, are sufficient for moral disapproval. Admittedly, we can also be taken aback, in our disapproval, by the consideration that the action in question was the necessitated outcome of necessitated antecedents. That is not to say that we cannot and do not in turn escape this constraint on our feelings and desires. We are not immured in the conception which enters into one attitude.

An anticipation of a kind of this central claim was noticed earlier.

(p. 103) The other one of which I know, which deserves more attention than it can have at a late stage of the writing of this book, is contained within a strong doctrine of freedom otherwise wholly different from our own. (G. Strawson, 1986) This doctrine, which contains the too strong idea that determinism does not need reflection since indeterminist views of the mind are futile or fatuous, does accept there is something called 'the ordinary strong sense' of the word 'free', and is in a way resolutely Compatibilist. Still, it speaks of us as being 'in some respects *natural compatibilists* in our thought about freedom, and . . . in other respects *natural incompatibilists.*' (G. Strawson, p. 19, cf. Ch. 2, p. 47, note 30)

It will have been noted of the third Incompatibilist contention (p. 104) that it is in a way vague. It is that all men have a belief *of some kind*. They have a belief *of some kind* that only voluntariness plus origination constitute a necessary and sufficient condition, in so far as the initiation of action is concerned, of moral disapproval and the like. This vagueness reproduces the actuality of the Incompatibilist tradition, as a look back at the quoted passages will confirm. What is suggested, but not explicitly asserted, is that we possess it as a literal truth, or something approximate to an ordinary truth, that something is a sufficient condition for something else. We have a belief in that fundamental sense.

The facts are otherwise. What we have is an attitude, which, to describe it one way, is a *taking* of voluntariness with origination together as sufficient for moral disapproval and the like. It is not the only attitude we have, but that is not the present point. The present point is that we do not have anything like a belief in a standard sense: *we do not have something that is true or false.*

Will it be suspected that too much distinction is being made, or too much weight being put on a distinction, between beliefs and attitudes? In the course of our inquiry so far into our attitudes and responses, relatively little of a general kind has been said of the nature of attitudes. It was taken that an attitude is typically an evaluative thought of something, feelingful and bound up with desire. (p. 14) It was noticed that we may speak alternatively of the same facts as (i) taking an attitude of moral disapproval with respect to an action, which attitude includes a conception of the action's initiation, and, as a moment ago, (ii) taking an attitude of disapproval on account of something separate, the conception of the action's initiation. (p. 81) Nothing important hangs on it, but let us here proceed in the second way.

What is it to take it that an action of a certain kind, of a certain initiation, is in a certain respect a sufficient condition of moral disapproval, of holding the agent responsible for it? Certainly this could not be a factual belief to the effect that the given facts—say facts having to do with voluntariness—are part of a *causal* or other *nomic* condition or requirement for moral responsibility. To suppose so would be a bizarre confusion, for a number of reasons. One is that the connection between the given facts and moral disapproval is not an explanatory but evidently a justificatory one. The facts provide a *ground*, not part of a causal circumstance.

Can it be, then, that in taking certain facts to be a sufficient condition of moral disapproval, in so far as the initiation of action is concerned, we take it that certain premisses of fact are a *logically* sufficient condition for that disapproval? That is, can it be that we take it that a certain entailment holds? Obviously not. If no complete account, as remarked, has been given of what it is to disapprove of a man in a moral way, it has been said that disapproval involves certain feelings and desires. Feelings of repugnance and desires for his discomfiture were mentioned. (p. 64) These feelings and desires are evidently to be understood in terms of what can be called evaluations and prescriptions. The desires, that is, can be rendered in some such way as this: 'Let it happen that he is discomfited or otherwise distressed'. There can then be no possibility that factual propositions about voluntariness can, so to speak, entail moral disapproval.

To come to the heart of the matter, and hence to show that what we have is properly described as an attitude, which thing is not a belief in the standard sense, or akin to one, it is clear that to say that we take certain facts as in a certain respect sufficient for moral disapproval can only be to say that we *regard* certain facts as providing reasons for certain feelings, desires and the like. What is in question here is in the ordinary sense not a belief at all, but rather something that is like moral and other evaluative judgements in not having a truth-value in the ordinary sense. If it can be called a belief, it is not a belief with a truth-value. Believing that certain facts are the sufficient condition of moral disapproval is precisely like, to take a random example or two, *believing that the existence of distress is a reason for a plan to end it*, or *believing that the length of time it takes to become a doctor is a reason for higher pay*. To have such a belief is not to have something which is true or false, but to have something which itself is properly described, as it has been, as an attitude or feeling.

Return for a moment to the scheming husband, who gives a large gift to his son in order to deprive his wife of her fair share both of the family money and the affections of the son. I may indeed take certain facts about the husband's action to be sufficient for my disapproval of him. But that can only be to say that I am disposed or inclined to take certain facts as reasons for feelings, desires, and related actions. I may take it that my desire that he be discomfited or distressed, and the judgement I may utter to that effect, rest on the good reason that his action was both voluntary and originated. At bottom what is in question is not a belief with a truth-value, but rather a ground-level commitment to the effect that certain facts support or justify feelings, desires, and so on.

If they are to be brought into distant reach of truth, what our Incompatibilists—and Compatibilists—must be converted into maintaining, although they certainly do not see this, is that virtually all men are alike in having a single attitude, in being of a single feeling. Incompatibilists and Compatibilists must be converted into exponents of the view that each of us is inclined to regard a certain set of facts, and these alone, as being good reasons for moral disapproval and related things. No doubt an overlooking of this necessary understanding of what is being maintained, or an avoidance of the question, has been of help to both parties of philosophers in their advocacy. It is easier to get the idea accepted that all men are of *one mind* about something—*each* man is of *one mind* about something—if the nature of the thing is left unexamined, and hence it is not made plain that what is in question is not a belief with a truth-value. The truth of a non-attitudinal belief—the facts which make it true—can be expected to produce in each of us a convergence upon it. The case is different with whatever gives rise to the *attitudinal* belief that something is a good reason for something else.

The true nature of the connection between the given founding-beliefs or founding-ideas and what they support, as we now understand it, reinforces what has been maintained, that each of us can take two conflicting attitudes, and make the response of dismay *and* the conflicting response of intransigence in connection with determinism. There can be no great surprise in the claim that we can entertain opposed 'beliefs' of the given kind, one which requires origination and voluntariness as a pre-condition for various things, and one which requires only voluntariness. It *would* be surprising if they were beliefs with truth-values, since the given claim would then be a claim as to the existence of a standard paradox, or something like one, and that would be an improbable claim. The nature of the given connection between founding-beliefs and what they support will be of significance in the argument to come, issuing in a conclusion about the choice between dismay, intransigence, and a third thing.

The fourth proposition and a further distinction of Incompatibilism is that moral responsibility was never a fact if determinism is true, since it excludes origination. Further, if a determinism comes to have general acceptance we can no longer persist in holding people responsible. To believe this, of course, is necessarily also to believe more, about more things than moral responsibility. While almost all Incompatibilists, as we know, have been overly concerned with the narrow effect on moral responsibility, and have given no attention to life-hopes and so on, some few of them—very few—have had a proper wider view. Some have been mentioned. (p. 102) The wider view does not save them from the present objection. Isaiah Berlin also takes a wider view, indeed a grand one. If we begin to take a determinism seriously, he writes, then

... the changes in the whole of our language, our moral terminology, our attitudes toward one another, our views of history, of society, and of everything else will be too profound to be even adumbrated. The concepts of praise and blame, innocence and guilt, and individual responsibility . . . are but a small element in the structure, which would collapse or disappear. If social and psychological determinism were established as an accepted truth, our world would be transformed more radically than was the teleological world of the classical and middle ages by the triumphs of mechanistic principles or those of natural selection. Our words—our modes of speech and thought— would be transformed in literally unimaginable ways; the notions of choice, of responsibility, of freedom, are so deeply embedded in our outlook that our new life, as creatures in a world genuinely lacking in these concepts, can, I should maintain, be conceived by us only with the greatest difficulty. (1969, p. 113)

It cannot be that this wider view, perhaps a touch more apocalyptic than is required, or the usual lesser proposition about moral responsibility, is correct. *Whatever* is to be drawn from the premiss that we have a single belief to the effect that both voluntariness and origination are required for something—just moral responsibility, or that and a great deal more—is drawn from a false premiss.

Given the possibility of the attitude having to do only with voluntariness, it is wholly false to suppose that a general acceptance of determinism must leave a void where moral responsibility had been. A future counterpart of the scheming husband, who goes about his wretched business in the era of determinism, will in the voluntariness of his action be open to a certain moral disdain. It has been implied already that I do not take it that our choice in the matter of responses to determinism is between only dismay and intransigence. However, the very possibility of what might be called the voluntarist attitude to the initiation of action is quite enough to falsify the claim that determinism must be regarded as destructive of moral responsibility and what depends on it.

What has been established, about attitudes and responses, conflicts as sharply with the fifth Incompatibilist commitment, that the principal questions about the consequences of determinism are questions of definition, clarity, logical relations, truth, and the like. Certainly the question of the truth of determinism is just that, a question of truth. However, that is precisely not the case with the fundamental question of the sufficient condition, with respect to the initiation of action, of responsibility, and like things. The issue of the sufficient condition of moral approval and disapproval is not one that is to be settled by *discovery*. Neither truth in the ordinary sense— contingent truth—nor logic provides us with a resolution of that issue. The resolution of that issue, which will be attempted in the following chapter, will have a character akin to that of *decision*. This follows from what has been said already, about the nature of our attitudes as to the necessity of certain facts to responsibility and so on.

The sixth commitment of Incompatibilism, an inclination or motivation rather than a proposition, is that men and women have a certain stature or standing only if they possess the power of origination. There is no determinate conception of an acceptable stature shared by all Incompatibilists. It can be said that for Kant it is the stature of entering into what is of ultimate value, the moral law, through originated actions. For some Incompatibilists, indeed many, it is a stature which has to do with a life true to the great reality asserted by religion, a reality which includes eternity. For others it is the lesser stature of simply being distinct in kind from the rest of what we experience, all of which is subject to causation. Not to escape this necessity, in Bradley's view, is to fall very low indeed.

For the moment, what can be said is that this sixth item in Incompatibilism is open to the reply that not all conceivable standings for men and women are dependent on their being originators. Needless to say, the general idea of an acceptable standing is vague. However, the intransigent response to determinism, a response which does not involve origination, can give some place to conceptions of nobility of spirit, gentleness, courage, and other great virtues and excellences which have always been among the objects of our moral and personal feelings. The idea that human lives which possess these excellences as conceived could none the less be absolutely without stature or standing may be taken as something like eccentric.

To come to the propositions of the Compatibilist Party (pp. 106 f.), we have already considered and rejected the first, which is shared with their adversaries, to the effect that virtually all men have a single common conception of the initiation of action in so far as moral disapproval and the like are concerned.

As to the second Compatibilist proposition, that this single conception has to do only with voluntariness, its falsehood follows from that of the first proposition. All of us find in ourselves a way of thinking which does not all accord with the given proposition. There can be no doubt that we are made to pause in our disdain of a man by the thought that his action was the necessitated consequence of a causal sequence whose initial items were either external to him, or else internal to him at the time of his birth. (pp. 63 ff.) It does not help to reflect that some items in the sequence were desires and intention for the action, and hence that the desires and intention were necessary to the action. It remains true that *no action but the action he performed could have been performed.* That is here to say, of course, no more than what has been said already: that the action was necessitated in a certain way. The use of the telling abbreviation, however, is entirely in place. Furthermore, if we are made to pause in our disdain by the given thought, and to turn to another conception, it seems as true to say that we would be made actually to halt if the thought was taken up by us unreservedly as a truth. We resist taking it up unreservedly because we see and are opposed to its consequence. (pp. 67 ff.)

We come to the vague third proposition of Compatibilism, that all men somehow believe that it is only voluntariness that is sufficient, in so far as the initiation of action is concerned, for moral disapproval and so on. Will it perhaps be objected that Compatibilists can be taken, despite all that has been said here, as having really been concerned with attitudes? The objection, of course, bears some similarity to the one considered in connection with the third proposition of Incompatibilists. (p. 110) The objection here, to repeat, is that Compatibilists have in fact not supposed or maintained that we have anything like a belief in the fundamental sense about the initiation of action. The objection runs afoul of a good deal, and cannot be taken seriously.

For one thing, this understanding of the Compatibilist enterprise would leave its degree of success wholly unexplained. Who would have been persuaded by the proposition here supposed to have been advanced, that *we have but one attitude* to the initiation of actions? *That* proposition, given what we know of the general possibility and fact of divergent attitudes in ourselves, would have been singularly unpersuasive. Secondly, this understanding of the Compatibilist enterprise would make almost incomprehensible its burden of complaint about want of clarity, confusion and so on. Finally, and most simply, to put it no higher, it is not what the language of Compatibilists implies or suggests. '. . . according to this proper, and generally received meaning of the word, a FREEMAN, is he that . . . .' (p. 88) 'For what is meant by liberty . . . ? . . . we can only mean. . . .' (p. 91) '. . . what I mean is simply after all that I could, *if* I had chosen . . .'

(p. 99) I accept that such claims are about a single conception of action-initiation we are supposed to have. They are not claims as to a belief about a sufficiency of that conception for something else. They do suggest or at the very least consort with such claims, partly because the conception and such claims are to some extent conceptually attached.

Have Compatibilists—and of course Incompatibilists—not been clear in their own minds as to what they were asserting, or must be taken as having been asserting? Have they not in their own minds distinguished between a claim about a standard belief and a claim about an attitude? No doubt this can be said of some or many of them. Perhaps few or even none of them have explicitly raised the question as to whether their subject-matter is a belief on our part or an attitude. None of this disturbs the proposition just defended, that what they have unreflectively assumed, and written, has to do with a belief.

That, however, is not what is most important in this connection. What is most important is that the main contention of the Compatibilists *requires* a standard belief rather than an attitude. Their main contention is to the effect that a certain sentence about a sufficient condition with respect to moral responsibility, a sentence about only voluntariness, is *correct*, and another sentence about the only sufficient condition, partly about origination, is *incorrect* or *mistaken*. Anything at all like the intended correctness and incorrectness are properties only of beliefs in the ordinary sense, not attitudes and the like. The usage 'correct attitude' does indeed exist, in political circles for example, but certainly does not denote something which has correctness in the sense that Compatibilists—and Incompatibilists—claim it in connection with their subject-matter.

The fact of our pairs of attitudes, together with the response of dismay, stands solidly in the way of the fourth Compatibilist idea, that a determinism does not touch the matter of moral responsibility, and that an acceptance of determinism would leave things exactly as they always have been. That cannot be true.

There is a further large reflection prompted by this supposedly anodyne idea about determinism's harmlessness, but a reflection that pertains as much to Kant and the other Incompatibilists as it does to Hume and his Compatibilist companions. It is a reflection which, to speak of my own thinking about the consequences of determinism, has been a particularly powerful one. It has contributed greatly to my confidence in what has been said of two families of attitudes and the two responses.

Hume and his companions, in order to sustain the idea that determinism does not touch moral responsibility, must offer some account of why the contrary has so persistently been supposed, no doubt more persistently than the other view. A suitable explanation of what is taken to be error is needed to deal with the anticipated and no doubt proper rejoinder that the idea in question owes its persistence to truth. The Compatibilists, to use a term lately introduced, do provide such an error theory. (Mackie, 1977) We have seen a good deal of it. To think about it is surely to conclude that it does not fall far short of being amazing. It reduces to this: what explains the persistence of the idea that determinism does affect moral responsibility is four or more centuries of *confusion*.

The reply must be that four or more centuries is a long time for a persistently discussed idea to be sustained by confusion. It is a stunningly long time if the idea in question, to remember Hume's words, and use them against him, has to do with 'any subject of common life and experience' (p. 91), and has been a matter not merely of persistent discussion but of acute controversy. It seems undeniable that one must find something better than confusion and indeed a kind of widespread weak-mindedness to explain the resilience of the idea that determinism affects responsibility. It seems undeniable that the only adequate explanation must undercut Compatibilism. *It is the existence of an entrenched attitude, widely or universally shared.* The attitude is to the effect that origination is needed for responsibility.

The same kind of reflection is entirely as pertinent to the counterpart error theory of the Incompatibilists. It is to the effect that it is unreflectiveness, or shallowness in reflection, or weak empiricism, or word-play that explains the persistence of the view that voluntariness does give an adequate foundation for moral disapproval and the like. That too is an extraordinary claim when it is taken as intended, and as it must be intended—as having to do with some sort of intellectual failing. Indeed, some might say that we have no need to mention four or more centuries of examination and cross-examination in order to cast doubt upon it. That is, to mention only Hume, it might be said that it offends against sense to consign him to the company of the unreflective, the reflectively shallow, the myopically empirical— or, God help us, *the muddled.* (Popper, 1982b, p. xix) Again, there must be a better explanation of the persistence of the view in question, and there is one which is nothing so congenial to Kant and his fellows. *It is the existence of an entrenched attitude, widely or universally shared.* The attitude is to the effect that voluntariness suffices for moral disapproval and the like. (Cf. p. 127)

All this is as relevant to the fifth commitment of Compatibilists, shared with Incompatibilists, to the effect that the problems we are considering are of standard intellectual kinds, and that our failings in considering them are intellectual failings. In particular, according to Compatibilists, there is the problem of understanding and keeping before the mind the distinction between causation and compulsion, the fact that causation does not entail a want of voluntariness. (p. 103) The truth that causation, being what it is, does not entail any want of voluntariness has been indefatigably asserted and elaborated by Compatibilists. So too have they been persistent in judging the obscurity of origination, and, to repeat a description, its 'obscure and panicky metaphysics'. (P. F. Strawson, 1968 (1962), p. 96) Certainly the issue of determinism and freedom raises intellectual problems. As remarked already, however, one principal question—what has been taken as *the* principal question—is not of this kind.

The sixth feature of Compatibilism, of the order of an attitude itself, is its subservience to determinism. Compatibilism is inclined to take determinism as rightly imperious. What I have in mind is not the conviction that determinism is true. Indeed, the attitude in question, or some close variant of it, can coexist with an uncertainty about the truth of determinism. Rather, the attitude is one which involves an acceptance of determinism as being, or as likely to be, *the very principle of reflection about all of reality*. What follows from this is a resistance to the perceiving of any recalcitrant fact. The main fact here is our common attitude having to do with origination. Compatibilists, notably those who are determinists, give the appearance of being incapable of registering or at any rate coming to grips with this fact. Their resistance to it will not make it go away.

It needs to be allowed that there is more speculation in ascribing this sixth feature to Compatibilism than in the case of the others. Also, what has been said of this feature is vague. It does seem clear, however, that there is at the basis of Compatibilism some counterpart of the Incompatibilist attachment to an aspiration with respect to the stature of mankind. There is a kind of commitment which contributes as effectively to what one is tempted to call one-eyed philosophy. The description of this Compatibilist commitment might be supplemented by a consideration of intellectual temperaments, these having to do with more things than determinism. As in the case of Incompatibilism and human stature, more will be said in what follows of relevance to Compatibilism and its subservience to determinism.

That concludes my main consideration of the long battle over the consequences of determinism between the two orthodox schools of thought. Before going forward with other matters, it will be worth while glancing back over the argument so far about the consequences of determinism.

Each of us can focus on either of two conflicting sets of propositions, ideas, or images about actions. One set of these things has to do with voluntariness or willingness—in one of several summary definitions, they have to do with action issuing from embraced desires. We can take these propositions as the only essential ones entering into life-hopes, personal feelings, knowledge, and moral matters. If we do this, we may make the intransigent response to determinism, that it does not matter. On the other hand, we can focus on a larger set of propositions and the like about actions. They have to do with both voluntariness and origination. We can take it that only all of these considerations together provide good reasons for life-hopes and so on. If we do this, we may make a different response to determinism—dismay. Neither facts nor logic by themselves, then, force us into either of the two responses. They are in part a matter of the mentioned focusing, the attitudes. What is true, as a matter of logic, is that a determinism is consistent with the first set of considerations and inconsistent with the second. It follows, if determinism is a fact, that the first set of considerations is undisturbed and the second is false.

This view of our situation, to repeat, was advanced before anything else partly in order to frustrate the philosophically conditioned reflexes of Compatibilism and Incompatibilism. If it is not all that is to be said of our situation, it constitutes a refutation of both those traditional views. Our situation is not one of a single conception as to the initiation of action, and anything like a true or false belief as to what is sufficient for moral approval and disapproval, or, to take the properly wide perspective, for that and the other mentioned things. The fundamental mistake of both Compatibilists and Incompatibilists has been to seize on one attitude with respect to the initiation of action, convert it into something else—a single conception of initiation and something presented as a belief—and to ignore another attitude quite as real. To reject the two traditional views is to leave the way clear for something else, to which we now turn. If the two traditional views were the only possible responses to the problem of determinism, that would not reduce it to 'a dead problem'. (Earman, 1986, p. 235) Given that they are not the only possible responses, it is very far from being such.

3

Affirmation

3.1 THE TRUE PROBLEM OF CONSEQUENCES

The true problem of the consequences of determinism, as will have become clear, is the problem of settling on a satisfactory response to it, involving our two families of attitudes. It is a problem of dealing with our feelings, feelings challenged by determinism and about things that are important to us—our futures, other people, and so on. It is most importantly a problem of desire. Life-hopes *are* a species of desire; desires enter into appreciative and resentful personal feelings; we desire to be able to have certain of the attitudes, notably a confidence in knowledge. Although we have yet to look at this, the problem also involves what we do in our societies as the result of our desires. It is not a problem to be settled by the discovery of truth, either truths of logic or truths of fact. The problem is partly raised by the seeming truth of determinism, but certainly not settled by it.

Our situation, as we have seen, is that each of us has or is prone to have two conflicting families of attitudes with respect to things important to us, and that the seeming truth of determinism gives rise in the first instance to two conflicting responses in us. If this is a situation that falsifies Compatibilism and Incompatibilism, it is also an unsatisfactory situation, or more than that, for a number of reasons. What it calls for, if it can be had, is a change in our feelings. Perhaps it is not too much to say that it calls for a change in our feelings about the nature of our existence.

To succeed in affecting a satisfactory change, if this can be done, will be to resolve the problem of the consequences of determinism. Nothing else will resolve it. This is so since, to repeat, the problem *is* that of settling on a satisfactory response to determinism. It can be said with absolute certainty that the problem is *not* a matter of extracting a correct definition of 'free' or whatever from ordinary language, or of contriving yet another in the long futile sequence of proofs and persuasions, however arresting or meticulous (Kenny, 1975; van Inwagen, 1983), each to the effect that we can properly mean only one thing by our relevant words. Nor is it a matter of establishing that we have some single 'belief' as to sufficiency, for moral responsibility and so on, of a free action somehow defined. The endeavour to move towards such a change in our feelings which will resolve the consequence-problem is our present business, the main business of the last part of this book.

One of the discomforts of the situation in which we find ourselves is the simple existence of our response of dismay, taken by itself. It is no satisfactory thing to have or to contemplate having life-hopes threatened, feelings about others and oneself put in question, confidence of knowledge undermined. Each is such a thing as to make us try to avert our attention from it. The discomfort, further, is not a problem which should exist only in one's study, or in one's personal emotional life, as distinct from the world outside, a dismay of philosophical reflection rather than ordinary or practical life. We *act* on certain of our desires, notably certain of our retributive desires. Hence there must be at least an unhappiness having to do with the morality of fundamental social institutions, practices, and habits. (Ch. 4)

Given an acceptance of the seeming truth of determinism, there is also another kind of discomfort involved in dismay itself: that of being aware of being adversely affected in a way that is unreasonable. This is the unsatisfactoriness of being troubled by desires for what, given the truth of determinism, cannot be had—origination and what follows from it. This cannot but strike one, or weigh on one, as in fact irrational. The irrationality, put one way, is that of having desires of which one accepts that they cannot be satisfied and hence are not a means to one's well-being.

A further and fundamental discomfort of the situation is of course the inconsistency it involves. We feel that only voluntariness with origination is enough to sustain hopes satisfactorily, and so on, and also that voluntariness by itself can do so. (This inconsistency has nothing to do, obviously, with the inconsistency claimed by Incompatibilists, between 'freedom' and determinism.) As for the two responses, we feel both that our hopes are dashed and that they can persist. It needs to be allowed that since no attitude and no response is a truth-valued belief, this inconsistency does not in itself involve us in falsehood. What is the case, rather, to speak in one way, is that we are involved in inconsistent *judgements*. If my inclination to take voluntariness alone as sufficient for life-hopes is not a matter of truth or logic, it does none the less issue in what it is proper to call a judgement, and such judgements stand in logical relations with other such judgements and indeed other things. My inclination issues in the judgement that the fact of voluntary action *in itself* is an adequate reason for life-hopes. If this is not true or false, not a proposition in the usual philosophical sense of that term, it none the less can be said to stand in contradiction with the judgement that only the facts of voluntariness *and* origination together are an adequate reason for life-hopes.

There is the same kind of contradiction with ordinary imperatives, which also lack truth-values. One account of such contradiction, although not an explanatory or fundamental one, is that two judgements contradict one another if someone's having the idea that both can be affirmed together is a reason for saying that he fails to understand them, that he does not grasp the meanings of the terms involved. (Cf. Hare, 1952, Ch. 2) A more fundamental account of such contradiction, although we need not pursue it, will have to do with the contradiction, in the most fundamental sense, of certain propositions related to the judgements.

The fact that the contradiction in which we are involved does not in itself commit us to falsehood does not much lessen the unsatisfactoriness of our situation in this respect. Being trapped in inconsistent judgements is as unsatisfactory as being prone to issuing inconsistent orders, or, more precisely, being *subject to* inconsistent orders. There is what can be called the instability of the situation: we cannot rest easy, but are pulled in two ways with respect to what is, in one sense, the same subject-matter. We are, for example, pulled in two ways with respect to the subject-matter of our futures.

Finally, if dismay in itself and the inconsistency are nothing agreeable, intransigence in itself, despite what has been said of its recommendations (pp. 31, 38), can hardly be satisfactory. If I can persist in intransigence for a time, I cannot by fiat become *unaware* of the different attitudes I am then rejecting—above all the desires in them—which issue in dismay. I cannot simply forever *subtract* from my thinking—about my own life and the lives of others—thoughts or images as to the origination of action. Intransigence takes *effort*, and not congenial effort. It takes the effort required to maintain a pretence, that I am only what I am attempting to be, someone concerned only with voluntariness. This is a point not about instability or movement of feeling, but of the unsatisfactoriness of *one* feeling while one maintains it.

If none of this goes against what was said earlier of our two families of attitudes and two responses, that they are natural to us (pp. 24, 30), it is indeed clear that our course must be somehow to escape or alter the situation of attitudes and responses that has been described. It is by doing so that we shall resolve the problem of the consequences of determinism, since it arises from the unsatisfactory situation of those attitudes and responses.

Will it be thought that the enterprise of somehow making an escape from or altering our present situation is somehow misconceived? Is there some fundamentality about a particular attitude or response which stands in the way of the enterprise? Is there a fundamentality which, if it does not make the enterprise misconceived, at least must *direct* or *govern* it? Is there, in particular, such a fundamentality about the particular attitude which involves both voluntariness and origination? Some may think so. If the view we now have of our present situation has not been advanced before, philosophers have said things which can be so altered as to be applicable to it, and tend in the given direction. Let us look at three.

(i) It was said earlier, in summary of one conception of what it is for an action to be voluntary, that it is one done out of embraced desires. (1.3) But, it may be said, it cannot be that one acted *because one desired or wanted to*—in any sense at all—unless in a certain sense one *could have acted otherwise*. The idea here, perhaps, is that acting out of desire is acting out of preference for one rather than another possible situation. What this comes to, it may be claimed, is that it cannot be that one acted because one wanted to unless there was an alternative: the action was *not* the upshot of certain causal connections. It cannot be, in fact, that one acted because one wanted to unless the action was an originated one. This could have been considered earlier, as an argument to the effect that we *cannot* take voluntariness alone as a ground for life-hopes, as it has been maintained we do, but we *must* and therefore do instead take voluntariness together with origination. Not to reopen what has been settled, but to stick to the present stage of our reflections, we can consider whether our present project must take into account that voluntariness does involve origination for the given reason. The argument is suggested by, but not the same as, one offered in a kind of defence of an indeterminist picture of the mind. (Kenny, 1975, pp. 142–3; 1978, p. 26)

The initial premiss for this line of reflection may have a persuasive ring. In fact, we can accept that it is true that if one acted as one did *because one wanted to*, then in some sense one *could have acted otherwise*. But that does not necessarily get us to origination. It is entirely persuasive to say that the report that a man did buy a punnet of strawberries *because he wanted to* comes to this: his wanting to buy a punnet of strawberries was explanatory of his action, or a part of the explanation of his action. Slightly more fully, his desire was an ineliminable part of the explanation of his action. In that case, *if he had not had the desire, he would have done other than he did*. But that latter conditional proposition is easily enough expressed by way of the capacious 'could'. It *can* be what we mean by saying that he could have done other than he did. What would have made the difference, if he had done otherwise, would have been a fact about him, the absence of his desire.

Such an understanding of 'could have done otherwise' was of course noted earlier, in connection with Compatibilism. (p. 99) Here, what is being maintained is not that it is or may be the only possible correct understanding, but that it is a possible understanding which deals with the given problem. In a sentence, doing something because one wants to may entail the existence of alternatives, but these may be a matter not of origination but only voluntariness.

(ii) A second consideration which may be thought to commit us to the ground of voluntariness together with origination, or to establish its fundamentality, has to do with what is called reflectiveness. It is maintained that reflective persons operate with the conception of voluntariness with origination, and unreflective persons operate with the ground of voluntariness alone. A reflective person is one who has an awareness of determinism, as a result of acquaintance with philosophy, science or religion. (Cf. C. A. Campbell, 1951) As will be apparent from what has been said already, this is false in its claim that many people—the unreflective as defined—lack ideas of the sort that issue in the indeterminist pictures of the mind, and so have ideas of voluntariness alone. It is not necessary, despite determinism's logical relation to origination, that our having ideas of origination requires our having an awareness of determinism, that our ideas of origination are somehow owed to an awareness of doctrines of determinism.

(iii) Differently, but again about something called reflectiveness, it may be said that each of us has reflective and unreflective moments in connection with moral responsibility in particular. When we are reflective we use the conception of moral responsibility which includes both elements, and when we are unreflective we use the conception which includes only voluntariness. This different reflectiveness is essentially a matter of emotional calm together with beliefs about the causal ancestry of a person's action, perhaps beliefs of a psychoanalytical kind having to do with experiences as an infant or child. Our unreflectiveness here is bound up with violent emotions, such as hate, anger, or indignation, typically having to do with an action of which we have been the victim. (Cf. Edwards, 1961; Hospers, 1961)

This is perhaps *more* arguable than the distinction between kinds of people, and evidently stands in some distant relation to the view about shared attitudes to which we have come. That is not to say, however, that these considerations establish that the wider conception of moral responsibility is somehow superior to the narrower. If there is some connection between strong feelings about an action and the narrower conception, it is certainly not true that we focus on voluntariness by itself as a ground for moral responsibility only if we are pushed by such feelings. We can focus on voluntariness as a result, for example, of calm thoughts about the function of morality. (pp. 70 ff.) In any case, if it is granted that there is some closer connection between strong feelings about actions and the narrower conception, that would not establish anything significant by way of superiority. It would not make it possible to draw the conclusion that the narrower conception is *false* and the wider *true*, certainly, and nothing else is suggested.

Unhindered, then, by any idea to the effect that one of the two attitudes, or one of two responses, is somehow fundamental, we can set about reflecting on the possibility of bringing about a change in our situation, which is to say a change in our feelings. What particular course shall we take? We can make a response which is best described as an attempt. It is, by way of a first very general description, *the attempt to free ourselves from the attitudes which carry thoughts inconsistent with determinism, free ourselves by various means, including reflecting on our attitudes having to do only with what is consistent with determinism, which is voluntariness.*

To succeed in some degree in freeing ourselves from attitudes of the first kind would be, to some degree, to avoid the discomfort of dismay. It would also be, to some degree, to avoid the irrationality of desiring what we cannot have. It would, further, alleviate our condition of contradiction, our condition like the condition of being subject to inconsistent commands. To make this attempt to free ourselves from attitudes which carry thoughts or images of origination is not to make the response of intransigence, and hence we may escape its unsatisfactoriness as well. This is so for the following reason.

The defining feature of intransigence is the assertion, so to speak, that determinism affects nothing—that it is true or can be true without anything changing. (p. 31) To this end it encapsulates a kind of dismissal or denial of attitudes involving origination. The present response is in part a meta-response, greatly more so than is intransigence—or dismay. (pp. 38, 23) The present response, crucially, allows the existence of those attitudes and attempts to deal with them. It is not an attempt to disavow them or to do anything like pretend they do not exist. It involves our accepting a certain loss, centrally a certain frustration of desires we do have. It involves our accepting that if we have desires having to do only with voluntariness, we do also have desires which rest in part on ideas of origination. We have the attitude to others that their actions are both voluntary and originated, and we also have this attitude to ourselves about our own actions. (Cf. p. 50)

Our third response to determinism, more particularly, will accept that we do indeed have life-hopes of a certain kind, which we must attempt to eschew, as well as hopes of another kind in which we can persist. My hope, say, that I shall overcome my various deficiencies and so achieve a distinction in my profession, in so far as the hope has to do with origination, rests on falsehood and I must seek to eschew it. My related hope, different in that it has to do only with voluntariness, may be taken to rest on a considerable truth or probability about voluntariness, and to be in no need of being eschewed. Reflection on the latter hope is one thing that may aid me in giving up the former.

Likewise, with respect to personal feelings, our response to determinism may be to accept that we do have feelings about others which carry ideas as to originated actions, and that we must seek to assuage these feelings, since the ideas are false—and the response will also include the fact that feelings about others which only carry beliefs as to voluntariness are often in place, since often the beliefs are generally true. So with the matter of knowledge, and with holding others and oneself morally responsible, and crediting others and oneself with moral responsibility. So too with the related moral matters. The attempted response to determinism in these connections will be one which accepts that we do have two kinds of feelings in this regard, one of which involves falsehood and needs to be eschewed, and one of which generally involves truth and so can persist.

The attempted response is better if still wholly generally and abstractly described as *the endeavour to give up certain attitudes, fundamentally the endeavour to accept the defeat of certain desires, by way of reflecting on the situation in which our success would put us.* It is *the endeavour to accommodate ourselves to what we can truly possess, mainly by seeing its value.* The two aspects of the endeavour, seeing the value of what we can have, and giving up with respect to what we cannot have, are of course intimately connected. The endeavour, as will be understood, is to arrive at attitudes beyond the pair involved in Compatibilism and Incompatibilism. (pp. 105, 106)

There is no supposing that we can satisfy ourselves about determinism and freedom without engaging in this endeavour. That is has not been much attempted in recent centuries within the dominant tradition of Western philosophy, is close to the explanation of the persistence of the problem of the consequences of determinism. That explanation, as anticipated in what was said of the 'error theories' of Compatibilists and Incompatibilists (p. 117), *is* the fact of our shared conflicting inclinations with respect to life-hopes, personal feelings, knowledge, and morality. We are pulled first in one direction, then in another. If we enter into the traditional Compatibilist and Incompatibilist misconception of our situation, a conception that mistakenly intellectualizes it, we are pulled back and forth between Compatibilism and Incompatibilism. Our attitude to the initiation of action which involves only voluntariness inclines us to Compatibilism, and our attitude which also involves origination inclines us to Incompatibilism.

The problem of the consequences of determinism has not persisted because of confusion, and it has not persisted either because the logical upshot of determinism is unclear—its consistency or inconsistency with other things. Compatibilists and Incompatibilists have maintained the former; many others have been inclined to the latter. The problem, as I hope it is a recommendation of this book to show, has persisted for the reason that determinism is unsatisfactory to the corpus of our desires—no matter which set of desires we concentrate upon—and not much attempt, and certainly no successful attempt, has recently been made to assuage that dissatisfaction.

To seek to do better—to seek to come to a certain judgement of our circumstance, and hence to seek to accommodate our desires to what we possess—is to try to arrive at a large part of what can properly be called a philosophy of life. A philosophy of life, in this understanding, is not rightly called an attempt to give meaning to life or to establish its meaning. It consists in a broad attitude to life, an attitude or group of attitudes which, most importantly, provides as much sustenance or support as can be had within the constraints of truth. The attitude or attitudes sustain or support one in the face of the defeat of our desires of various kinds, including those pertaining to the initiation of action which enter into life-hopes, personal feelings, and so on. The attitude or attitudes, further, encompass fundamental valuations, and, if the terms are not too diminishing, fundamental policies and strategies. The responses of dismay and intransigence, if either could be persisted in to the exclusion of the other, could also be advocacies of parts of philosophies of life, in the case of dismay something other than a satisfactory one.

Attempts to provide philosophies of life or parts of them have not been common in the dominant tradition of Western philosophy. It is the tradition which can be quickly identified as having Aristotle, Descartes, Hume, and Kant as exemplars, and as giving a priority to roughly that kind of argumentation which has been the stuff of our inquiry so far into determinism. Indeed, within the recent part of that tradition, there has been something like a disdain for philosophies of life. This may owe something to the obscurity, excess, idiosyncrasy, and in general the intellectual weakness of views of our existence offered by many who do not attempt to satisfy the usual standards of the dominant tradition—for whatever reason.

It is plain enough, however, that philosophies of life in the relevant sense have been of great importance in the work of some of the great philosophers within the tradition. Plato, Aristotle, Spinoza, Kant, and Russell have in different ways recommended philosophies of life. So too have able contemporary philosophers. (Klemke, 1981; Edwards, 1967a) My reason for attempting to arrive at a part of one, however, has nothing to do with any inclination to carry on what is mainly a philosophical practice of the past, and nothing to do with any inclination to be free of the usual standards of the dominant tradition. My reason, as has been explained, has to do with the nature of the final problem of this book. *Nothing but* the relevant part of a philosophy of life can complete our inquiry with any chance of success.

The attempt to come to such a thing can get some help from at least a part of what has been a subsidiary philosophical tradition, a variegated one of some depth and strength. It has Spinoza in it, and in a way Kant, Rousseau, and Hegel. Three other groups of members of it are Cicero, Marcus Aurelius and others of the Stoics; Duns Scotus, Luther and Maritain; and Comte, Marx, Engels, and Bakunin. Some would add Freud. The tradition is said to concern freedom. A full account of it has characterized it as concerning 'the acquired freedom of self-perfection'. (Adler, 1958)

It has to do, in fact, with the renunciation of some of our desires, and the embracing of what is right, good, true, natural, rational, wise, righteous, necessary, or historical. Despite what has been maintained earlier about the ambiguity of 'free' and about attitudes (p. 107), Bentham was perhaps not wrong to abuse the tradition, to abuse above all those who have said only *right* acts or the like are 'free' acts. 'They pervert language; they refuse to employ the word *liberty* in its common acceptation; they speak in a tongue peculiar to themselves.' (1950 (1840), p. 94; cf. Nozick, 1981, pp. 326 ff.) The tradition of thought in question cannot really be said to have to do with any freedom distinct from voluntariness and origination. It will be of some use none the less.

What has been said so far has been no more than programmatic. Let us now set about the attempt to resolve the problem of the consequences of determinism.

3.2 LIFE-HOPES

The least tractable issue is that of life-hopes. We *do*, as we have seen, have hopes of the kind which rest on and contain images or ideas of a self and of its activity in escaping environment and character, in securing for us an open, alterable, or unfixed future. (p. 17) These hopes, depending on and carrying these particular images or ideas of the initiation of actions, are in conflict with the theory of determinism. The hypotheses of the theory make our future actions the effects of certain causal sequences, by definition unbroken, whose initial items are bodily items at the time of our birth and environmental items then and after. There can be no doubt about the inconsistency. Given the theory of determinism, my feeling that my life so far has not gone so well as I hoped cannot be dealt with by means of the thought that I have a certain radical capability of achievement in the future.

Nothing can be contrived, consistent with determinism, that will actually *preserve* the life-hopes which get their identity partly from the given images or ideas—the germs of doctrines of origination in the indeterminist theories of the mind. It is possible, perhaps, to be attracted for a time to Kant's determination to have it both ways, to have a determinism and also to have what is inconsistent with it. In the end, his 'two worlds' enterprise (p. 94) is yet less satisfactory with life-hopes than with moral responsibility. Moral responsibility may seem to offer the possibility of *etherealization*, so to speak, but my life-hopes, very definitely, are *of this world*, the world of which we are taking determinism to be true. Nor is there any chance of going even any significant way in the Kantian direction. We shall not actually save our hopes of the given kind, by regarding them as involving *useful fictions*. (Cf. Vaihinger, 1924)

The question must be not whether we can preserve these hopes consistently with a determinism, but rather, in part, whether we can go towards *abating* or *diminishing* them. The attempt to do so will involve various things: consideration of the content of these hopes, several possible compensations of determinism, a number of reassurances, and finally a certain prospect having to do with belief in determinism.

3.2.1 Conceptual Thinness

Any strong inquiry into indeterminist theories of the mind, and the widespread philosophical scepticism about those theories, suggests a first possibility. The hopes with which we are concerned rest in part on what we can now call images of origination. For an action to be originated is (i) for it not to be a matter of certain nomic connections, such as those asserted in our theory of determinism, and (ii) for it to be somehow in the power of the agent. The first or negative part of this conception is clear. In one respect it has to do with an intention we form, the forward-looking intention to perform an action. It is the idea that this intention is not a certain effect, not a product of a certain kind of causal sequence.

The second or positive part of the conception includes the image or idea of a self, as well as some image or idea of its relation to the intention. An attempt may be made to characterize the relation by way, say, of notions of teleology. Such notions, at bottom, have to do with an earlier thing's being explained or determined by a later. They are unsatisfactory. Roughly the same is to be said, as is evident, of other attempts to give effective content to talk of the creative or productive relationship between the self and its intentions and the like.[1] It may be said that in so far as the positive part of the conception of origination is concerned, we are left with a referring term that does not do much referring— *the self*—and a collection of verbs of doubtful content. The self *has a power* with respect to intentions and the like; it *controls* decision-making; it *acts*; it *gives rise to* choice; it *causes* things, but not in the standard way, such that its so-called effects are ordinary effects. The referring term and the verbs, it may be said, pass through the mind without leaving a great deal of trace. It can be argued that as they are used they are sounds to which not much by way of actual conceptions is attached.

The upshot is that it approaches being true that the relevant content of the given life-hopes can be articulated only negatively. To have a life-hope which involves thoughts of origination is to have a hope whose content having to do with the initiation of action is not much more than a proposition denying certain causal connections, connections expressed by certain conditional statements. My hope, perhaps, is to write another novel, and I take it that the necessary means to this end is a campaign of reflection and invention, which campaign will depend on my keeping various of my inclinations in control. My hope, being of the kind we are considering, is in its clear content for little more than the non-existence of certain causal connections. The little more is expressed by an ineffectual designator and the various verbs. What they reduce to, it seems, is a power-I-know-not-what.

To come towards the main point, can we make use of the thought that less is taken from us by the denial of such hopes than might have been supposed? My denied hope is less contentful than it might have been, far less contentful than the free-speaking and free-writing defenders of origination have pretended. They have often assumed that we all have some full and determinate conception of origination, but we have not. Can we then not set out to take the defeat of our hope as a lesser thing? To come to the main point, can we not with reason address a certain exhortation to ourselves? Let us, we can tell ourselves, seek to care less about being deprived of what is near to a mystery, care less about the absence of what is near to inexpressible. Let us try to escape being troubled by being denied what is conveyed by only a shuffle of elusive verbs with an evanescent subject.

The exhortation, to my mind, is not greatly effective, for four reasons.

The first is that it rests on a judgement or idea as to contentfulness, and such a judgement or idea is no very secure foundation. It did not turn out to be true, certainly, despite the considerable contributions of Logical Positivism to philosophy, that that movement succeeded in formulating a principle of contentfulness. (Ayer, 1936) It is all very well to speak of a shuffle of verbs with an evanescent subject, but they are not *nonsense*—actually without sense. Used in the elusive way, they are intimately connected with discourse of several kinds, which connections may themselves be taken as giving them significance. What is most important at this point is not the consideration of certain relevant doctrines in the philosophy of language, having to do with contextual meaning and the like. What is most important is that we *do accept* that the verbs and the like do bring into view something of importance to us.

A second reason why the given exhortation is less than persuasive is a general truth to the effect that our feelings do not depend so much on content as might be expected, or perhaps hoped. The example of a nameless or shapeless fear is relevant. There seems little reason to think that feelings which in some respect have little content are likely to abate on that ground alone. It is at least sometimes possible to argue in precisely the opposite direction.

Thirdly, the exhortation presupposes a certain possibility of managing our emotions, of managing hopes of the given kind. Certainly we can in some ways and to some extent control our emotions—if this were not possible, the whole enterprise on which we are now engaged in connection with the consequences of determinism would be pointless. We can, for example, sometimes forcibly turn our thoughts from a dark subject, and so alter our feelings. But can we by a rather intellectual consideration—about want of contentfulness—move far towards giving up something as fundamental to our lives as hopes of the given kind?

That is unlikely. There is a common intellectual temperament which easily withdraws from or even revolts against the conceptually unsatisfactory when the subject-matter does not touch on our lives so closely as the present one. The subject-matter of the nature of numbers will do as an example. There is also an intellectual temperament, not common, which withdraws or revolts even when the subject-matter *does* touch on our lives as closely as the present one. This latter temperament, perhaps exemplified by some of the Compatibilist philosophers, is not one which is anything like widely distributed among men and women. It is not widely distributed among philosophers, or, as can definitely be added, scientists.

There is a fourth reason why there is little use in the exhortation to care less about being deprived of what is near to a mystery, near to inexpressible. We have it that hopes involving origination have to do with (i) with a denial of certain nomic connections and (ii) with a peculiar power on our part. It is the second and positive element that is obscure, and whose obscurity we are contemplating as an aid to abating the hopes in question. However, the second element, the conceptually slight element, is absolutely essential. It is this remainder that makes the difference between mere chance—a denial of determinism—and something else, which is what we do want. The second element is what is to save us from being victims of mere randomness. What we are being exhorted to do, then, is to free ourselves from certain hopes by way of denigration, if that is not too strong a word, of exactly something that is essential to them. It is at least as fundamental to them as the other element.

There is nothing irrational in the exhortation we have been considering—to try to eschew certain hopes by reflecting that they are in a certain respect minimally contentful, that they are not *for* something clear. It is hard to see that it can carry us far forward. It cannot be of much significance in the attempt to arrive at a satisfactory philosophy of life in so far as life-hopes are concerned, and in so far as the other matters having to do with the initiation of action are concerned, personal feelings and so on.

Before turning to a consideration of a second strategy, there is a general point that calls out for emphasis, although it has been in view already, and can be introduced by a certain similarity.

We are looking into possibilities with respect to the characterization of a certain response to determinism. Or, as it is as proper to say, we are seeking to *make* this response. The first possibility we have been considering is an exhortation having to do with a conceptual thinness of essential ideas which enter into life-hopes inconsistent with determinism. Any reader with our past journey of inquiry in mind must have the true thought that there exists a certain similarity between the proposal we have been considering and something which was specified as part of the response of intransigence. A part of that response, it was said, is resistance to the unsatisfactory image of origination. (p. 31) Here in particular, therefore, there arises the question of the distinctness of the response with which we are now concerned and the response of intransigence. *Are they distinct?*

One part of the answer has already been given: that the response of intransigence is by definition a rejection or denial of certain attitudes, as distinct from an attempt to deal with them (p. 125) The forceful frame of mind which is intransigence can make more use of the charge of conceptual thinness than the frame of mind we are now considering. A second and connected thing to be said is that our present enterprise is the self-conscious search for a *settled* state, an escape from a kind of oscillation between inconsistent things.

A third thing to be said in answer, which takes us to the general point that needs emphasis, is that we must not fall into the error or pretence that the matters with which we are concerned are so distinguished in the reality of our lives as they have been on the page. Distinguishable responses are not unrelated entities, anything like unique. The truth, rather, is that there are likenesses and continuities between what we distinguish. The response to determinism we are considering is *not* wholly different from intransigence. It is quite as true, however, that it is not wholly different either from dismay. We are in this part of our inquiry concerned with a spectrum of feelings. It is not a subject-matter that in itself is made up of wholly contrasting phenomena or entities. (Cf. pp. 31, 125)

3.2.2. *Escape from Chance*

Comte serves as an example of a considerable number of philosophers, many of them traditional Compatibilists, who see in determinism the compensation that it rescues us from mere chance. (cf. Foot, 1957; Hobart, 1966) Comte takes it that the alternative to a world in which we are subject to determinism would be one in which my actions and the actions of others are owed to chance, which is to say owed to nothing. He also has something else in mind, having to do with the seemingly unlikely subject of politics. If a determinism 'may seem to chain us to external necessities', it has the recommendation of 'the elimination of the element of caprice, ever favourable to the worst instincts', the recommendation that it saves us from 'arbitrary will', 'arbitrary personal dictation'. (1875–7, Vol. iv, p. 194, Vol. i, p. 296, Vol. iii, p. 294, 1885, p. 435)

The main thing to be said of any such idea about chance alone is of course that we do not suppose that the alternative to a determinism is no more than chance, a denial of nomic connection. If a determinism saves us from being subject to chance, it equally deprives us of that which involves the absence of nomic connection but also involves control or agency. It deprives us, that is, of a self's origination. If our aim is to accommodate ourselves to a determinism's defeat of our life-hopes in so far as they rest on the idea of origination, we shall not much succeed in it by reflecting that determinism also defeats the idea of mere chance. We are not much compensated for the loss of a good by the reflection that what goes with it is something undesirable but never much contemplated by us.

With respect to Comte in particular, as distinct from other philosophers who have seen determinism as preserving us from chance, it is evident that he brings together an absence of nomic connection with such other things as wilful political authority or mindless tyranny. He thus also provides us with an example of confusions—there have been other kinds of them—that do not help. As is plain, what he speaks of is as consistent with a determinism: it cannot be that a determinism, in compensation for the loss of origination, gives us political freedom and rational societies. It does have certain political implications, but not necessarily these. (Ch. 4)

More generally, if one has in mind chance by itself, it is something less than clear that we would take *all* forms of it to be undesirable. That is, if we forget entirely about origination, there remains the fact that determinism in excluding *all* chance is not necessarily reassuring. Certainly we do desire the power of origination, clearly, and we cannot conceivably desire a world of chaos, one with very little or no order. It can be supposed, however, that that having subtracted origination from our world, determinism does us a separate hurt in ruling out what would be desirable, a world of *limited real uncertainty*. The idea is a vague one, but there seems the possibility that the fixity of a determined future is not preferable to the conceivable alternative of a future without origination but with limited kinds and degrees of want of necessity.

It must seem, therefore, that there is nothing to be gained from contemplating the idea that a determinism excludes chance. There is little more to be gained from related ideas that determinism gives us an intelligible world or that it provides us with a sense of security. (Snyder, 1972; Trusted, 1984, p. 49; Pagels, 1983, pp. 18–19) Nor does there seem to be anything like relevant truth in something which may be taken to be opposed to a fundamental proposition of our own inquiry, Sartre's famous theme to the effect that what we want is an escape from freedom, freedom to which we feel condemned and which issues in our 'bad faith'. (p. 98; M. Warnock, 1965, Ch. 2; Danto, 1975) There is a very different idea of determinism as compensatory, which calls for more consideration. It has a long history.

3.2.3 *Nature*

We have been concerned with the fact, as it can be described, that in certain of our life-hopes we desire a certain disconnection. We desire a disconnection from our own past lives and also from nature, where the latter is conceived as the non-human world. To have the power of origination would be to escape or to rise over nature. In a way, incidentally, it would be to have an ability to escape or rise over that part of the world which is constituted by one's own body. By contrast, it is true of all decent determinisms that they put us into connection with nature.

Each of the three hypotheses of my own theory contributes to this. Our conscious lives consist in effects of certain causal sequences whose initial conditions are constituted not only by our bodily endowment at birth but by our environments then and thereafter. The same sequences are in the causal histories of our actions. There is the further proposition of this determinism, necessary to its completion, that mental events are in the connections with simultaneous neural events specified in the Union Theory.

The compensatory idea must come to mind that a determinism in clearly asserting *a close and unproblematic connection with nature*, can be conceived as a source not only of frustration but of reassurance or even elevation. The unproblematic closeness is that of nomic connection. This particular idea about reassurance or elevation, tied to a determinism, is of course related to others. The taking of oneself as somehow but more loosely connected to nature, perhaps with nature more vaguely conceived than as just the non-human world, is something essayed and celebrated in a good deal of literature and in some religion, most familiarly in the literature of Romanticism. The particular recommendation of a determinism, if it is a recommendation, will have to do with its assertion of a close and unproblematic relation between ourselves and the natural universe.

If a determinism is true, it may be said, I cease to be a trivial existence. I cease to be what by contrast with the universe is a momentary and insignificant thing, the antithesis of anything of grandeur. I can, through my perceived *membership* in nature—my relation to it is properly so described, rather than as an external relation—escape the mereness of myself. I escape an isolation from the natural world. In place of triviality and isolation, I can identify with the greatest of realities. There is the satisfactory possibility, further, of having a certain view of my own species and its history, a view which brings it together with other species and so rises over a petty anthropocentrism. Determinism, therefore, may be claimed to be far from being 'the hideous hypothesis' (Hampshire, 1951, p. 179) and in fact the source of a deep satisfaction.

This internal connection with nature asserted by determinism, further, does not make me nature's slave. I can see, with Bakunin, that in my existence there 'is indeed no slavery at all, inasmuch as every kind of slavery presupposes two beings existing side by side and one of them subject to the other. Man being a part of nature and not outside of it cannot be its slave.' (1895, Vol. iii, pp. 213–4; cf. 1953) There is another related thought. It is that rather than being the creature of what must be regarded, in the context of the universe, as my footling series of desires, I go forward in the greatest of processes.

If this several-sided perception is a means to giving up my hopes, it may be said, it is also a compensation, or rather more than a compensation, for doing so. Furthermore, it may be said, if I have the sustenance of this several-sided truth, there remains a still larger truth, of greater sustenance. It is not only that I have what follows from clear internal connection with the natural universe, with the latter taken as the great *fact*. My membership, rather, is in that alone which is of *value*. My membership is in that alone which matters, and which matters supremely. Both the several-sided perception and the larger proposition about value have behind them a considerable tradition. Let us glance at four diverse parts of it, the thoughts of Zeno of Citium, Spinoza, Shelley, and Hegel, Marx, and Engels.

Zeno of Citium, in the early part of the third century BC, conceived of nature, of which he took us to be part, as material and deterministic, but also as suffused with Spirit or the Divine Fire. He took us to have the possibility, in our awareness of determinism, of what can be described as a life in harmony with nature. This is also the life of virtue. Diogenes Laertius, speaking of the end or goal of man, records that 'Zeno was the first . . . to designate as the end "life in agreement with nature" (or living agreeably to nature), which is the same as the virtuous life, virtue being the goal towards which nature guides us'. (1925 (c.225), p. 195) To achieve this virtuous harmony or agreement with nature, and hence with the divine, is to have a life such that health, possessions, success, and indeed all the objects of ordinary life-hopes become of no account. I not merely abate but am *freed from* my hopes. It was Epicurus who supposed that the good man could be happy while being racked, but the idea is also in accord with Zeno's teaching.

According to Spinoza in his *Ethics* we are parts in a certain sense of the sum and system of the single substance that there is, God or Nature, and wholly subject to a determinism which is somehow a matter of logical necessity rather than the natural necessity of nomic connection. Through a certain kind of increasing knowledge of the single system, we can to some extent escape our passions, one of them being hope, which Spinoza defines as 'unsteady joy arising from the image of a future or past thing about whose issue we are in doubt'. (1910 (1678), p. 123) In particular, we escape our passions through knowledge of the necessity which governs all things. One of Spinoza's propositions is this: 'In so far as the mind understands all things as necessary, so far has it greater power over the passions or suffers less from them.' He adds: 'For we see that sorrow for the loss of anything good is diminished if the person who has lost it considers that it could not by any possibility have been preserved.' (1949 (1678), p. 258)

Spinoza also supposes that if our knowledge of the necessities within God or Nature increases, we achieve 'the highest possible peace of mind', 'the highest joy', which appears to be identical with what he famously called 'the intellectual love of God'. (1949 (1678), pp. 273 ff.) From a determinism, then, there comes the prospect of enjoying the most fulfilled of ways of life. It is, certainly, the life of virtue. Increase in the knowledge of the necessity of all things, and its culmination in the intellectual love of god, is entirely bound up with the life of virtue. (1949 (1678), p. 205) Determinism thus offers the overwhelming compensation—the word, of course, does not catch the great value in question—of identification with the divine and hence with the most fundamental goodness.

If it is in general true that Romanticism celebrates a lesser and more obscure connection between ourselves and nature than is asserted by a determinism, and perhaps by Spinoza, there is the exception of Shelley. *Queen Mab*, the poem of his youth which to some extent he later disavowed, explicitly celebrates a doctrine of determinism, which doctrine is expounded in his notes to the poem. The impersonal divinity of nature, as he is very certain, is not to be confused with the inferior manlike God of Christianity. What is apostrophized, further, is not the universe in its substantiality, however divine, but necessary connection itself.

> Spirit of nature! all-sufficing power,
> Necessity! thou mother of the world!
> Unlike the God of human error, thou
> Requir'st no prayers or praises; the caprice
> Of man's weak will belongs no more to thee
> Than do the changeful passions of his breast
> To thy unvarying harmony; the slave
> Whose horrible lusts spread misery o'er the world,
> And the good man, who lifts, with virtuous pride,
> His being in the sight of happiness,
> That springs from his own works; the poison-tree,

> Beneath whose shade all life is withered up,
> And the fair oak, whose leafy dome affords
> A temple where the vows of happy love
> Are registered, are equal in thy sight:
> No love, no hate thou cherishest; revenge
> And favouritism, and worst desire of fame
> Thou know'st not: all that the wide world contains
> Are but thy passive instruments, and thou
> Regard'st them all with an impartial eye,
> Whose joy or pain thy nature cannot feel,
> Because thou hast not human sense,
> Because thou are not human mind.

To move on quickly to Hegel, Marx and Engels, there is the theme prefigured in Spinoza that what is called man's freedom consists wholly or partly in knowledge of necessity. In the case of Hegel, the necessity is run together with the Rational, the Absolute. 'We are free in recognizing it [the Absolute] as law, and following it as the substance of our being.' (1944 (1840), p. 283) Engels gives credit to Hegel for seeing that 'freedom is the appreciation of necessity' and that 'necessity is blind only in so far as it is not understood'. Freedom, for Engels, 'does not consist in the dream of independence of natural laws, but in the knowledge of these laws, and in the possibility this gives of systematically making them work towards definite ends.' (1978 (1934), pp. 128–9)

There is in Engels the familiar idea that knowledge of necessities has an instrumental value in the advancement of human history: through knowing natural laws, whether of the non-human world or our own natures or society, we are enabled to achieve certain ends. It is of course a truism that knowledge of the working of natural laws is of great value to us. It increases voluntariness, in that it decreases obstacles to the realization of desire. However, as the quoted passages indicate, there is also a quite different idea in Engels. The freedom in which knowledge of necessity issues is evidently neither voluntariness nor origination, but a certain state of mind and feeling. This freedom, so called, consists in an *acceptance* of our existence. It consists in something approximate to a *tranquillity*, and indeed related to Spinoza's intellectual love of God, which, of course, is also properly named intellectual love of Nature. This state of mind and feeling is owed to that which a determinism can be said to assert, man's membership of nature. If nature is not made divine or god like, by Engels, it inevitably retains a grandeur. There is the same compensation of determinism offered to us by Marx, although it is not the first of his conceptions of freedom.

Of what strength are such assurances as the four at which we have glanced, those offered by Zeno, Spinoza, Shelley, and Hegel, Engels, and Marx? Is the compensation of membership in nature, in one of these forms or another—perhaps Russell's (1917b) or Santayana's (1930)—something which can assuage the defeat of our life-hopes in so far as they are informed by images of origination? Can it be that a determinism in this way gives us more than or as much as it takes away, and so enables us to come to tolerate the loss of what it takes away? I suspect, despite the existence of a venerable tradition, that readers will not have been reassured.

What determinism itself gives us is no more than a nomic connection with the non-human universe. Assuredly a determinism in itself does not include any conception of the non-human universe as spiritual, divine, or godlike, let alone any deification of necessity itself in Shelley's way. However, the attempt can be made, as it is by Zeno, Spinoza, Shelley, and many others, somehow to identify the universe with something personal, spiritual, or divine, or to ascribe to it such a character. Nothing in a determinism precludes such an attempt. There is an evident consonance, in fact, between religious ideas of omnipotence and omniscience and the idea of perfect nomic connection. It is a consonance exemplified by Calvinism and predestination.

However, it is evident that ascribing a spiritual, divine or godlike character to the universe, at least in the late twentieth century, is what might unkindly be called a minority inclination. Whatever has been true in the past, very few of us are now given to anything like Spinoza's vision, or to such approximations to it as forms of pantheism or panpsychism—philosophical defenders though they have. (Sprigge, 1983) The different mysticisms of Zeno and the youthful Shelley are yet more remote from the attitudes of almost all of us. Nor are many of us likely, by whatever sort of exertion, to change our attitudes—to bring ourselves to feel that the universe is spiritual or personal. Those who have such a feeling, it seems safe to say, have acquired it by some other means than philosophical or religious argument or instruction. If such aids have sometimes been involved in the genesis of such a feeling in individuals, that genesis has had greatly more to do with something which cannot be acquired through argument or instruction, or decided upon, or summoned. It is a temperament or susceptibility of a certain kind, one which is uncommon. In its direction on to the external world, it is distinct from any ordinary religious inclination.

That is not to say that a distantly related thing is uncommon. Almost all of us, in conceiving of the physical universe, have a conception of its grandeur. Awe is inevitable. It is explicitly expressed, often enough, in scientific descriptions. Here what is in question is nothing so rare as the mentioned temperament or susceptibility having to do with spirituality, but rather a common disposition of very nearly all men. Is it possible that the disposition to awe of nature can be put to use? Can a determinism's connecting of our existence with the grandeur of nature serve us in the endeavour of seeking to give up that character of our life-hopes which has to do with origination?

It is hard to think that we can have much success by this means. One reason is partly that the enterprise cannot be much different in effect from certain related ones mentioned at the beginning, say the enterprises in Romanticism of more loosely identifying with nature, which related enterprises do not include a clear idea of a close connection between ourselves and the non-human world. That is, we are unlikely to get much more sustenance, in whatever sort of frustration or melancholy, by contemplating nomic connection rather than some lesser relationship—and contemplatings of some lesser relationship have surely not often been significantly efficacious in dealing with the large challenges of life. (It might indeed be argued, as in the case of the vagueness of the idea of origination, that we are *more* moved by the unspecific (p. 131), and yet not moved much.) It is one thing to write odes and quite another to deal effectively with such experience as Samuel Johnson's in his recurring contemplation of death. (Boswell, 1934–64 (1791)) To suppose that men as they have been, and as they now are, can very often put aside such darkness, when it comes upon them, by the means of identification with the universe, is surely to confuse poetic or philosophical reverie with life itself. It is indeed hard to think that determinist identifications with nature, even if they do offer *more* hope, can do much to assuage the defeat of life-hopes having to do with origination. Still, at least one of the ideas which turn up in identifications with nature can be separated out and needs more consideration. (3.2.8)

3.2.4. Failure

A different possible compensation of a determinism is more intimately connected with it than are thoughts of nature. It has little tradition behind it, and can be set out quickly. To have a life-hope, to recall, is either to hope that one will achieve a certain thing, or else that some state of affairs will come to obtain. At least typically, with respect to the second kind of hope, one believes that the desired state of affairs will only come about through one's own doing, and so in both cases the realization of the hope *depends on oneself*, on one's own endeavours. Life-hopes therefore carry with them the possibility of personal failure. A hope is indeed to be characterized as an unsteady joy or like feeling about something of whose occurrence one is uncertain. (p. 137) At least typically the aspect of doubt in my hopes, as Spinoza might have added, is doubt as to whether I will succeed or fail in my endeavours. Will I win or lose, rise to the challenge or not, measure up or not, secure what I want or instead secure disappointment, embarrassment, grief, or disgrace? The contemplation of failure is no light thing. The experience of failure is likely to be a darker one.

Consider life-hopes of the two kinds in so far as they carry ideas as to origination. The prospect of failure and the actuality of failure are here a prospect and actuality having to do with origination. More particularly, our subject is the individual power of origination which each of us is inclined to attribute to himself or herself, and the possibility of its being insufficient to some challenge or project, or the fact of its having been insufficient.

My supposed power of origination is one which I obscurely identify with *myself*. That very claim is in itself obscure, but it is a claim which seems impossible to deny. The prospect or experience of failure, then, in so far as it has to do with origination, is absolutely the prospect or experience of *my failure*. This particular prospect and experience of failure are different from others which can be distinguished, those which involve a view of myself as fundamentally a corpus of dispositions. My experience of failure, if I put my failure down only to a less rational desire having carried the day over a more rational, brings with it a lesser self-accusation, a lesser diminishment or disgrace, than if I put my failure down to myself in the other sense, the very centre of my existence. The 'I have failed' which carries no idea about origination, and hence no failure in it, also carries less hurt.

Indeed, some will want to say more, by way of a certain question. *Is there* an 'I have failed' which carries no idea about origination? Can we, as we are, have something properly describable as an experience of failure which does not have in it the self-accusation which attaches to an idea of origination? The thought that a temptation has triumphed, or that a less rational desire has carried the day over a more rational, may seem to be more a dismayed report on what has happened than a self-accusation. Despite what was assumed above, some will say, it seems not really to be the thought that I have failed. This seems to me an understandable inclination, but incorrect. More will be said of it in due course in connection with the issue of determinism and personal feelings, on which we are now verging. It *is* correct, however, and the point that is now important, that the sharpest sense of failure is one which has to do with origination. It might be mitigated by reducing our sense of ourselves in a way that has been admirably expounded and indeed recommended. (Parfit, 1984, Chs. 10–12) but we have not yet done that.

All of this, as must be allowed, is impressionistic. The subject-matter of the self is one of which it is impossible to get a clear view, and it is as impossible that our conceptions for dealing with it can be very satisfactory. To speak of something that *is* possible, more might have been done to give a more specific account of many things that have been bundled into the two categories with which we are concerned, anticipation of failure and experience of failure. A certain conclusion can nevertheless be attempted.

If a determinism deprives us of certain life-hopes, all our life-hopes of a certain character, it can also be said to offer us *some* compensation. It saves us a certain apprehension and sharp experience of failure, a peculiarly sharp apprehension and experience of failure. It offers us, in place of certain fears of failure and self-accusations of having failed, a certain composure or tranquillity. This, in its calm, is related to such feelings as might be produced by a successful identification, if that were possible, with ongoing nature. However, the given composure or tranquillity is a quite different thing in having a quite different ground. Its ground has to do with me, and the lack of a conceivable power that I might have had, and not with the external world.

It is hardly possible to discuss our present subject without feeling uneasy, as I have before now, about falling into a kind of autobiographical reflection lacking a general relevance. Perhaps something of this kind is inevitable, since the enterprise we have in hand is in a way personal. It is an enterprise, by its very nature, which should not issue readily in confident generalizations. I propose, however, that the consideration about failure offers to all of us a *greater* aid than anything else considered so far. We can go some way towards abating certain of our life-hopes by persistence in the thought a determinism can preserve us from the anticipation and experience of a certain kind of failure. We can go some way in the given direction, which is not to say that we turn a corner, that a determinism in so far as it touches on life-hopes becomes a tolerable thing.

3.2.5. *Unbounded Hopes*

Let us, to consider the possibility of a certain reassurance, look back to our very first reflections on life-hopes. We took it that very often they are hopes that we shall achieve certain things, and, when they are not, they are likely to be hopes for states of affairs that will in fact depend on what we do. It is possible and natural, as we saw, to have in mind in either case life-hopes which depend on the idea of originated actions. I thus have the idea of a series of future moments of challenge in my life. At each such moment, according to this idea, I will be subject to two desires, one of them being a desire which will not serve my life-hope, no doubt a desire for immediate gratification. The outcome at each such moment will *not* simply be the result of the strength of this desire and that of the opposed desire to achieve my life-hope. It will not be the case, according to this idea, that what I do will be the effect of only these pulls. Rather, given both these desires, and all else that is true of me, I shall have a kind of possibility of two courses of action, the one serving my life-hope and the other providing only immediate gratification. (1.2)

On the other hand, as we saw, it is possible and natural to think that life-hopes do not depend on an image or belief about originated actions, but on the belief that our actions will flow, not from reluctant desires we shall have, but from our embraced desires. Our future circumstances of action will be enabling rather than frustrating circumstances. Thus a man's life-hopes may be taken to depend on what was called the way of his world, on the ascendancy in him of desires that do serve the realization of his hopes, on his independence of others, including their threats, and on the absence of such bodily constraints as illness or disability. His life-hope, say, to come to have some distinction in his profession, may be taken by me as depending on such things. (1.3)

Given a determinism, it is hopes of the latter kind that we can have, and the question now is their worth. A first thing to be said of them is that they are in a certain sense *no more limited than* life-hopes of the former kind, involving origination. Let us have in mind what can be labelled as the *object* of a hope, an action of achievement, with nothing said of the initiation of the action, or a certain state of affairs. For any life-hope involving origination, there can be a life-hope with the same object involving only embraced desires. Any object of a life-hope involving origination—professional distinction, to be an actress, the achievement of a certain peace—can be the object of a life-hope involving only embraced desires. This is of great importance.

If I contemplate my future first with origination in mind and then without it, it makes sense to say that whatever possible goods turn up in the first contemplation can also turn up in the second. It is not as if some *sector* of goods is closed off by a determinism. Any fantasy of grandeur, any vision of success, any picture of personal security, any thought of personal relationships or of the avoidance of disappointment or disaster—any of these can as readily be the stuff of the second kind of hope as the first. In a clear sense, hope can be as unbounded in the second way as in the first.

It may be objected that hopes are not only a matter of what have been called their objects. That is true enough, as we know. Hopes can be for actions expressly conceived as originated. They can be for states of affairs taken to depend on actions conceived as originated. If such ideas of origination are thin ones, as we have seen, that does not greatly matter. There is the fact of which we know, that something of value is subtracted from a hope by subtracting ideas of origination from it. It remains a truth, despite the objection, that such subtraction deprives us of no object of hope, and it can be said that objects of hopes are the great constituents of hopes. Any summation of objects, say Byron's in *Don Juan* (II, clxxix)—

> Glory, the grape, love, gold, in these are sunk
> The hopes of all men, and of every nation

—any summation of objects, however shallow or profound, is as true of a deterministic human world as it is of a human world of origination. It can be added, certainly, with respect to the constituent of hopes having to do with the initiation of action, that to take it as only voluntariness does allow us certain thoughts to the effect that what is to come is not inevitable, is within our control, and does contain opportunities. (Dennett, 1984)

3.2.6 Uncertainty

There is something else that is virtually as much a part of hopes which depend on beliefs that one's future actions will flow from one's own embraced desires. There is evidently a difference, already noticed, between hope and something else, the anticipation or expectation of a happy circumstance with the *certainty*, in so far as we can have it, that it will occur. There is a difference between hoping that I will get an award of merit and *knowing* or *fully* expecting that I will. Is it possible to feel that hope, when it is full and strong, is the better thing, a better species of happiness? One can take it, surely, that a life wholly informed by *certainty* as to the having of future goods would be a lesser life than one informed by good hopes, or at any rate one which was partly a matter of hopes rather than wholly undoubted expectations. No doubt this line of thought needs examination and more qualification, but is hard to resist the idea that a part of the value to us of our hopes is owed precisely to the uncertainty of our actually getting what we hope for.

To come to the essential point, there is virtually as much room for uncertainty—a desirable degree of uncertainty—with respect to the second kind of hopes. If my hope for fame rests on the belief that my future actions will indeed flow from my embraced desires, there is virtually as much room for uncertainty in this case as with hope when it involves origination.

Assuredly a hope involving only voluntariness is one which is consistent with the truth of a determinism, a fixed future. It thus is consistent with the logical possibility of a man's certainty as to what will happen. There is not the same logical or conceptual possibility of certainty, based on nomic connection, with hopes that bring in origination. However, this makes little difference. Whatever logical possibility of certainty may attend the former hopes, there is uncertainty enough about them. It is very far from true that my world becomes in fact a predictable place by way of the truth of a determinism. I can be reassured that the flavour that is given to life by the possibility that good or great things will happen is not taken away by a determinism.

3.2.7 Credit

Perhaps there is also a reassurance that is as much a matter of the category of personal feelings as of life-hopes. Among my personal feelings towards myself, as remarked earlier, I may have the satisfaction of giving myself credit for something. (p. 35) A part of my hopes may be the anticipation of such credit. A larger part may be the anticipation of having the good judgements and feelings of others. What credit can I anticipate, from myself and others, by way of hopes which do not involve origination?

It needs to be allowed, consistently with what was said above of the tie between origination and failure, that there is a kind of credit that I cannot anticipate. I have no chance of the credit that could be mine if I had a power of origination. But that is certainly not the only credit conceivable. To say but a word here, I can in my future actions have the credit of rational action, action in accordance with desires that serve my fundamental end. Or I can have the credit of strong character, or sensitivity, or judgement, or decency, or of rising over mere conventionality. The list continues. Life-hopes having nothing to do with origination, therefore, can be hopes to do what will secure me the good feelings and judgements of myself and others.

3.2.8 Acceptance of Determinism

It is possible to conclude that a theory of determinism is very strongly supported. To go beyond that, it is possible to be *convinced*, as I myself am, of such a theory, although with the reservation that this conviction goes beyond the sum of evidence for and against. As was none the less remarked, in the course of an argument having to do with moral responsiblity and dismay, it is true that almost all of us, at least in one great tradition of culture, do not in fact believe a determinism. (p. 67) It was added that we do not disbelieve it either.

To say more of this majority, it includes some or perhaps many who accept that all the evidence and argument on offer tells on balance in favour of a determinism, and yet do not believe it. To be in this position is not both to take it to be true, *simpliciter*, and yet not believe it, which is logically impossible. Rather, perhaps, it is to think that all the known evidence and argument supports it on balance, and also that contrary evidence or argument may turn up. The agnostic majority, secondly, also includes some or many who are inclined to think that all the known evidence and argument on balance supports determinism, but entertain a suspicion that there is error in that evidence and argument. The suggestion of contradiction in this position, surely, is a problem that might be dealt with if philosophers were to turn their hand to providing a perspicuous philosophy of the propositional attitudes, in part a differentiating account of kinds of assent to propositions. The agnostic majority, finally, must contain some or many people who are somehow still closer to dissent than the two groups mentioned.

It is possible to feel that the explanation of the existence of the agnostic majority is owed to rootedness of images of origination in our lives, where that rootedness is not to be identified with truth or conceptual necessity. It is not too much to say, as it seems to me, that in our reflection on determinism we are apt to be prisoners of culture. We are bound by our inherited ways of feeling. These get expression in our language and are given a reality in many fundamental practices both individual and social. That is not to say, to repeat, that we have *reasons* for thinking determinism false. We do not have rational grounds of opposition.

There is the possibility that further reflection on determinism, including reflection on the non-rational sources of opposition to it, will issue in a more settled and unqualified belief that it is true. *It is such belief that is certain to be more effective than anything we have so far considered in enabling us to abate life-hopes having to do with origination.* To approach the same conclusion by a slightly different path, there is a distinction between hopes and wishes. One can wish for the impossible, it seems, but not hope for it. At least a majority of us do not take origination to be impossible, whatever our attitude to evidence and argument. We hope for it. We shall move effectively towards ceasing to hope that it exists, and come merely to wish for it, when we come closer to a settled and unqualified belief in the truth of determinism and the impossibility of origination. We can move towards such a state by an awareness of what has been impeding it.

To express the matter from the point of view of one who *is* persuaded by the evidence and argument for a determinism, the best strategy for dealing with one's recalcitrant life-hopes is further persuasion of the truth of determinism. Spinoza was considered above in connection with the possible compensation having to do with membership in nature. As was noted, however, he also maintains that it is increasing knowledge of the necessity which governs all things which enables us to escape our passions. (p. 137) One can object to his general claim that sorrow over the loss of a good is diminished by the perception that the having of it was impossible. It does not seem that one can object to the proposition that certain of our hopes, if they can be abated somewhat by the consideration having to do with failure, can only be cured by a final acceptance of determinism. That, to repeat, is importantly a matter of rising over our history.

Of course, one cannot just *choose* or *decide* to believe anything, and so there is no possibility of abating our hopes by choosing or deciding to believe a determinism. The most that one can do is to consider that one's want of final assent to a determinism is owed not to evidence or argument against it, but to one's being a prisoner of inherited desires. To begin to do this—to suspect oneself—is to do something which may have effect. In this there is the greatest likelihood we have so far discovered of abating one's hopes having to do with origination.

What has just been said may be misconceived, and so seem curious or worse. It *would* be bizarre to attempt to prove the truth of a determinism by way of the idea that a desire gives rise to opposition to it. It would be perfectly proper to reply to any such attempt that the fact that determinism is unsatisfactory to a rooted desire is consistent with there also being good reason for not accepting it. What has been under consideration, however, has not been an irrelevant and necessarily failing attempt to prove or confirm determinism. The idea, rather, has been to try to ameliorate a certain effect which a theory has on life-hopes, rather than to confirm the theory. The idea has been to make a certain recommendation.

The recommendation comes to this: *let us try to escape certain hopes by coming fully to believe what is in fact true, a determinism.* It is the recommendation that we come to *accept* what can independently be seen to be a likely truth, by escaping a certain cultural inheritance, and so abate our life-hopes in so far as they involve origination.

3.2.9 Affirmation

It is at this point in this inquiry into the consequences of determinism that we come to its principal conclusion, although not a full awareness of the breadth of that conclusion. The latter cannot be had until we have looked again at the matters of personal feelings, knowledge, morality, and certain social institutions and practices, all of which are touched by a determinism, and have also glanced at things of great value to us which are not touched by it at all.

We have been considering a third response with respect to determinism and our life-hopes, a response different from those of dismay and intransigence. It is *the response of affirmation.* As anticipated (p. 125), it has several parts.

First, it accepts that a determinism does affect our life-hopes. It defeats those which have a character which they cannot have if determinism is true. This must be at least a deep disappointment. It is not as if we can submit ourselves to the commanding fact of causation—which submission is the attitude included in Compatibilism as defined. (p. 106) If there is assuagement to be had from certain things, and relief to be had in the future from one of them—a fuller or deeper belief in determinism—it remains a truth that we cannot escape being affected in our life-hopes by a determinism. We are far from the mistake of a Compatibilist who considers life-hopes and asserts that nothing changes with respect to them as a consequence of determinism. Nor is our response the response of intransigence.

The response of affirmation in a second part asserts that a determinism does not destroy life-hopes. We can in a fundamental way persist in them. It is entirely a mistake, the mistake of an Incompatibilist who considers life-hopes, to think that a determinism must end them. Nor is our response the response of dismay. We take it that if our life-hopes must have one character rather than another, that does not come close to saying that a determinism ends them.

There is a third part of the response of affirmation, separable from the propositions that a determinism at least touches our life-hopes but does not destroy them. The response is importantly that our life-hopes, conceived as they can be, remain at least sustaining things, life-sustaining things. They have at least that large value for us. This is owed to the facts we now know. They can be unbounded in a clear sense. The goods which are their objects are made no less good by a determinism. They can have what distinguishes them from foreknowledge of a good, the feature of uncertainty, which is a recommendation of them. They can be hopes for honour, standing, and in general all the forms of credit to which we so much aspire.

Thus, if a determinism touches my life, taken as consisting in a line of hopes, it none the less may leave my life a great deal more than merely tolerable in this respect. My life, in so far as it consists in a line of hopes, does not become dark. The line of my hopes supports me, and it may enlarge, delight, and enrich me. My life, as a line of hopes, can be a life of full anticipation and fulfilment. My hopes can enter importantly into a philosophy of life which is not one of resignation or defeat, such as to burden me, but rather can be one of celebration.

Will someone ask at this point for more precision, perhaps for a definition of what it is for something to be life-sustaining, or of what it is for a life to be one of full anticipation and fulfilment? There is nothing unreasonable about the request so long as it is not accompanied by unreasonableness about what can be done to satisfy it. It would be unreasonable, for example, to think that the conception of that which is life-sustaining is wholly a matter of discovery of facts. It is not, but is in good part a matter of decision or resolution. It would also be unreasonable, as always, to demand a kind of precision which the subject-matter does not allow.

Let us finish here by having clear the relation of affirmation to Compatibilism and Incompatibilism. Affirmation differs wholly from both in that it recognizes the existence of two attitudes where Compatibilism and Incompatibilism assert a single conception and a single connection with moral responsibility and the like. Affirmation does involve reliance on a single attitude, having to do only with voluntariness, which of course is related to the single conception of initiation which Compatibilists assign to us. Affirmation also has to do with the other attitude, pertaining also to origination, related to the single conception which Incompatibilists assign to us. It is not much more like Compatibilism than Incompatibilism. (Cf. p. 112)

3.3 PERSONAL FEELINGS

What is to be attempted with personal feelings, as with life-hopes, is the response of affirmation. Personal feelings were divided into the appreciative and the resentful or accusatory kinds, the former being reactions to having the good feelings or judgements of others, the latter being reactions to having the bad feelings or judgements of others. Both kinds have large, fixed places in our lives, and the former enrich our lives. Resentful feelings were illustrated by the example of my bitterness about an adversary who makes trouble between myself and my friend and patron, thereby depriving me of support in something important to me. The appreciative feelings have gratitude at their centre, and might in fact be regarded as consisting in forms of gratitude.

Suppose, to elaborate the example just mentioned, that a woman comes to see my adversary's action as I do, and understands that I stand to lose by it. Perhaps out of affection owed to a past connection, and not because she has anything to gain, she goes out of her way to try to put matters right, and does so. I may feel that it was not merely that she had nothing to gain by her intervention, that for good reason she found it disagreeable to mix in the business. My gratitude to her is considerable.

In what does gratitude consist? To feel grateful is in part to have certain ideas or the like about the initiation of another's action, an action which one values as having benefited or been intended to benefit oneself, and in another part to have a desire or inclination to benefit one's benefactor. One wants to repay or at least recognize a good turn. More can be added, in line with the general conception of the attitudes or feelings noticed earlier. (p. 81)

My gratitude to my benefactor, then, includes ideas or the like about her initiation of the action which put matters right with my friend and patron. What are my ideas as to the initiation of the action? Evidently they must include beliefs as to voluntariness. There would be no possibility of my feeling gratitude to her if I took her action to have been the result of an effective threat or to have had some related inception. In short, it needs to have been an action which flowed from her embraced desires.

It may be that I also have an image or idea of origination in connection with her action. I may regard the putting-right of my connection with my patron as other than something that was inevitable, an event fixed by the past. A very natural expression of my gratitude to my benefactor, my saying that she need not have done what she did, is naturally taken as expressing not only my belief as to her voluntariness in her action but also its not having been the upshot of certain nomic connections. The image in my mind's eye is of my benefactor out of her own originative volition settling on doing the thing, resolving to seize an opportunity, or pressing on with her defence of me. As noticed already, such an image or thought of origination, in so far as the clear and the literal is concerned, reduces to not much more than a denial of determinism. Still it is of no small importance to my feeling.

If the relations between the components of gratitude are unclear, it seems at least arguable that the ideas or whatever about initiation have a certain consequence for other components. The *character* of the evaluation, and of the inclination or desire, owe something significant to the given ideas or whatever. If that claim is abstract and general, it seems none the less to contain a truth. What we come to, then, is that gratitude, in so far as it involves images or ideas as to an originated action, as it certainly may, is in other parts different from what it can be without those images or ideas. One is tempted to say that in so far as gratitude carries images or the like as to origination, it is more profound, perhaps what can be described as a more moving emotion. It is, to recall another component of an attitude, also different in feeling in the narrow sense.

It may well be, then, that there is more than one way in which an effective determinism conflicts with gratitude of a certain kind. Certainly it conflicts in being inconsistent with the image of origination which may be part of our gratitude. However, in the case of this gratitude, it seems to make sense to say that it conflicts with the character of other elements of the feeling. The same is to be said of the resentful personal feelings. Here a determinism fights with feelings which we do not esteem in anything like the way that we esteem their appreciative counterparts, partly as a consequence of the fact that the resentful feelings have in them desires to return a hurt. (p. 33) However, there can be no denying that the resentful feelings are deep-rooted. Here, if a determinism is not a challenge to what we value, it is a challenge to what we may feel we cannot succeed in giving up.

Given all this, we must accept that a determinism cannot leave our personal feelings untouched. How can we be helped to eschew the personal feelings which are inconsistent with determinism? What was said of identifying with nature in connection with life-hopes (p. 135), which enterprise was anyway judged unpromising, can hardly be transferred to the personal feelings. The reflection that determinism excludes a certain sort of failure is at least germane to life-hopes (p. 140), but hardly germane to giving up the relevant kinds of appreciation and resentment. There is a possibility, obviously, of reflecting on the impossibility of a certain failure in connection with *reflective* personal feelings, feelings about oneself (p. 35), but they are of lesser importance than other personal feelings. Gratitude to oneself, or resentment directed to oneself, are surely rare phenomena. What is to be said is much the same as what was said of giving credit to oneself. (p. 145)

A stronger idea that must come to mind in connection with the personal feelings is the idea that there would be no loss to our lives, but rather a gain, in withdrawing from *resentful* feelings in so far as they contain ideas of origination. One side of this several-sided idea of gain is that certain feelings of hatred and the like involve false accusations, which is to say false propositions to the effect that a person not only intended out of embraced desires, but also originated, a hurtful, damaging, or vicious action. There is thus a general unfairness in our feelings, the unfairness of being disposed to vengeful action on the basis of falsehood. (There is also the unfairness of *action itself*, of course, which will be attended to in Chapter 4) We escape the falsehood and the resulting unfairness by eschewing the given feelings.

Another side to the idea of gain does not have to do with the possibility of our coming to have a better moral standing, but the possibility of serving self-interest by escaping the relevant part of the experience of hatred and the like. Such feelings are not a satisfaction to us. They are not a satisfaction in themselves, and there is also the fact that they must often be frustrated, sometimes for reasons of prudence. The situation is greatly different, certainly, with the appreciative feelings.

It seems to me, although there is again the danger of falling into the merely autobiographical, that there is some hope of making the acceptance of a determinism more tolerable by such a means. If it is said, in opposition to this, that being deprived of appreciative feelings of a certain character could not be compensated for by way of a withdrawal from like resentful feelings, there is a certain rejoinder. It is that there is also falsehood in the given appreciative feelings, if a determinism is true, and an unfairness. Here, the point is not so much that those to whom we feel grateful are unfairly benefited, but that those to whom we do not feel grateful are unfairly deprived. If origination is a fiction, true of no one, then to distinguish in our feelings between persons in terms of origination is essentially unfair. However, this rejoinder can at best give us no more than was claimed, the idea that a determinism in so far as it affects the personal feelings may be made *more tolerable* by reflection on the escape it offers from an aspect of the accusatory feelings.

One more fundamental strategy for accommodating ourselves to the necessary alteration of our personal feelings must be the attempt to accept determinism. (3.2.8) Another such strategy, of which more can usefully be said, has to do with those personal feelings that remain to us, those based on voluntariness, most importantly the appreciative ones. The situation *is* in this respect like that with life-hopes. (p. 142) We can persist in a full spectrum of appreciative personal feelings, and they are not to be underestimated. They are based on and informed by things which are of great value to us: the love of others for us, their loyalty, perseverance in forwarding our lives, humanity, tolerance in dealing with us, and also their admiration, esteem, and approval with respect to our natures and our endeavours.

A determinism does not wholly subtract any of these things from our existence. A determinism does alter a perception of mine of my sister's tenderness for me. It seems to make sense to say, none the less, and may be true, that in my remaining perception of her she is not made *less tender* towards me. The possible degrees or shades of tenderness would not be greater in a human world containing origination than in a human world without it. So with, say, the sagacious admiration of someone for me, if I happen to earn it. He is, it seems, not *less admiring* in virtue of the truth of a determinism. There is in a sense no level of admiration that is possible if determinism is false, but not possible if it is true, no level of praise that is possible in the first case but not in the second. To return to the earlier example as elaborated, my adversary's act of unscrupulousness does not come from lesser or different motives if a determinism is true, and the goodwill of the woman who helps me out is not in itself reduced by the fact of a determinism. There is obscurity and uncertainty here, but surely also a fact.

It is a fact which is part of what can tempt one to embrace intransigence, to declare that a determinism in no way affects our feelings for others. What we are attempting now is something else, more secure and in general more satisfactory. It includes accepting, despite what has just been said, that there *is* a kind of personal feelings to be given up. It also involves the assurance that we can persist in personal feelings of another kind. It involves, further, the assurance that these remain a great source of satisfaction to us. An unoriginated act of love is an act of love, an unoriginated act of magnanimity is an act of magnanimity, an unoriginated true assessment of our worth is a true assessment of our worth.

3.4 KNOWLEDGE

The response of dismay, with respect to knowledge, is that a determinism undermines or constricts it, condemns us to an agnosticism or scepticism. The response derives from the attitude that for us to have what are good reasons for a claim to knowledge, they need to be owed to mental acts and ordinary actions which are not only voluntary but also originated. For facts or propositions to be good reasons they must have in their background originated acts and actions. That is, there must have been a certain possibility of discovering whatever might have unseated these facts and propositions as good reasons. It needs to have been the case, as was remarked, that we have explored reality rather than been guided on one tour of it.

The attitude need not include the idea that my belief now, that the paper I am writing on is white, is owed to a nearly simultaneous originated mental act or action. It *is* arguable that my belief, involuntary as it is, is owed to an act of attention, and that without such an act I would have a kind of awareness that falls short of belief, but let us pass by that matter. I do require with any belief, if I take the attitude in question, that voluntary and originated acts and actions lay in the further background of the belief, in the growth of my knowledge and of a conceptual scheme. The attitude is stronger in the case of knowledge-claims not having to do with immediate experience, where we take acts of judgement as very much part of the recent background of the knowledge-claims.

The conflicting response of intransigence is that a determinism does not at all trouble our existence as knowers. No significant change need occur in my view of my own beliefs, my confidence in them, if I come to accept a determinism. The response rests on the attitude that facts or propositions, if they are good reasons for a claim, need be owed only to acts and actions that are voluntary. More fully, I take the attitude that for reasons to be good ones, what is required is only that they are wholly owed to my desires for information, as distinct from reluctant desires, and furthermore that my mentioned desires for information were themselves partly owed to acts and actions which themselves issued from desires for information.

The consequence of determinism for knowledge is different in detail from its other consequences, as they are different among themselves. This difference includes one having to do with the identities of the agents in question. My life-hope of either kind that I shall achieve some rank or standing is a feeling whose content includes beliefs or the like pertaining to *my* future actions, beliefs that they will be both voluntary and originated, or simply voluntary. With respect to personal feelings of either kind, except the reflexive ones, they have to do with initiation of *others'* actions towards me—say the action of the woman who remonstrates on my behalf. My moral disapproval of the husband facing divorce also has to do with his action, although not towards me. There is a related fact about the rightness of particular actions, such as his, and a different related fact about particular judgements as to moral standing over time, judgements on such specific individuals as the husband, but not judgements with respect to a single action. (p. 53) As for general judgements or principles as to good men and women, and right actions, they carry presuppositions about the initiation of acts and actions generally, assigned to no persons in particular.

In the case of my beliefs or claims to knowledge, to return to them, what I take to be good reasons are conceived by me as facts or propositions owed to the acts and actions related to those reasons, *my* acts and actions but also those of *indefinitely many other persons*, those in the history, so to speak, of my beliefs or knowledge-claims and also my conceptual scheme.

It may be that the indefiniteness of the class of relevant acts and actions has something to do with a more important proposition about the distinctiveness of the consequence of determinism for knowledge. The proposition is that despite what has been said, the consequence of determinism for knowledge is a lesser consequence than others, and hence that there is less obstacle to the response of affirmation. Other consequences of determinism, it might be added in support of this, have to do with my life where it has a pressing emotional content— consider life-hopes and resentment—but the consequence for knowledge has to do with what touches me less, my reflective or philosophical life. It is a consequence, more particularly, tied up with reflection on the nature of reality, with metaphysics. The consequence is most importantly one for those of a certain philosophical turn of mind, and for them when they are subject to it or indulging it.

Still, there is at least aspiration and a kind of desire in such reflection. The affirmative response accepts that an aspiration is defeated, that our access to reality is in a way limited. We have a thin but significant conception of what may exist and be forever beyond our reach. A parallel can be seen. We take it without hesitation that our knowledge is different from, and greater than, that of lesser species. It seems we must accept the thought that our access to reality stands to another conceivable one as knowledge of lesser species stands to ours. The consideration that underlies the former difference, a determinism, is of course different from the consideration that underlies the latter. Our position, therefore, is related to those to which we are assigned by Plato, Kant, Spinoza, and other philosophers who bar us from *a reality beyond*. It is my own feeling that the determinist argument for a conclusion of this kind may well give us more pause than arguments of a more metaphysical or wholly metaphysical kind, including those phenomenological ones which regard our immediate experience as a kind of screen between us and reality.

Can we assuage the defeat of an aspiration by a certain reflection? We considered, as a means of dealing with the defeat of certain of our life-hopes, the thinness of our ideas or images of origination. The stratagem, it was judged, could not be very successful. There is the same conceptual thinness in connection with knowledge, of course, but also another, noticed a moment ago in passing and also earlier in connection with the response of intransigence. (p. 51 f.) There is a particular sparseness about my conception of what I might now possess, a wider or deeper knowledge, if the history of my present beliefs had been a matter of acts and actions that were originated as well as voluntary. I can have no *grip* on the possible *reality beyond* from which I am excluded. The objects of my hopes are clear, as are the actions I resent or am thankful for, but that which origination might have provided with respect to knowledge is beyond my sight. Is renunciation therefore easier here? It is possible to think so.

Can the compensation having to do with membership in nature be specially shaped or adapted so as to work better with knowledge than with life-hopes? The contrary may seem more likely. Is there then some small compensation to be had having to do with the impossibility of a certain kind of intellectual failure? Perhaps. What may be more important is another consideration of which we know, that determinism does exclude chance. This has to do with the clear fact that a world of causal and nomic order offers a possibility of knowledge that is absolutely denied by a chaotic world, a world of widespread chance. There is the difficulty, however, that what we are contemplating, as an alternative to a world of determinism, is one which is nomic except for the origination which would, if it existed, serve the end of knowledge.

The response of affirmation must rely not so much on what has been called assuagement or compensation but on a recognition of what knowledge we possess despite determinism. What we have is the present state, the continuing growth, and the large future of knowledge —conceived as the product of no more than desires for information. (It may also owe something significant, no doubt, to what is distantly related to origination, which is causally determined but in a sense 'random' searching. (Dennett, 1984, pp. 66 f.)) If our good reasons lack a certain character which we may, in one mood, aspire to have for them, that is not near to allowing that our reasons have no recommendation. After all, truth and evidence, or anyway ordinary truth and evidence, are defined *within* the existence we have. Further, no particular reason, and no particular set of reasons, is thrown into question. As we need abandon no particular object of hope on the premiss of determinism, so we need abandon no particular belief on that premiss, other than any which is in the ordinary way inconsistent with it.

Finally, and relatedly, we need not on balance succumb to a dejection. One large point here must be that we need not suppose that the arrays of our desires and inclinations, including our life-hopes, are devalued by the true consequence of a determinism for knowledge. We need not suppose, that is, that our desires and inclinations have no decent foundation in our knowledge as it is. Yet more fundamentally, perhaps, we need not suppose that great satisfactions of what we can properly continue to call knowledge, satisfactions in knowledge itself, are denied to us. It is not as if philosophy and neuroscience, to mention only two bodies of knowledge, become anything like dreams. We need not suppose we are in anything like the situation of illusion to which Plato among others assigns us.

3.5 MORALITY

The burden of what was said earlier about moral responsibility is that to hold a man morally responsible for an action, to disapprove of him morally for it, is to have one or the other of two complexes of feeling about him. (1.7) This simplification ignores variations of several kinds, but catches hold of what is fundamental. The response of affirmation has to do with both of the things distinguished.

To speak again of the husband preparing for his coming divorce, the first complex of feelings includes as one of its elements a repugnance for his desires and intention to cheat his wife of their son's affections and of a fair share of the monies of the marriage. He himself is also repugnant as the tolerator and indeed the forwarder of the desires and intention. The first complex of feeling also includes the element of retributive desires. We are disposed to act against him, to subject him to some degree of distress, perhaps so little as the discomfiture produced by an expression of our disapproval, perhaps more. Our retributive desires are in fact attached to a third element of our disapproval, images or ideas of origination—his origination of his intention and action. There is no logical connection linking our retributive desires to our ideas of origination, but it is nevertheless true, as we now are, that the desires do depend on the given ideas. If we reflect on holding the man responsible in the way in question, we will take our ideas of origination to be a necessary part of the reason we can offer for our desires. The truth of a determinism, then, conflicts with these retributive desires, which we must seek to escape.

There is a like complex of feelings in crediting someone with responsibility, approving of him morally for an action. To do this may not only to be attracted to his desires, rather than repelled by them, and hence attracted to rather than repelled by him, but also to be disposed to benefit him for a particular reason, at least by offering him

the satisfaction of one's expressed moral approval, one's commendation. These desires are as linked to ideas of origination. They too are
vulnerable to the truth of a determinism, and we must seek to deal
with them.

We may have an inclination to resist the latter uncongenial
conclusion, about moral approval. This is to be explained, it seems, by
what is taken to be a lesser need to justify desires to benefit as against
desires to distress. The inclination can hardly be defended. It needs to
be noted that what is under consideration is not at all a further element
in the first complex of feelings, which is desires to direct future
behaviour, desires to serve the ends of morality. What is under
consideration is the question of whether a discriminably different
desire to benefit someone by at least commendation for an action can
persist if the action, the intention in it, and so on, are perceived as
effects of causal sequences of the kind specified in the theory of
determinism. If one clearly distinguishes the given desires to benefit as
we now have them from other things, it seems that they are in place
only if there was a certain possibility of the agent's having acted in
other than in the creditable way he did. The desires to benefit are in
place only if he possessed a power of origination.

Retributive desires are deep-rooted in us, and desires to benefit are
both deep-rooted and more satisfactory to us. The response of
affirmation with moral disapproval and approval, to repeat, is in part
the attempt to give up both categories of desire. Here, as with the
resentful personal feelings, we may have the help of an awareness of
the unfairness of such desires. We can look to an escape from a certain
moral guilt. We can, with respect to desires to benefit, escape the
unfairness of rewarding some, and thus depriving others, on the ground
of a fiction, that all possess a power of origination.

Can we, despite much that has been said, indeed despite what has
been a refrain of this inquiry, contemplate a certain possibility, certain
very different strategies of affirmation? We have it that the connection
between our images or ideas of origination and our desires to benefit
and desires to distress is a contingent one. To repeat, it is not as if there
were a logical connection between the ground for the desires, so to
speak, and the desires themselves. The situation, rather, is that we
regard a certain conception of the initiation of action as a reason for
the desires. We are disposed to this. This is the way we are. (p. 111) The
fact of contingency can give rise to certain questions.

Why should we found retributive and the related desires on
origination? Why should we desire the distress or benefit of a man on
the ground of his having originated a malevolent or otherwise wrongful
action, rather than on the ground alone of his having acted out of

malevolent or otherwise wrongful desires, desires which he embraces? If it can be said to be reasonable on either, does it not seem as reasonable to do so on the latter ground—the ground of voluntariness or willingness—as the former? There is a second and different question. Why should we not attempt the radical course of eschewing desiring-to-distress but persisting in desiring-to-benefit?

Consider desiring to benefit a woman on the grounds alone that she is a moral exemplar, which is to say someone whose commitments, desires, inclinations, and so on give rise to our overwhelming admiration, and are wholly voluntary. There would be no *mistake* in the impulse to reward such a person. Would there be unfairness in it? Would it be unfair in that the existence of the desires of the moral exemplar are as fixed by antecedents as the desires of a moral monster? It might be said in reply, of course, that the charge of unfairness would have to be based on the supposition that the kinds of benefit in question had to be *earned*, in such a way as to bring in origination. But why should we be overborne by this thought?

There is, of course, the suggestion of inconsistency in the idea of attaching desires to benefit to voluntariness but not desires to distress. As elsewhere, it is possible to consider escapes from inconsistency. It might be said, for a start, that distress and satisfaction are different in such a way that desires for the satisfaction of some persons carry no implication about desires for the distress of other persons. That origination is a reason for doing one thing does not commit us to its being a reason for doing another, given that the two conceivable actions are different as well as alike.

Both prospects—attaching both kinds of desires to voluntariness, or only desires to benefit—are attractive. But to contemplate them, surely, is to fall into a kind of utopian thinking. I cannot with any optimism *resolve* to change what is my nature. Perhaps the most that can be said of the two prospects has to do with a possibility noticed in connection with life-hopes. We may come, or we are likely to come, eventually, to a full and true belief in determinism. It is that which will be a cure for the problem of the consequences of determinism. (p. 145) Along with a final acceptance of determinism might come a more real possibility of alteration in our dispositions having to do with desires to benefit and desires to distress.

We have so far been considering moral approval and disapproval when they consist in one complex of feelings, a complex which includes images or ideas of origination. The other part of the response of affirmation with our present subject has to do with moral approval and disapproval when they consist in a second and different complex of feelings. This complex is the same as the first in desires and feelings except that it lacks the retributive desires. What we have here is in no way inconsistent with determinism. What we have here rests only on beliefs as to the voluntariness of actions. We are in no way prohibited by a determinism from approving and disapproving of others and ourselves where what is in question is no more than actions which flowed from embraced desires.

What we have is of value to us. We may persist in approving of actions which are truly describable as fair, human, tolerant, or otherwise commendable. We are not prohibited from disapproving of those whose actions flow from unjust, prejudiced, vicious, or otherwise unacceptable desires. In a clear sense a morally splendid act becomes no less morally splendid for not being originated. In a clear sense, having to do with voluntariness, it is an act of self-denial, or kindly perception, or courage. In this sense, likewise, a monstrous act remains monstrous, despite not being originated. We can persist, further, in prevention and encouragement—in general, in desires to affect the future. We can seek to promote non-maleficence, beneficence, fairness, and truth. (p. 72) there is the large fact that the truth of a determinism does not conflict at all with the purpose of morality. In this alone we have a thing of great value. It is perhaps not too much to say that determinism would be a calamity or somehow unthinkable if it conflicted with the very purpose of morality. It does not do that.

What we have, in sum, is that a determinism forces us to give something up in connection with moral responsibility and leaves us with much. It leaves us with certain immediate reactions to the desires and intentions of others. It leaves us with the possibility of acting in accordance with the purpose of morality. It leaves us with the possibility of which much is made, as we have noticed in passing, in the tradition of thought having to do with 'the freedom of acquired self-perfection'. (p. 128) The situation is the same, of course, with respect to what we have not had in mind, moral responsibility and oneself. If I cannot in a certain sense be a moral agent, given a determinism, that carries with it an escape from a kind of guilt and self-torment. I do none the less have the possibility of regarding myself morally. My desires and intentions, in my own view of them, are things which can morally sadden or gladden me. They can be seen by me as obstructing or furthering the purpose of morality.

So much for the response of affirmation with respect to the bearing of a determinism on moral responsibility. Let us now quickly consider the remainder of morality, the connected issues of right actions and good agents. The first is the question of what actions are right, its general answer being a moral principle or a set of moral principles. The second question is that of the nature or standing of the good man or woman, and its general answer will be in terms of certain dispositions. An answer to either question, as we saw, also provides an answer to the other, and in fact the two questions can be expressed in this one way: How ought the world to be, in so far as we can affect it? (p. 55)

Right actions and good men or women, it was maintained, presuppose judgements about responsibility. Only an action for which an agent can be held responsible or credited with responsibility can be right or wrong. This is so since morality has to do with the world in so far as we can affect it, in so far as our actions are within our control. As for the judgement as to standing that someone is, say, morally sensitive, this is a judgement as to a disposition of the person. The disposition is one to perform certain right actions. In the absence of responsibility, there would be no right actions and hence no such dispositions. There would then be no men or women who were good in any moral way.

According to one of our conceptions, a responsible action is one that is both originated and voluntary. The other conception of responsibility is such that a responsible action is one which is no more than voluntary. It is evident that the conceptions of right actions and good men and women cannot be said actually to *depend on* the first conception of responsibility. It is not as if right actions and persons of moral standing cannot exist without origination, and hence do not exist if a determinism is true. Right actions can be taken as being within the class of actions that are controlled in the sense of being voluntary and no more than that. Good men and women can be taken as those who are disposed to perform right actions of this kind of initiation.

It is at least arguable, however, that the permissible conceptions of right action and good men and women—the conceptions consistent with a determinism—have a cast or character different from the conceptions that are related to the moral responsibility tied up with origination. The fact is a counterpart of facts having to do with life-hopes, personal feelings, knowledge, and moral responsibility itself. There is little doubt that we all have a sense of right actions and moral standing which is akin to that which moved Kant to tie morality to a moral self, at bottom to origination.

The response of affirmation, here as before, can involve a consideration of compensations, including an escape from a certain guilt and sense of moral failure. The response of affirmation must rest, however, on perceiving the value of what we have, the remaining possibility of right actions and of good men and women. It is not as if a determinism subtracted fair or just decisions from the world, or the possibility of celebrating morally great persons. A determinism does not consign me to a world from which moral grandeur has been removed. It has in it, to mention one principal category of moral grandeur, those men who have kept in sight their knowledge of the wretchedness of the lives of others, and have given over their lives to political struggles whose goal was to end or reduce that wretchedness.

There are two principles, or rather a possible principle and a principle, both mentioned earlier, that are affected by determinism. One is the idea, of a Kantian kind, that part of what makes an action right is that it was originated. (p. 69) That is, it is a right-making feature of an action, on a par with fair consequences or the like, that the action was originated. This is distinct from the idea, already rejected, that it is a logically necessary condition of an action's being right or wrong that it be a responsible one in the sense of being both originated and voluntary. The principle, if it can count as such, is obscure. It conflicts with a determinism but its loss, it must seem, is tolerable.

The other loss, although perhaps for an unexpected reason, is what can be named the Principle of Desert, if the name does not suggest something too determinate. (p. 69) It is, roughly, that every man is to get what he deserves. We are to act in such a way that this happens. What this comes to, in one part, is that each man is to be morally commended when this is deserved, and blamed when that is deserved. What the principle actually has to do with has long been a matter of mystery and dispute, but it must appear to be bound up with origination. It will be considered in the last section of this inquiry— into the consequences of determinism for fundamental institutions and the like in our societies, notably the institution of punishment.

3.6 THE POSSIBILITY OF AFFIRMATION

The response of affirmation, it was said earlier, is a part of a philosophy of life. By one possible reckoning, or in terms of one sense of things, it can better be described as entering into one large part. It enters into that part of a philosophy of life which has to do with a sector of our lives which is bound up with attitudes to action and its initiation. The response, a response to determinism, is that despite a certain defeat, the defeat of expectations which the history of our culture forces upon us, we can persist, at least satisfactorily, on the basis of one conception of the initiation of actions. We can persist in kinds of hopes, personal feelings and so on, resting on actions taken as no more than voluntary.

The response of affirmation, to repeat, does not in itself constitute all of an attitude to this sector of our lives bound up in the given way with action and its initiation. Two other things required, to fill out this part of a philosophy of life, are one's own appraisal or choice of goods, and a morality. (Cf. Rawls, 1972) One's choice of a set of goods can be seen as an evaluation of, and selection from, the range of possible objects of life-hopes. As we know, a morality when brought into clarity and order is a principle or set of principles which provides a conception of right action, of the moral worth of persons, and of the grounds of approval and disapproval with respect to particular actions. A morality brings with it, implicitly or explicitly, a politics.

It is one thing to come to see and feel, in general, that voluntariness by itself provides at least an adequate foundation for an outlook on our existence in so far as the initiation of action is concerned. It is another to build on that foundation, It can be built upon in diverse ways. I begin, so to speak, with the commitment that voluntariness is in a way sufficient in so far as the initiation of action is concerned, and then add some or other conception of the good to be pursued for myself and one of various possible moralities. Not much constraint is put upon me by the foundation. One constraint that is put upon us has to do with the Principle of Desert, whose consideration has been postponed, and not much else.

A philosophy of life, to mention one other part, cannot be complete without an attitude to the ending of life. A determinism has very little logical consequence with respect to death. There is nothing in it inconsistent with doctrines and aspirations having to do with immortality, and there have of course been religious and theological determinisms. (Adler, 1958) On the other hand, there is a particular consonance between an acceptance of determinism and an acceptance of mortality. To accept the first is surely to be more able to deal with the second. It may be that the tight connection between determinism and nature is more sustaining as a part of one's attitude to death than it is as a part of one's attitude to life. The contemplation of oneself as a part of ongoing nature seems to be of more sustenance in connection with the end of one's life than in the acceptance of adversity within it.

I have not attempted to recommend a completed philosophy of life, but only a constituent of the part most concerned with action and its initiation. It is the acceptance of this constituent of many possible philosophies of life that is recommended in the response of affirmation, and which, it can be believed, will end the history of the problem of the consequences of determinism.

Are there good reasons for resisting the recommendation and doubting the prediction? My own explicit answer, certainly presupposed in what has been said already, can be approached by way of an essay mentioned several times already. (P. F. Strawson, 1962; cf. 1985,

Ch. 2; G. Strawson, 1986, Ch. 5) It is supposed in this essay that Compatibilists or some of them take a determinism to have the consequence, which they may recommend to us, that we must eschew absolutely the personal and moral feelings, and limit ourselves to taking *the objective attitude* to everyone. The objective attitude, as described earlier (p. 78), is a disengagement from ordinary connection with other persons, an attitude of a detached kind. It is the attitude that we now ordinarily have only to individuals who are grossly abnormal, those whom we treat, control, guard ourselves against, detain for their own good, and so on. It is in reaction to this rebarbative proposal assigned to some Compatibilists, it is supposed, that other philosophers have produced the obscure metaphysics of origination, ideas thought to be needed in order to rescue us from the threat of being imprisoned in the objective attitude.

My interest, however, is not in the speculation that Compatibilists have proposed that a determinism has such a consequence, and that it be accepted, but rather something else: something related to the questions of (i) whether it is actually possible that we should ever come to take up the objective attitude in a general way, as a consequence of accepting a determinism, and (ii) whether, if it is possible, it would be rational to do so. The questions suggest related questions. Is it the case that a different proposed alteration in our lives—the alteration that is proposed in the response of *affirmation*— is possible? If it is, would it be rational to make *it*?

It needs to be emphasized that the alteration proposed is *not* one which would limit us to the disengagement or detachment of the objective attitude. There is, admittedly, an analogue to the objective attitude in one part of what has been said of affirmation and the moral attitudes. It was said that several categories of feeling can enter into the approval and disapproval which is consistent with a determinism, and that one of these categories is of desires to direct or influence future behaviour, desires to gain the ends of morality. There is a partial analogue to the objective attitude in these particular desires, but no more than that. (A similar partial analogue was noticed earlier between the objective attitude and the attitude which enters into the response of intransigence in connection with morality. (p. 79)) To be disposed to attempt to influence the behaviour of others in the given way is *not* necessarily to detach them from the human community in the way that we now detach grossly abnormal individuals from that community. The desires in question have *all* men as their objects, and are consistent with accepting that we ourselves are suitable objects of such desires on the part of others. Related remarks can be made in connection with affirmation and the personal feelings.

That is one significant distinction between advocacy of affirmation and advocacy of the objective attitude. There is another. The alteration to our lives proposed in the response of affirmation—an alteration which subtracts ideas of origination and their concomitants—allows for a further category of feeling in connection with morality. We can persist in certain responses to the desires and intentions of others, and hence to them. There is no obstacle to my abhorrence of the desires and intention of the treacherous husband foreseeing his divorce, or, more important, to my abhorrence of him, a man whose personality and character are consistent with these desires and intentions, and support them. There is no obstacle to the related but very different feelings about those who behave well or better. Related remarks pertain to affirmation and the personal feelings.

A third distinction, although one not in view until now, is that affirmation in no way involves taking others as non-rational, as not open or less than fully open to rational considerations. Taking the objective attitude, it seems, does centrally involve regarding others as beyond the reach of ordinary argument and persuasion.

Affirmation, then, is far from recommending a retreat into the objective attitude. It recommends no such bloodlessly managerial an attitude to others. Still, it may certainly be thought to raise the same questions. Is it possible that we should come to live, in so far as moral responsibility and the personal feelings are concerned, in the way prescribed in the response of affirmation? If it is possible that we do live in this way, would it be rational to do so?

It may well be that there can be no real question of our retreating into the objective attitude with respect to all people. It may well be, as is said, that if it is not absolutely inconceivable, it is 'practically inconceivable' that we go over to a general objectivity. It is indeed close to certain that 'the human commitment to participation in ordinary inter-personal relations is . . . too thoroughgoing and deeply rooted for us to take seriously the thought that a general theoretical conviction might so change the world that, in it, there were no longer any such things as inter-personal relationships as we normally understand them. . . .' (P. F. Strawson, 1962, p. 197) It is close to certain that our natural human commitment to ordinary inter-personal attitudes may indeed be 'part of the general framework of human life, not something that can come up for review as particular cases can come up for review within this general framework.' It may be true, further, in connection with rationality, that 'if we could imagine what we cannot have, viz. a choice in this matter, then we could choose rationally only in the light of an assessment of the gains and losses to human life, its enrichment or impoverishment; and the truth or falsity of a general thesis of determinism would not bear on the rationality of *this* choice'. (1962, p. 198; cf. Ayer, 1980; Bennett, 1980; G. Strawson, 1986, Ch. 5)

What is *not* true, to consider affirmation rather than objectivity, is that there is no practical possibility of our making the response of affirmation, and living in accordance with it. To do so, admittedly, will involve an acceptance of the defeat of a large aspiration which gives a character to our moral and personal feelings as they are, and also to our life-hopes and our confidence in our knowledge. It is also to be admitted that no argument or book will produce a general acceptance of affirmation. It would be innocent to suppose that the alteration of our outlook in question could be affected by what, given the rootedness and pervasiveness of that outlook, is so slight a thing. That is not to say that the cumulative and no doubt very indirect effect of philosophical argument and the advance of the relevant sciences, to mention the principal considerations, will forever fail to produce a general acceptance of affirmation, and consistent ways of life. It is not to say, putting aside the matter of a future general acceptance, that the response of affirmation and what follows from it are not within the capabilities of individuals now. While it is a mistake to minimize what is involved in this renunciation, it is equally a mistake to maximize it in certain ways.

The idea of 'the general framework of human life', something not open to review or reconsideration, is certainly of use in thinking of the possibility of affirmation. There are facts about our existence—say the fact of desire itself, the fact that we are desiring creatures—which for whatever kind of reason cannot be supposed missing from anything that could count as human life. Such facts are in an obscure but very strong way essential. By contrast, ideas of origination and the considerable concomitants of these ideas cannot be regarded as such a fact about our existence. Compare the fact that we have and act on ideas of origination with the fact of our being desiring creatures, and the facts in past epochs of pantheistic ideas, or religious hopes and fears, or ideas of an individual's God-given place in the hierarchy of a society and indeed a universe. It seems clear enough that the fact having to do with origination is more to be put with the later three facts and not the fact of desire. It would be at least audacious to look back into the past and by some conceptual stipulation tie the emergence of 'recognizably human life' to that time at which ideas of origination emerged. The enterprise, surely inevitably, would depend on an arbitrary conception of human life.

Ideas of origination and what goes with them are a part of human history, however long a part, as distinct from some sort of condition of that history. It is tempting but it is surely mistaken to take ideas of origination and the structure of life which goes with them, however developed, extensive, and substantial that structure, as some foundation of our existence that cannot be thought away, some primordial *given* which always was, is, and will be. The emergence of ideas of origination and associated facts was a long historical event, an event with an explanation. The persistence of these ideas has also been such an event, with an explanation. It would be strange to suppose that there could not possibly occur conditions issuing in the decline of ideas of origination and their consequences. A general decline of desire, or, perhaps, a change to a universal objectivity of attitude, are things such that it is difficult or impossible to think of causal circumstances for them. This is not the case with ideas of origination and their consequences.

The second question has to do not with possibility but with rationality. Might it be other than rational to make the response of affirmation and to try to live in accordance with it? Might it be that an assessment of the gains and losses to human life, its enrichment or impoverishment, leads us to reject affirmation? Certainly it involves accepting what is reasonably regarded as a loss, a kind of impoverishment. There is succour in ideas of origination, most notably in connection with our life-hopes.

The question is that of the rationality of affirmation as against something else in the situation where determinism has been accepted, but it will be as well to notice, first, the absence of alternatives with respect to such an acceptance. One truth that bears on this matter, a truth which has entered our inquiry before now, is that belief in the fundamental sense is involuntary, that we cannot choose between believing and not believing, decide between thinking of a proposition that it is true and that it is false. We can of course choose to act as if such-and-such were true, or to accept such-and-such as an hypothesis. The fact of the involuntariness of belief in the fundamental sense, it seems, is not much put in doubt by the most relevant phenomenon which can be adduced against it, that of self-deception. The latter is best regarded not as successful lying to oneself, which might be taken to involve choosing to believe, as well as the logical impossibility of believing and not believing, but as choosing to remain in a state of ignorance, typically by taking care not to come to have the experience or evidence that will settle an issue.

No question can then arise of choosing to believe whether such a determinism as the one that has been expounded is true. No question can arise, further, of choosing whether such a determinism is inconsistent with ideas of origination. With respect to these two matters, then, we do not have alternatives, and so no question of rationality of a certain fundamental kind can arise. Such a question of rationality, of choosing the best course in terms of gains and losses, can arise only if there are two possible actions between which one can choose. The rationality in question, differently described, is of course the rationality of efficiency, as it is sometimes called—choosing effective and economical means to an end.

One way in which an issue of rationality as efficiency might be thought to arise, consistently with what has been said, is by way of the possibility of self-deception where that is not doing what is logically impossible, but choosing to remain in a certain ignorance. That is, most importantly, there can be the question of whether it would serve our human lives if we were to take care to avoid that which may settle the question of the truth of a determinism. It may be contentious to describe such a course as one of self-deception. Perhaps, with the aid of certain philosophical assumptions, it could be given a better name. Certainly such a course would offend against typical commitments to truth. There is, however, a more telling consideration. Most of us are such that it is not within our powers deliberately to take such a course. It is not the ignobility of it, but rather the impossibility or great difficulty of it, that is decisive. If the explanation of this fact is hard to come by, as it seems to be, it seems none the less a fact.

To come to the main question, that of what it is or would be rational to do given a full and clear acceptance of determinism, it is of course important to have the right alternatives in mind. The choice we have, given what has been claimed in this inquiry into the consequences of determinism, is between affirmation on the one hand, and, on the other, the discomforts of our situation as described in the first part of our inquiry—the discomforts of being settled in two inconsistent attitudes to the initiation of action, and the two inconsistent responses of dismay and intransigence. The alternative to affirmation is not something contemplated earlier, in connection with morality. (p. 158) We do not have the possibility of attaching to voluntariness by itself the feelings which were previously attached to voluntariness and origination.

Certainly the situation of inconsistency and conflict, although it includes dismay, cannot be regarded as so intolerable as would be a retreat into the objective attitude. But it is far from agreeable. It is this disagreeable situation which is to be weighed up against affirmation, or which will in the future be weighed up against affirmation. The choice concerns not only matters of which we know—life-hopes, personal feelings and so on—but also social matters to which we are coming. (Ch. 4) It will be clear already, however, that affirmation arguably can be taken as the more rational course, the course to be chosen in the light of an assessment of gains and losses for our lives.

3.7 RECAPITULATION

The argument about the consequences of determinism has been a long one, and can usefully be brought into a succinct form. The following paragraphs are derived from sections of the previous two chapters and the present one.

1.2 All our life-hopes involve thoughts to the effect that we somehow initiate our future actions. Some involve not only beliefs as to voluntariness or willingness but also an idea, or what is more an image, of our originating our future actions. To think of life-hopes of this kind, and their manifest inconsistency with determinism, and to accept the likely truth of determinism, is to fall into dismay. We are deprived of the hopes.

1.3 We also have life-hopes involving only beliefs as to voluntariness —that we will act not from reluctant desires and intentions, but from embraced desires and intentions, that we will act in enabling circumstances rather than frustrating ones. These circumstances have to do with at least the way of my world, the absence of self-frustration, independence of others, and absence of bodily constraint. Thinking of hopes of this kind, and noting the clear consistency of a determinism with them, may issue in intransigence. These life-hopes are not at all significantly threatened by determinism.

1.4 We have appreciative and also resentful feelings about others, owed to their actions deriving from good or bad feelings and judgements about us. Both sorts of personal feelings involve assumptions somehow to the effect that others could do otherwise than they do. It is natural in one way of thinking and feeling to take the assumptions to amount to this: others act with knowledge, without internal constraint, in character, and in line with personality, not out of abnormality, not because of constraint by others. This second one of a set of fundamentally like conceptions of voluntary action, wholly consistent with determinism, may lead us to make the response of intransigence with respect to personal feelings. However, we also have other personal feelings, having a certain person-directed character and including an assumption as to a power or control of their actions by others. The assumption is inconsistent with determinism and may lead to dismay.

1.5 We accept that our claims to knowledge derive in part from beliefs and assumptions as to our mental acts and our ordinary actions, by which we come to have evidence and the like. We may take it that originated acts and actions are necessary, and, taking them as ruled out by a determinism, suffer a want of confidence in our beliefs, a dismay having to do with the possibility of a further reality. Inevitably, however, we can have a different kind of confidence, owed only to an assumption as to voluntariness, the possibility of our satisfying our desires for information. Hence intransigence about knowledge. These are facts which the Epicurean tradition of objection to determinism has greatly misconstrued.

1.6 One fundamental question in morality is that of how the world ought to be in so far as we can affect it. However, it allows us to concentrate either on the nature of good men and women, or the nature of right actions. The other fundamental question is that of moral approval and disapproval of agents for particular actions, the responsibility they must have for their actions. An action's being right, and a person's having a good moral standing, presuppose that we do somehow have responsibility for our actions. Hence determinism's effect on all of morality can be considered by way of its effect on moral responsibility.

1.7 What feelings enter into our moral disapproval of the vicious husband and father anticipating his divorce? We may have tendencies to act against him, retributive desires for at least his discomfiture. These desires, by a kind of direct reflection (pp. 66) can be seen to be vulnerable to a determinism. The result may be dismay. However, reflection on the purpose of morality brings into view a kind of moral disapproval, and approval, which rest not on an image of origination but only certain beliefs as to voluntariness. There is no conflict between them and determinism. Intransigence with respect to determinism and morality is as possible and natural as dismay.

2.1 There are two traditional views of the challenge of determinism, Compatibilism and Incompatibilism. Considering them throws into greater definition the fact that each of us has two families of attitudes, including two sorts of life-hopes and so on, and may respond to determinism with at least dismay and intransigence. The two traditional views also demand consideration as the principal alternatives to the correct resolution of the problem of the consequences of determinism.

2.2 Compatibilist philosophers ascribe to us a single conception of the initiation of action, and a kind of belief as to the sufficiency of this initiation in so far as moral approval and disapproval are concerned. The conception is that of a voluntary action, and hence a determinism is taken to affect moral responsibility not at all. Incompatibilists also ascribe to us a single conception of the initiation of action, which includes origination, and a belief as to its role. They take it that the truth of determinism would destroy moral responsibility. Both philosophical parties take the problem of the consequences of determinism to be of an intellectual or theoretical kind, to which can be added that Compatibilists are in a way overwhelmed by the great fact of causation generally, and Incompatibilists are greatly desirous of our having a certain stature, of elevating us.

2.3 Our two families of attitudes, and the two responses, establish the falsehood of both Compatibilism and Incompatibilism. We do not have a single conception of the initiation of action, or a single belief as to the role of such a conception. Our circumstance is not either that a determinism leaves moral approval and disapproval untouched, or that it destroys it. To suppose that it destroys it, as Incompatibilists do, is to ignore our attitudes which may issue in intransigence. To suppose that a determinism leaves moral approval and disapproval untouched, as Compatibilists do, is to ignore our attitudes which issue in dismay. Compatibilism and Incompatibilism are as mistaken in other respects, not least in offering what are very nearly absurd explanations of the persistence of the problem of the consequences of determinism.

3.1 The true problem of the consequences of determinism is to escape the unsatisfactory situation in which we find ourselves, prone to two inconsistent families of attitudes, and two inconsistent responses. It is fundamentally a problem of dealing with desires. In trying to make this escape, we are not restrained by some fundamentality of origination as against voluntariness. Our endeavour must be to accept the defeat of certain desires, by reflecting, in part, on the satisfaction of others. It is an endeavour which enters into arriving at a philosophy of life.

3.2 In so far as origination is a fiction, life-hopes which we have are affected, and the damage cannot be assuaged by the reflections that ideas of origination are faint ones, or that a determinism saves us from chance. There is little solace in the fact that determinism gives us a particular membership in nature. There is more in the escape from failure which it allows. There is also the fact that our life-hopes in a deterministic world are no more bounded in their objects than life-hopes would be in a world of origination. If these hopes also have other recommendations, a final acceptance of our situation will depend on *full belief* in a determinism. We may respond to determinism, nevertheless, in so far as our life-hopes are concerned, with affirmation rather than dismay or intransigence. This includes the endeavour to accept what must be accepted, by several means, and also the recognition that our life-hopes can be life-sustaining things. They can enter into a celebratory philosophy of life.

3.3 A determinism conflicts with personal feelings of the kind that involve an image of origination, and an acceptance of this is included in the response of affirmation. The renunciation, particularly of the appreciative personal feelings of this kind, is made more tolerable by a related escape from the resentful ones. The response of affirmation also includes an assertion of the great value of the personal feelings as they can exist in a deterministic world. To make the response is to keep one's balance, which balance allows for a recognition of the great worth of an existence enriched by facts of personal relationship.

3.4 We can be said to be barred by determinism from knowledge of a possible reality. Thus there is a truth distantly related to propositions of Plato, Spinoza, and others. That is not to say that our lot must be a kind of unhappy agnosticism. Affirmation, as elsewhere, gives a place to both considerations.

3.5 Moral approval and disapproval, since they may rest partly on origination, are affected by a determinism. Our specifically retributive desires are affected. There is more consolation here than with life-hopes, however, and perhaps more than with personal feelings. The moral responsibility untouched by determinism is of a large significance. For one thing, each of us has a moral standing. There are corollaries having to do with right action, and good men and women.

3.6 The response of affirmation enters importantly into a number of possible philosophies of life. It may be asked if it is possible for us really to make the response, since it involves a significant change in our lives. It may be asked if it would be rational to make the change. In fact the change is possible, and the question about whether it would be rational can be answered in the affirmative.

These answers effectively give the main ideas of a resolution of the problem of the consequences of determinism, the problem which has most exercised philosophers. What remains is a consideration, for which we now have some guiding principles, of certain fundamental social and political facts.

4

Punishment, Society, Politics

There is unavoidable greater complexity with respect to each of this set of subjects to which we now turn. More differentiations need to be made with each of these subjects than with life-hopes, personal feelings, knowledge, moral responsibility, right actions, and the moral standings of persons.

This is so for three reasons, the first being that it would not be at all effective to proceed in a general way, to think of any of the institutions, practices or habits with which we shall be concerned as one thing, a single type of thing. It would not be at all effective to ask what the consequence of determinism is for this type, since, given our interests, it has importantly different instances or tokens. To speak of punishment, there now exist discriminably different institutions of punishment by the state. There have been others in the past, and perhaps there are more to come. What we have is a range of possible institutions, several of them now actual. To try to settle on a satisfactory response in the matter of determinism and punishment is to do something which involves a choice or choices from this range of possible institutions.

The second reason for complexity has to do with the fact that punishment, like the other institutions, practices and habits, is a matter of action and the result of action, not of attitude taken more or less in itself. It has thus been the subject of moral and other reflection and argument in a way that life-hopes and so on have not. The given range of possible institutions is inevitably subject to moral judgement. We necessarily value one or some, defend it or them, and do not value or defend others. To try to settle on a satisfactory response in the matter of determinism and punishment, then, is to do something which is complicated by moral commitments and arguments. One result is that we may be able to give up something inconsistent with determinism by way of becoming convinced of what we take to be true independently of determinism, that it lacks a moral defence. More important we may have the support, in limiting ourselves to something, that it is by our lights in accordance with fundamental moral principle. Here then there are particular aids, if that is not too small a word, to affirmation.

To be more specific, we can and indeed must conceive of punishment in ways which make for moral disagreement: as a matter of a man's getting what he deserves, as the fulfilment of an agreement, as something whose aim and recommendation is Utilitarian, as an institution having a Utilitarian character but also features having to do with desert, as an institution serving fairness somehow conceived, and so on. That is not to say, of course, that we can conceive of our *actual* institutions of punishment in our present societies in all of these ways, but that we can conceive of different possible institutions, one or several of them identical or more or less identical with one or more of our actual institutions. Each of these possible institutions will be described by and justified by one particular *theory of punishment*, as such things are called.

There is no real counterpart to these facts with, say, life-hopes. Life-hopes, at any rate, have not been in such a way distinguished into kinds, kinds discriminated by means of general moral principles and necessarily also a matter of possible moral disagreement. Personal feelings have not been and could not in such a way be the subject of differentiating moral theories. So with confidence in knowledge. Nor is the situation in fact greatly different with the moral matters we have been considering, although to be sure we might have looked into the aid to affirmation provided by moral conviction. It was possible and effective, certainly, to proceed in the general way we did with moral approval and disapproval, right actions, and moral standing.

Our project, then, first with respect to punishment, must be to consider from a certain point of view—although out of a concern for our present state of affairs, for actual institutions—each of a number of theories and associated possible institutions. What, we need to ask, is determinism's consequence for it? This consequence will be fixed by the fact of what is required by each theory or possible institution in terms of the initiation of action. Above all, does it depend on the assumption that men and women are not only voluntary in their actions but also originate them? Is it the case, with a possible institution of this kind, inconsistent with determinism, that it is anyway morally indefensible, that determinism's inconsistency with it is no loss? Is it the case that a different institution, taken independently of determinism, *is* morally defensible? Is it the case with this institution, or this with another, that it can properly be the subject of, or enter into a response of, affirmation? Where do our actual institutions fall in this range of possibilities? If necessarily we must consider possible institutions, it is our actual institutions which must be our main concern.

So—the enterprise is complicated for the reason that punishment is not effectively conceived as a single type of thing, and the further reason that we are in an area of moral dispute. It is also complicated for a third reason, related to the second. If we have been urged by a long line of moral advocates to conceive of punishment in various ways, and to act on the conceptions, it is far from clear what some of this advocacy comes to. What *is* the nature of the advocated possible and perhaps actual institution in question?

It is far from clear, above all, what it is to conceive of punishment as *deserved*, what it is to conceive of the possible or actual institution of punishment whose nature is fixed wholly or partly by desert. For this to be unclear, of course, is for the moral recommendation of the institution, if any, to be unclear. Talk of desert, using the word itself or a variety of equivalent locutions—the locutions have become more popular than the tainted word itself—has always been pervasive on the part of judges and other officers of punishment by the state. It remains so. That is not to say that the talk is clear. There are similar difficulties about punishment taken as a matter of the fulfilment of agreement, punishment taken as a matter of fairness, and so on.

Our inquiry into determinism's consequences for punishment, then, and for other institutions and the like, must have large parts different from our inquiry into the previous consequences considered. We need to clarify certain lines of moral advocacy, thereby coming to see what possible institution or practice is being recommended, and have some view of its worth. The endeavour is a large one, and cannot be organized and carried forward with as much confidence as those which have been completed. It will involve quickness, generality, and selectiveness in dealing with large subjects which themselves call for, and have often had, close and extended attention.

What is true of punishment, to repeat, is as true of the other six institutions and the like to be given less consideration. Each is in fact best regarded as a set of possible institutions or whatever. Let us quickly survey the six, however, in terms of what are most important to us, their instantiations in our contemporary societies. These instantiations are like our present institution of punishment in raising moral questions. In particular, they seem to have to do significantly with desert.

Some say that punishment has no counterpart institution of *reward*, an institution of the same social fundamentality. That is at least misleading, but not because of the relatively unimportant fact that specific rewards are offered for information in connection with particular criminal offences, relatively few of them, or because of other special inducements to actions of one kind and another. Rather, it is misleading since a society can properly be said *generally* or *systematically* to reward law-abiders, law-abiders in general, for their obedience to law. They are rewarded in that they are left to themselves, in peace, which is to say not subjected to the attentions of the criminal law. Certainly we can and do say that they deserve this, whatever argument or consideration may be conveyed by that, and whatever else may be offered in justification of this reward.

It can be said, thirdly, and often is, that our actual institution or practice of different *incomes* for different jobs, positions, and ranks is justified by desert, or has desert as a part of its justification. A managing director or a doctor deserves more money than a plumber or salesgirl, a more cunning policeman more money than a less. Those who think that the great disparities of income, and the great disparities in things of real value attached to them, are not defensible, or think that the scale is in one part mistaken or in several parts mistaken, may still suppose that some or even many disparities can be defended at least in part by some consideration of desert. Alternatively, advocates and critics of income-distributions may depend on other propositions, perhaps having to do with agreement.

Fourthly, partly for reason of the connection of income with *wealth and property*, limited though the connection is, it is not uncommon partly to defend our distribution of wealth and property by means of such talk of desert. It may also be defended as deserved by the idea that some of those who have wealth and property have used it for the common good, or have been patrons within a community, or simply by the idea that they have protected or preserved it. It is said of those who do not have it, or many or some of them, that they do not deserve to have it, or indeed that they deserve not to have it.

A fifth practice or institution, again in a somewhat extended sense of those words, has to do with positions of *relative power* of several kinds. If we put aside democratic decision-making, in a society as a whole and in greater or lesser parts of it, where we are at least in some distant approximation to being on a level, and also put aside much of private life, it is perhaps reasonable to say that the rest of our existence falls under relations, systems, or hierarchies of power. We have positions in systems of seniority, chains of command, or authority and the like. It is often suggested, in one way or another, that we deserve our positions of relative power. It is also suggested, for example, that they have a Utilitarian justification or something like it.

So too, sixthly, with what can be distinguished from power, if uncertainly, which is *rank, authority, standing, respect,* and the like.

Here there are precedences and offices of various kinds, public awards and honours, and also grades in examinations and prizes in competitions and games. There are also impeachments, dismissals, cashierings, discharges, failings, and disqualifications. These too are said to be deserved.

There remains a seventh item, related to what concerned us earlier in this inquiry, moral disapproval and approval, holding people responsible for things and crediting them with responsibility. Moral approval and disapproval in this sense, as we know, consist in feelings. They do not consist in actions of *commendation or condemnation, praise or blame.* (pp. 11, 53) These latter things, it can seem, are of the stuff of much of our social life, a seventh and last practice or habit to be considered. It includes the actions of praise and blame, often directed to social groups, in which officers of a society and other public persons engage. Moral condemnation by judges is distinct from the punishment they impose. There are also politicians, industrialists, economists, churchmen, leader-writers, and other overt or covert praisers and blamers. There are also the various forms of praise and blame in private or more private life. In all practices and habits of praise and blame, it is common to speak of them as wholly or partly explained and justified by desert.

It is clear then, as philosophers have needed to be reminded (Feinberg, 1970), that desert has to do with a good deal more than punishment—or punishment and reward, and praise and blame. Indeed the list of relevant things might be extended further than we have, to such items as practices of compensation and reparation for injury or loss, and habits of gift-giving and denial as a consequence of such personal feelings as gratitude and resentment. There are also such social provisions as old-age pensions. Let us go no further, however. It is safe to say that much of the nature of our societies is owed to the seven institutions, practices, and the like. Each of them, and hence our societies, are in *some* degree shaped and defended by considerations of desert, whatever those may come to.

To come to a principal if anticipated point, it is at least natural to think that some claims that someone deserves something for an action, which I shall call *desert-claims,* and practices that are affected by such claims, depend on taking the action to have been not only voluntary but also originated. On the other hand, the idea that there is this dependency has often been denied. It has been denied, although in the course of their misunderstanding of the problem of the consequences of determinism, by some Compatibilists, who take morality, including a principle of desert within it, to require only voluntariness. Mill's words quoted earlier might be taken to suggest that desert is independent of origination. (p. 95) Also, and as important, various analyses of desert-claims—including several at which we shall look— seem not to require the assumption of origination.

That it would be rash to draw conclusions quickly about the issue of whether desert-claims and practices into which they enter do depend on ideas of origination is also indicated by other facts. It is not only *we* who are said to deserve things, but also other animals, and also such entities as problems, theories, proposals, and works of art. Some problems deserve close attention, some hypotheses deserve reconsideration, some bills of legislation deserve to be passed, and a portrait or a still life by Monet or Coldstream deserves admiration. Nor is it evident that these latter sentiments can be reduced to claims about the desert of some person or persons. In any case it seems not absurd to say that a piece of natural beauty, perhaps a sunset on the Alberta prairies near Lethbridge, deserves looking at or even contemplation. Given that things other than persons can be deserving, it cannot be certain that when persons are taken as deserving, this is so in virtue of a proposition about them which is threatened by determinism.

If it is the case that some claims of desert do depend on taking actions to be both voluntary and originated, and that these claims do affect or shape our actual institutions, then we must, as with other things of which we know, attempt the response of affirmation. We must escape what will be our situation here as elsewhere, dismay and intransigence. Affirmation here, unlike affirmation with most of our previous subjects, may have somewhat more to do with the seeming necessity or unavoidability of things—above all punishment—than the warmth of our feelings for them. The situation is rather like that with *one* previous subject, the resentful personal feelings, which do not improve our lives but are entrenched in them.

The nature or size of the enterprise of affirmation in connection with the seven social institutions, practices, and the like will depend importantly, as already implied, on what view we have, or come to have, of the worth or defensibility of arguments having to do with desert, taken independently of determinism. The nature and size of the enterprise of affirmation will also depend as much on something else, the *extent* to which the seven things are affected by desert-claims. Certainly they are *significantly* affected, but that is not to say a great deal. It *may* be that they are greatly more affected by other feelings, claims, principles, or whatever. To speak differently, are we or are we not to draw a general conclusion to the effect that the truth of determinism, given its relation to desert, has great consequences for our societies as they are, that great changes are called for? That has been declared by philosophers opposed to or sceptical about determinism. They have sometimes supposed, as it seems, that our societies as we know them could barely survive a general acceptance of determinism.

The principal subject-matter of this chapter is in fact determinism and punishment. More particularly, as explained, it is determinism's effect on theories of punishment and their associated possible institutions, above all the theories associated with our actual institutions. Our conclusions about determinism and punishment, when we have them, will be a guide to what will get very much less attention, the other mentioned institutions and the like. If punishment is of great importance itself, and the subject of ongoing controversy, we can by considering it also come to have much of the means of dealing with the other institutions and the like, and also some of the means to a final speculation, about determinism and politics.

Desert-claims in themselves and the problem of their analysis, as already indicated, cannot be near to all of our subject. It is evident, to repeat, that desert-claims do somehow affect our present social institutions, that some institutional facts do derive from them. How large these facts are will depend on the extent to which our existing institutions derive from quite different claims or propositions. We must ask to what extent they do. There is also another question about these different claims—separate from the question of their relative effect. It is the question of whether any of these claims not having to do with desert are none the less affected by determinism. One category of them in particular, already noticed in passing, is both like and unlike desert-claims, and needs to be thought about in this connection.

They can be called *agreement-claims*, and are to the effect that someone has agreed to do or to accept a thing. They can be offered as reasons for his doing or accepting the thing. Agreement-claims are like desert-claims in that they enter into a defence or justification of something which can seem to rest wholly upon a past action, in the case of agreement-claims the past action of making an agreement, giving consent, or the like. Agreement-claims are unlike desert-claims, to mention one way, in that they do not essentially involve any moral or evaluative appraisal of the past action—that of agreeing. Whether I think you ought or ought not to have signed the lease making me the tenant of your cottage, and indeed whether or not I have any moral view at all about it, I may think that the fact that you did sign it is of importance. You ought to give me the keys. The distinction between desert-claims and agreement-claims issues in the linguistic fact that I cannot naturally say you deserve to give me the keys because you signed the lease, let alone deserve to do so *for* signing the lease. I may allow, without prejudice to my argument, that there is no way in which you do deserve to give me the keys.

We shall at first follow a certain procedure in dealing with what, as will now be evident, is a large and not easily manageable subject. Our sequence of questions, to be followed with a number of propositions about punishment, will be roughly as follows.

(1) How are we to understand or analyse a given agreement-claim or desert-claim about punishment, and what reason or argument for the institution does it in fact involve?

(2) Is the latter really a significant or prima-facie reason or argument for punishment?

(3) If so, is it affected by a determinism? That is, does it involve origination?

(4) If the reason is affected by a determinism, is it none the less the case that other justificatory propositions untouched by a determinism are of greater importance in logically sustaining the proposed institution of punishment, perhaps our actual one?

The latter questions in this sequence arise only if certain answers are given to those before. It is mainly at the end of each sequence—if we reach it—that we shall consider the response of affirmation.

4.2 PUNISHMENT AND AGREEMENT-CLAIMS

There is a certain advantage in beginning not with desert but with the considerable tradition to the effect that all offenders have somehow agreed to their punishment, or even that they want or choose it for themselves. The penalties which we now impose on offenders in our actual systems of punishment, it is said, can be justified, partly or wholly, by certain defensible agreement-claims. Let us look at two strong and recent examples of the tradition. Certainly they have recommendations lacked by their predecessors.

The first begins from the nature of consent in ordinary agreements or contracts in civil law, perhaps the agreement one makes by getting into a taxi-cab and giving an address to the driver. (Nino, 1983) That example illustrates that an act of consent need not be in a certain sense explicit. No taxi-driver expects to hear from the back seat 'I consent to pay the specified fare if you will take me to Ritson Road.' Indeed we can with a little trouble imagine a taxi case, in line with the case of a nod at an auction, or handing the ice-cream man a coin and pointing to the chocolate, where no words at all are spoken. What is required for consent in law, so long as two other things are true, is a somehow free action *of any type*. In particular, it need not be an action of speaking or writing. One of the other two things required, if it is proper to separate it from the requirement that the action be somehow free, is that the agent in question knows of consequences of a certain kind of his action—for example, that the taxi-driver will have a legal right to the fare. The other, it is said, is that the relevant law is somehow morally defensible.

It is important that for the passenger to have consented, certain other things are *not* required. It does not matter if he believes he can avoid paying, intends not to pay, or does not want to pay, either at the time he consents or when he gets to his destination. None of these things affects the fact that he has in law consented. Nor, it is said, does any of these things affect what importantly follows from his consent, more particularly from his consent to undertake a legal obligation, which is that others acquire a moral right to enforce the obligation he has acquired.

Now consider an offender. His very action of breaking the law— pulling the trigger, or diverting the funds, or cheating the client—can be regarded as his giving a certain consent. This has nothing to do with any prior social contract which some philosophers deem him to have made, simply as a member of the society. His offence *is* his consent. What he consents to is said to be the giving up of his legal immunity to punishment. This is an immunity which we all possess if we do not offend, a matter of our individual legal rights.

His consent, to be more exact, is said to consist in his acting with the knowledge that loss of his legal immunity to punishment is a legal consequence of his action. He acts with this knowledge, which is to say nothing of his moral culpability or moral blameworthiness. The *Consensual Theory*, to give it a name, has nothing to do with moral culpability or blameworthiness. (Nino, 1983, p. 293) The general idea of consent of this kind is only that one is said to consent to all of what one knows to be the somehow necessary consequences of one's action. Thus the offender is not said to consent to his actual punishment, which itself is not a necessary consequence of his action. It may not happen.

As in the case of an ordinary legal agreement, it does not matter if the offender believes he will not be punished, intends to avoid it to the best of his ability, and wants not to be punished. He has nevertheless consented to give up his legal immunity to punishment, and it follows from this that we acquire a moral right to enforce the agreement he has made. We need not exercise our right, as with any right, but we may also choose to do so, for the reason that we suppose his punishment will have the effect of preventing future offences, perhaps by him.

What justifies us in making use of him to this end, in short, is not that he deserves it, but that he has in the given way consented. It is part of the view we are considering, as it is of others, that the preventive reason by itself would not justify punishment.

The Consensual Theory has the remarkable recommendation, not had by other theories in its tradition, of struggling to give a specific account of agreement-claims with respect to our actual institution of punishment and other possible ones. Does it, however, to pass on the the second question to be asked, give us a significant or prima-facie reason for punishment?

There are several grounds for saying no. One has to do with what we need to keep clearly in mind, which is that *no* claim has been made that the offender consents to his *punishment*. One reason the Consensual Theory does not claim this, foreshadowed above, is that if it did, it could provide no reason for punishment whatever where offenders *believe*, as some certainly do, that they will not be punished. A man cannot conceivably be said to consent in the given way to something he does not believe will happen or be the case. Thus the essential claim of the theory must indeed be the weaker one, that he consents only to the loss of his immunity to punishment. Despite what has been said so far, what exactly does this come to? What are the details of this consent? That is uncertain, partly because his loss of immunity is repeatedly said to be a 'normative' consequence or a 'legal normative consequence'. (Nino, 1983, pp. 296–7) Perhaps his consenting to lose his immunity comes to something so strong as this, which is favourable to the Consensual Theory, that he acts with the knowledge that the law is such that if he is apprehended, and if the authorities make no mistakes, he will not be regarded as having an immunity to punishment.

We might reflect a good deal on this matter but we need not. Evidently whatever he consents to is wholly consistent with his precisely *not* consenting, in any sense whatever, to *his punishment*. He will not foresee *it* as a necessary consequence of his offence. Further he will not consent to it in another more ordinary and fundamental sense, difficult to specify clearly. Here, very roughly, to consent to a thing is not merely to see it as a necessary consequence of one's act of consent. Here, to consent is to be more willing and decisive, or at any rate more desirous or happy, with respect to the very thing itself. I consent to pay in this ordinary sense, as well as the other, when I point to the chocolate ice-cream. In this ordinary sense, to repeat, the offender does not consent to his punishment. On the contrary, he is against it, attempts to escape it, and so on. With respect to his punishment, he in both senses and indeed every sense *dissents*.

The general idea of the Consensual Theory, and all theories of punishment having to do with agreement-claims, is that in punishing a man we have the defence that somehow we are acting in accordance with *his* past or present will, volition, autonomy, self-determination, end, or desires. In the Consensual Theory, it is said in particular that we are treating him as an end. This is understood with commendable clarity as our acting *in accordance with his ends*. But if we take into account both his consent of a kind to lose his immunity, whatever the details of that consent, and his dissent in every sense with respect to his punishment, it is at least arguable that in punishing him we are acting against what are his ends. We are certainly acting against his predominant ends. We can be said, as well, to be acting against his predominant will, volition, self-determination, desires, or whatever.

It is to take a partial view of the situation, to say the least, to focus upon his consent in a secondary sense to what is less significant to him, and to overlook his dissent in every sense from what is greatly more significant to him. He consents in a secondary sense to some necessary condition of his punishment, and dissents in every sense from his punishment itself. It is false, or as near to it as makes no difference, to say that punishment among other things 'is the product of the will of the person who suffers it'. (Nino 1983 p. 297)

Should we suppose that the consent which consists in the offender's acting with knowledge of a certain consequence is none the less somehow decisive because, after all, it is the kind of consent which is entrenched in the ordinary law of contract? Should we suppose, for this reason, that the objection that has just been made must somehow be ill-judged? One might well resist the assumption that the kind of consent which is decisive in contracts is also decisive with punishment. There is another consideration, however. It bears not only on the question of whether an offender's consent to lose his immunity is somehow decisive, but also on the prior and basic idea of the Consensual Theory, that there is a close analogy between that consent which is given in an offence and, on the other hand, ordinary consent in the law of contract.

What we have with respect to punishment is an action done with knowledge of some legal consequence, but also an action done, at least typically, in the perfectly apparent desire, intention, and determination to avoid punishment. We are given every evidence of this. What is the proper analogue of this action in terms of the law of contract? It is too quickly assumed that the proper analogue is a standard or ordinary contract. On reflection, it must instead be a curious case which has the feature among others that someone successfully conveys from the beginning that he has no intention of doing or accepting a certain thing.

Consider the remarkable case where I get into the taxi cab, give an address, and then beyond doubt really do persuade the driver that I intend not to pay. For whatever reason, none the less, he takes me where I want to go. Have I consented to pay in the relevant sense, and do I have a legal obligation to pay when we get there? The answer is surely no. Or, certainly, it cannot be that the answer is a simple yes. If *this* curious case is the analogue to the offender's consent, then the offender's consent is *not* the kind which enters into ordinary or standard contracts.

More generally, what we are given in the Consensual Theory is a certain account of what it is to consent in connection with an ordinary contract. This does not include anything about intending to keep to the contract. That is held not to be necessary—in anticipation of what is going to be said about consent in punishment. But what if we find an accurate analogue of the offence? What if it is such that the consent-condition is satisfied *and*, in the judgement of all parties, the person in question successfully convinced the other person that he intended not to keep the contract? It may be that there can be no such case, that there is incoherence in the speculation. But surely *any* tolerable response to the question must put into question the line of argument that an offender's action is somehow decisive consent because it has an analogue of consent within the law of contract. There is room for more argument (Nino, 1987), but it remains difficult to accept the idea of the Consensual Theory that there is an effective analogy between punishment and ordinary contracts.

There is a further ground for saying the Consensual Theory does not give a prima-facie or significant moral reason for punishment. Suppose a man sees the possibility of an action profitable to him but greatly harmful to others, one which will ruin their lives. It is by any moral test an action of viciousness. He sees too what is also true, that it is not illegal, although it is indubitably of the moral gravity of illegal acts. How it has happened that it is not illegal—there are various possibilities—does not need detailing. The Consensual Theory of punishment does not apply here at all. In performing the awful act, he cannot be said to have consented to lose his legal immunity to punishment. That is precisely not a foreseeable consequence. Here, then, the theory gives no reason whatever for punishment.

This is unfortunate for the theory, for a particular reason. The theory assumes, as all such theories do, that there is *some* moral reason for punishment in an offender's past action, taken by itself. The assumption has been hard to resist. The theory, so to speak, recommends its reason for punishment partly on the ground that there is wide agreement that there does exist a reason of the given sort. However, *its* reason is *not* of the given sort. This is so since anyone at all inclined to think there is such a reason will take it that it somehow *does apply* to the imagined case. But the analysis in terms of consent has the consequence that in this case there is *no* backward-looking reason for punishment. There might be attempted the reply, among others, that the imagined case is not one of an *offender*, and hence not one where *punishment* is in question. To that kind of reply there is a rejoinder. (Honderich, 1976, pp. 62 f.)

Let us not pursue the Consensual Theory further, however. If the objections to it have not been fully developed, and certain complexities and difficulties glossed over, it is difficult to avoid the conclusion that although the theory gives a novel account of agreement-claims in connection with punishment, it can hardly be taken as providing a significant or prima-facie reason or argument for it. It purports to apply to our actual system of punishment, but it cannot be said to give us a morally defensible institution.

Is the reason for punishment offered by the Consensual Theory consistent with determinism? Does the reason necessarily bring in origination? That third question is apposite since the reason requires, as remarked, a somehow *free* action, a free action of consenting. (p. 180) We shall not consider the question, or the further one, to which an answer has been implied, of the relative weight of other propositions pertaining to the defence and nature of the institution. Thus we do not come to the matter of the response of affirmation. That matter does not arise. It is not the case, for example, that we here have a kind of justification on which we might be able to depend if we are forced by determinism to give up another kind.

To turn now to a second and large view of agreement-claims in connection with punishment, it is one clearly suggested but not developed in an impressive and greatly successful political philosophy, a theory of justice. (Rawls, 1972) This second view of agreement-claims is best approached by way of something it includes, the Hypothetical Contract Argument about justice. If we take time to get both things clear, it will not take much more to come to a judgement on what is important to us.

The Hypothetical Contract Argument is in limited analogy with a certain simple method of reflection, whatever its nature and worth. That is the method whereby in an attempt to solve a moral or other problem, I ask what view would be taken of it by a person or persons with certain attributes. Suppose my problem is about divorce. I may suspect that my personal history prejudices or clouds my judgement. It will be useful, I suppose, to ask what view would be taken by a different person of another history. He or she—the less prejudiced person—does not need to be an existing person, but can be a matter of my own imagining. The less prejudiced person, real or imagined, is of course not identical with me.

Suppose the less prejudiced person in fact or in my reflections takes the view that the proper ending for marriages of a certain kind is an equal division of property between husband and wife. This may now seem right to me. Notice, however, whatever is to be said of that opinion, that there obviously is no possibility of a certain line of thought. Partly since the less prejudiced person is not me, there is no possibility of a certain *agreement-claim* pertaining to me. I cannot later be said to have *agreed* to a 50/50 division, or *consented* to it, or made any kind of *contract*, in virtue of the fact that the less prejudiced person took that view, or was imagined as taking that view. None of this is the case although it is irrelevantly true that I can be said to *agree with* the less prejudiced person.

So much for the analogy. The Hypothetical Contract Argument, in sum, is that imaginable persons or persons in an imaginable situation would make a certain contract or agreement as to the society they are in process of establishing. It is a hypothetical contract in the sense that it is not one that ever was or ever will be made, in actuality, but one that would be made if certain imaginable conditions obtained.

One of the conditions is that each of the contractors in what is called the Original Position is equally free to propose principles for the governance of the society to come. A second condition is that each is rational. That is to say that he will choose principles which are effective means to securing his end, which is the possession of certain goods, and that he is not envious—he will not worsen his own position, in absolute terms, in order to reduce the difference between himself and someone better off. Thirdly, each contractor is self-interested, concerned for himself. Finally and importantly, the contractors have a good deal of *general* knowledge or belief about people and societies, but each is entirely in ignorance as to his—or her—own individual future in the society to come. Each is in ignorance as to his or her own future position and personal characteristics. This ignorance is complete, and so extends to each person's future wealth, power, standing, sex, race, physical well-being, intelligence, desires, interests, even moral beliefs. The imagined situation, then, is one which absolutely precludes any contractor's being influenced by the contingencies of personal good fortune and natural advantage which in ordinary life guide or distort an individual's choices as to principles and policies.

Taking into account all the enumerated conditions, the situation is a *fair* situation for making an agreement. The principles of distribution that are agreed upon will be owed to a fair agreement: an agreement made under conditions of fairness, a recommendatory situation. This is what we want. True principles of justice are those that would issue from an agreement arrived at in such a situation of fairness. We see justice rightly when, for what a much-used abbreviation is worth, we see *justice as fairness*.

According to the Hypothetical Contract Argument, we can reason that the imagined persons would in fact reject certain alternatives and agree on what are perhaps best described as three fundamental principles of justice to govern the institutions of their coming society. The principles have to do with (i) certain traditional liberties, (ii) equal opportunity, and (iii) socio-economic inequalities.

The argument as a whole is of course directed to us. It seeks to persuade us that given principles are correct for our actual societies. Despite the imagined agreement, and as with the less prejudiced person and the question of divorce, the argument as we have it has nothing to do with agreement-claims bearing on us. Certainly we can speculate, about our imagined contractors, that *they* will be subject to certain agreement-claims in their coming society which we imagine. That is nothing to the present point. We may or may not be persuaded to act in accordance with the three principles, to support or struggle for actual social institutions in our actual societies which are in line with the three principles. That is not to say that any of *us* is subject to any agreement-claim having to do with the Original Position. None of us is or was a person in the Original Position.

A little attention is given, in this theory of justice, to certain other arguments analagous to the one just sketched. That is, we can imagine our contractors, having settled in the first stage on the fundamental principles for their society, moving into a second, third, and fourth agreement-making positions or situations. (Rawls, 1972, pp. 195–201) The second is called a constitutional convention, the third the legislative stage, and the fourth a stage in which rules are applied to particular cases by judges and administrators. The four-stage sequence involves, among other things, an increase in individual knowledge— knowledge of the attributes and positions of particular persons. In the fourth stage it is complete. In each of the three later stages of this process there arises the matter of the institution of punishment. Indeed the institution is literally a part of the fourth stage.

Clearly we are to suppose that our imagined persons decide on an institution of punishment, although little is said of it. Further, given their situations, that decision may be argued to have a certain recommendation. Just as the moral view about divorce of the less prejudiced person can be taken to be an argument for my conduct, and the choice of the original contractors an argument in favour of certain fundamental principles for our societies, so their choices in subsequent stages can be taken as arguments for our guidance with respect to particular actual institutions, including punishment.

What is important now is only the same point as before. We can, to repeat, imagine certain persons, or persons in certain situations, who would opt for an institution of punishment. That they would do so, given their imagined attributes or situation, may lead us to think that the institution has a certain justification. What is also true is that *none of us*, by engaging in just this method of inquiry or argument, becomes subject to any agreement-claim whatever.

So much for the Hypothetical Contract Argument in general and specifically with respect to punishment. It is not in itself our present concern, but I have given time to it partly since it is essential to distinguish it, and whatever strengths or virtues it may have, from a larger and yet more speculative argument into which it enters, and with which it is run together. The larger argument, which *does* have to do with a supposed agreement by us, is referred to as 'the Kantian interpretation of justice as fairness' or 'the Kantian interpretation of the Original Position'. (Rawls, 1972, pp. 251–7) It might better be named the Kantian use of the Hypothetical Contract Argument, or, as I shall name it, for reasons which will be clear in a moment, *True-Nature Consensualism*.

It is proposed or implied in the paragraphs below. In them, as needs to be noted, the persons referred to are not the imagined contractors but we ourselves, at one point we ourselves imagined as being in the Original Position. The reasoning referred to in the third paragraph is the reasoning that the persons in the Original Position would choose the three principles of justice having to do with liberty, equal opportunity, and socio-economic inequalities.

. . . there is a Kantian interpretation of the [Hypothetical Contract] conception of justice . . . . This interpretation is based upon Kant's notion of autonomy.

. . . he begins with the idea that moral principles are the object of rational choice. They define the moral law that men can rationally will to govern their conduct in an ethical commonwealth. Moral philosophy becomes the study of the conception and outcome of a suitably defined rational decision. . . .

. . . Assuming, then, that the reasoning in favour of principles of justice is correct, we can say that when persons act on these principles they are acting in accordance with principles they would choose as rational and independent persons in an original position of equality. The principles of their actions do not depend upon social or natural contingencies, nor do they reflect the bias of the particulars of their plan of life or the aspirations that motivate them. By acting from these principles persons express their nature as free and equal rational beings subject to the general conditions of human life. For to express one's nature as a being of a particular kind is to act on the principles that would be chosen if this nature were to be the decisive determining element. (Rawls, 1972, pp. 252–3)

If this is not wholly clear, and perhaps gives less than the most effective statement possible of True-Nature Consensualism, as to my mind is the case, an explicit argument can certainly be derived from it. It is, to repeat, a larger argument which includes the Hypothetical Contract Argument within it.

(i) The fundamental premiss is that each of us can be and should be autonomous. That is, we should be free makers of rational choices. This is our shared *true nature*. It is not to be confused with our merely individual properties, either our personal attributes or our inclinations owed to our positions in society, both of which are contingencies.

(ii) It is this true nature which is the only source of true morality, including correct principles of justice and justified institutions, including punishment.

(iii) If we wish to distinguish these principles and institutions, we can do so first by fixing on our true nature, and then noting its deliverances. More particularly, we can imagine certain persons, those in the Original Position and subsequent positions. In the Original Position and to some degree subsequently, none is distracted by his or her particularity. At least in the Original Position the contractors are, so to speak, true abstractions of ourselves, imagined beings who have only our true natures, or rather are forced to proceed as if so.

(iv) Given that they would agree on certain principles of justice and in particular on an institution of punishment, what attitude are we to take to the principles and the institution? We must conclude *more* than that the principles and institutions are supported by the Hypothetical Contract Argument in itself. Given, so to speak, that we in our true natures are identical with the contractors, we must conclude that punishment, to speak of it in particular, is something to which *we* can be said to have assented and to which we do now assent. If we are also offenders, and so resist it in our own cases, we nonetheless in our true natures or autonomy consent to it. *The offender agrees to his punishment.* In punishing him, we do his own rational bidding. In the words of another proponent of True-Nature Consensualism, we *respect* him. 'Respecting a man's autonomy, at least on one view, is not respecting what he now happens, however uncritically, to desire; rather it is respecting what he desires (or would desire) as a rational man.' (Murphy, 1973, p. 229)

It is possible, despite the great attention paid to the Hypothetical

Contract Argument by political philosophers, to remain unimpressed by it (Honderich, 1975), and hence by this larger sequence of argument, True-Nature Consensualism, which contains it. Many objections do not pertain directly to our present concern, which is the given doctrine about agreement-claims advanced in justification of punishment. Let us here try to consider the larger argument.

Its first premiss is that we have a true nature, as free makers of rational choices, and the second is that this is the only source of true morality, and in particular any correct moral view about punishment. The initial and indecisive description of our true nature—we are free makers of rational choices—is first given some content by contrasting that nature with our individual properties, our personal attributes, and our inclinations owed to social position. Our true nature is further specified, in the third premiss, as that part of ourselves which would issue in moral choices if we were in total ignorance of our individual properties in the given sense. That is not and cannot be the end of the specification. Our true natures, since they are brought into view by what is said of the imagined contractors, *also* involve our having certain general knowledge, or general belief, about persons and society. Such knowledge or belief is obviously wholly necessary to what follows.

On the assumption that our true natures, so called, have been adequately specified for the purposes of the argument, together with the assumption that our true natures produce true morality, we can now ask in particular what their upshot is in connection with punishment. To put the question differently, as we are advised, we can ask what the imagined persons would decide. It can indeed be supposed that if they would in fact decide on the three principles of justice, this decision itself implies support for an institution of state punishment. It can be supposed, further, on the same assumption as to their initial decision about principles, that they would explicitly establish such an institution in their subsequent constitutional and legislative stages.

Indeed, as in effect is allowed by the proponent of the view we are considering, it can be *guaranteed* that the contractors would decide on the three principles and on punishment. We can do this by adjusting our conception of them, in fact by adding to it. To be plain, we can be more specific about the general beliefs which we have given them. We can add one to the effect that the lack of an institution of punishment in almost any society would be disastrous. That it can be a guaranteed conclusion that imagined contractors would opt for punishment is an instance of a wider possibility. It is in fact possible to produce a proposition, about any moral or political view whatever, from Apartheid to Zen Buddhism, to the effect that a certain imaginable assembly would agree on it. It is one of the fundamental contentions we are considering, of course, that only the Original Position is an imagined assembly that should lead us to accept what it decides on.

We are here in the neighbourhood of the general objections to the Hypothetical Contract Argument mentioned above, not pertaining precisely to our present concern. There are reasons for doubting the worth or the relative worth of all arguments based on hypothetical contracts. However, let us stick to the matter of agreement-claims about actual persons and punishment. If we do so, we can in fact also ignore something else, the mysterious second premiss about right morality. That I have agreed to something does not depend on, and is independent of, the thing's actually being morally right. True-Nature Consensualism can in fact be reduced to this argument:

(a) Imaginable persons would opt for or approve of an institution of state punishment bearing on themselves.

(b) Those persons are in a sense identical with our shared true natures.

(c) Hence all of us in our true natures opt for the institution of punishment.

(d) The offenders among us therefore agree to their punishments.

Two questions arise, and the answer to each of them, to my mind, defeats the argument. Do all *offenders* have the given true nature? That is, in part, do all of them have the necessary general beliefs—do they have just the general beliefs that must be assigned to the hypothetical contractors? That is the first question.

No reason is given for thinking its answer is yes, and in fact the answer must be no. Admittedly it is arguable that most or all offenders are inclined to have beliefs about *some* conceivable society, with punishment in it, such that they would opt for punishment in that society. In that society it would without exception be essential. Consistent with this is the fact that almost all offenders, like very many non-offenders, are inclined to have beliefs about their own actual society, and the punishments in it, such that they would *not* opt for all the punishments that are imposed. Nothing is more common on the part of offenders than general beliefs about their societies to the effect that some members are allowed by law to have agreeably large shares of what is going, while others, including the offenders themselves, must break the law to have the hope of anything like such a share. They precisely lack a belief which they must have if their true natures, so called, are as True-Nature Consensualism requires. Since at least many offenders lack beliefs which they would need to have in order for the given agreement-claim to be put upon them, True-Nature Consensualism fails.

It fails, I think, even if that objection is waived. The second question about the doctrine can falsely presuppose that all offenders *do* have precisely the true nature which the doctrine assigns to them. They have exactly the properties, including the general beliefs, which can be assigned to the imagined contractors so as to guarantee their support for punishment by the state. On the assumption that all offenders have the specified true nature, does it follow that they consent to their punishments? Do they agree to them?

It is impossible to say so. My agreements with other people are not agreements between *certain of my properties* and other people. They are not agreements between certain of my beliefs, commitments, inclinations, etc., and other people. No doubt I may be subjected to a good deal of argument and pressure to the effect that *really* I do accept something, perhaps to make a donation to the National Union of Mineworkers, or that in my true self I do agree with doing so. This may be true, and moreover I can agree that it is true. That is, it may be true that certain grounds which I accept, or certain feelings which I have, or certain other facts about me, should incline me to make the donation. They may indeed be grounds, feelings, or facts that are somehow central or fundamental to the person I am. I can agree with all this. It does not follow that I have agreed to, or do agree to, give the donation. The situation, rather, is that there are others of my beliefs and feelings, or other facts about me, that tell against it. Hence, I do not agree or consent, whether or not that can be described as going against my better judgement. I do not perform an act of agreeing, in words or on paper, or in any other way. I do not do a thing of which I know certain necessary consequences. Nor do I agree or consent in the other more ordinary and fundamental sense mentioned in connection with the theory considered earlier, the Consensual Theory. (p. 182) That is, it is not true that I consent in the sense, difficult to specify briefly, where I am more willing and decisive and also more desirous with respect to precisely the thing consented to.

True-Nature Consensualism is in fact a large elaboration of an ordinary response to an offender. It is that if he were not facing a penalty himself, he would agree that punishment is necessary, justified or whatever. That may well be true, and it is conceivable that something of interest can be discovered to follow from it. What is not true is that he has agreed or does agree to his penalty.

It was anticipated earlier (p. 180) that a sequence of questions arises about agreement-claims and desert-claims with respect to punishment. The very first question was that of the understanding of such claims, and the reason or argument for the institution which they involve. True-Nature Consensualism does not establish that our actual or indeed any possible institution of punishment does involve agreement-claims, or that these claims give rise to a significant or prima-facie reason for punishment. Therefore we need not go forward with questions about the effect of determinism on such a reason and the relative weight of such a reason. We shall not here consider the response of affirmation with punishment.

Our general conclusion is that neither the Consensual Theory nor True-Nature Consensualism establishes that agreement-claims are important with respect to punishment. Many related theories about offenders' agreeing to their punishments are as unpersuasive. This is so, certainly, of the classical theory of this kind, owed to Hegel (1942 (1840)) and discussed elsewhere. (Honderich, 1976, pp. 45-8) If agreement-claims are not of importance in the justification and nature of punishment, however, they may be so with other social institutions, practices and habits. In fact they are. We shall consider the question in due course, but let us now turn to desert-claims in connection with punishment.

4.3 PUNISHMENT AND DESERT-CLAIMS—TRADITIONAL VIEWS

Desert-claims are to the effect that someone deserves something for something else. In connection with punishment, they are to the effect that someone deserves a particular penalty, or something bound up with a particular penalty, for a particular offence, or something involved in a particular offence. As in the case of all desert-claims, at least as standardly made, these are somehow to the effect that there exists a certain *relation*, which relation serves as or enters into a reason or justification for something, the thing said to be deserved. We shall take sufficient time—which is no little time—to understand what in general is involved in desert-claims before looking at the particular theories of punishment in which they issue or to which they contribute.

What, more clearly, is the thing for which an offender deserves something? The still inexplicit but correct answer must be a culpable action, which, by way of initial description, is an action somehow open to moral disapproval. In the ordinary course of things, this will also be an illegal action, but it seems plain enough, despite a common view to the contrary, that it is not its character as illegal which is essential to its being deserving of something. I may of course suppose that many penalties are justified for reason of being deserved for actions that are among other things illegal. But I shall also refuse to accept that all penalties visited on persons in connection with illegal actions have been deserved, or that certain conceivable actions, if made illegal, would deserve any penalty whatever. I shall refuse to accept this of actions for which I am convinced there is moral justification or no need of moral justification.

That is not to claim that we suppose all actions rightly punished are morally culpable actions, or that all actions rightly punished deserve to be punished. There are offences prohibited under statutes of strict liability, and hence, in effect, actions defined specifically without reference to intention in the ordinary way or to any negligence or failing. (Hall, 1960; G. Williams, 1961) They can be, despite suspicions about many offenders, actions whose intentions and degree of care do not in any way call for moral disapproval. Strict-liability offences include the unintentional selling of bad food under certain circumstances, certain motoring offences, some actions in contempt of court, the possession of drugs under certain circumstances, certain financial transactions, and a great many other actions. A large part of the given rationale of strict liability is that it is difficult or impossible to prove intention or negligence with respect to certain actions, and yet essential to secure the prevention of more of them, to reduce their incidence. It is commonly allowed in the law that at least some penalties under strict-liability statutes, however defensible the penalties, are not deserved.

A culpable action, to repeat, can be described as one for which we feel moral disapproval, hold the agent responsible. Somewhat better, a culpable action is one for which we feel moral disapproval and which we take to be sufficiently grave that it ought not merely to be blamed or condemned but ought to be illegal and therefore open to punishment. It may well be that our moral disapproval is in part or importantly owed to the belief that the agent knew the action to be illegal, but that is not to say that our relevant view of the action, in so far as desert is concerned, is that it was illegal. Nor is the fact that it is the culpability which is important to desert, and nothing but the culpability, affected by the fact, if it is one, that we take the act to be culpable partly because illegal.

To recall what was said earlier (1.7) of moral disapproval, it involves repugnance for an agent's desires and intention, repugnance typically owed to our awareness of the consequences of his action, of which we also take him also to be aware. We may also have desires for his distress in some degree, at least for his discomfiture. These may be at least as fundamental to our state of feeling. We may also have desires pertaining to the future and prevention. We want to prevent like actions. These and other elements of moral disapproval are raised in us by two properties of the action, one of them being its wrongfulness. The other is the agent's initiation of it or, as we can say, his responsibility for it. This is the fact that it was a matter of his voluntariness, or his voluntariness and origination. A culpable action in itself, then, is one of wrongfulness and responsibility, the wrongfulness such as to call for legal prohibition of the action. This familiar truth can be usefully elaborated. (Fletcher, 1978; Nozick, 1981)

What is the other term of the relation involved in desert-claims about punishment? The standard answer is a penalty, but the answer requires clarification. Does a rapist get what he deserves in the barely conceivable case where his gaol sentence is what he wants above all, something which causes him no distress? It may be correct, it seems, no doubt depending on *why* he wants it, to say no. Does he get a penalty? It is certainly possible to say yes. What emerges from this, evidently, is that if a penalty is given as one term of the desert-relation, it must be a penalty in the sense of a distress itself, rather than a penalty in the more standard sense of an alteration in his circumstances, which alteration is specified independently of its relation to his desires. A penalty in the latter sense, further, is an alteration which typically but not necessarily gives rise to a penalty in the former sense. What can be said to be deserved, then, if we are more careful than to refer to an end by its typical means, is a penalty in the non-standard or less standard sense of a distress.

If a culpable action and a distress are the terms of the desert-relation in the case of punishment, what is the relation? It is this fundamental question of analysis which has received many conflicting answers. Let us look at four of them, in several cases very quickly. Others have been considered elsewhere. (Honderich, 1984b) All of them, in terms of a certain contrast, can be described as of *traditional* kinds. (p. 203)

The most common and least reflective answer, the *Uninformative Answer* as it might be called, is to the effect that there is some factual relationship of *equivalence* between an action of a certain culpability (c) and a certain distress (d) of a penalty. It is in an ordinary sense true or false that a particular culpability is in this relation of equivalence with a particular distress—as it is true or false that I am of the same height as you. The factual relation is also described as one such that d with respect to c is *proportional, corresponding, fitting, commensurate, reciprocal, merited, owed,* or *retributive.* Or, d is *according to* c.

In the absence of an analysis or account of this factual relation, as distinct from still more synonyms as unenlightening, this answer to the general question of the nature of the desert-relation is useless. It is a useless answer which very few pieces of jurisprudential writing (N. Lacey, 1988) have the great merit of avoiding. Certainly there is no commensurability in the literal sense of that term between culpability and distress taken by themselves, and hence no such possibility of a literally equivalent or non-equivalent penalty in an ordinary sense. If common units can be contrived for the direct measurement of culpability and distress, no one has yet done the job.

A second and better answer to the general question of the content of desert-claims, and a possible analysis of the one just glanced at, is that *c* and *d* are so related that persons of somehow standard *preferences* would be indifferent between being the victim of the culpable act and having *d* imposed upon them—indifferent, say, between being assaulted in a certain way and having the distress typically caused by a certain gaol sentence. (A. H. Goldman, 1979) There are certain standard difficulties in this line of thought, the *Indifference Answer*, having to do with theory about preferences, but let us ignore them. Let us accept, that is, that we do here have an adequate *content* given to desert-claims with respect to punishment. What is the value of a desert-claim, so construed, when given as a reason for the distress? Do we, to pass on to the second question (p. 180), have a significant or prima-facie reason for punishment?

It seems plain that we have no reason at all. To speak generally, suppose I do so act as to satisfy or frustrate another person's desires, and it is possible for someone to act so as to satisfy or frustrate my desires. Suppose further, and crucially, that in terms of the preferences of standard persons, there would be indifference between having the satisfaction or frustration of the person I affected, and having the satisfaction or frustration which I might experience. Does this equivalence in itself give any reason whatever for someone to act in the given way, so as to satisfy or frustrate my desires?

Who can think so? I please the waiter to a certain extent by a generous tip. There is, we can suppose, standard indifference between having his experience and having my experience of getting to the shop in time to buy batteries for my bicycle lamp. The fact of indifference is no reason why someone should secure that I get to the shop on time. Yet, *ex hypothesi*, there obtains precisely the stipulated equivalence. There can be no more force, evidently, where the indifference involves two undesired experiences. Indeed, if there *were* a recommendation in indifference-equivalence in itself, then there would be a recommendation in causing a certain experience to Green even though he had absolutely nothing to do with the causing of an earlier experience of Brown's.

The objection has gone unnoticed for a particular reason. Here and elsewhere, proposals as to the content of desert-claims, and arguments that if they are so understood they constitute reasons for imposing distress, are bound up with other quite different considerations about punishment. The doctrine of punishment on offer, as in the present case, may also contain the recommendation of it that it is preventive of offences, something regarded as essential to justification, or the definitional constraint that punishment is the work of an authority. It is plainly essential that these surrounding propositions do not distract attention from what is in question. That is a proposal as to the sense and argumentative worth of desert-claims, and nothing else.

The third answer to the question of what relation holds between a culpable action and a distress, when the latter is said to be deserved for the former, is a more long-running and a puzzling one. It requires more attention. The *Intrinsic-Good Answer*, as it is given, is just that the relation is such that *the suffering of the guilty* is intrinsically good. (L. H. Davies, 1972) In the terms we have been using, what we have is that the relation is such that it is intrinsically good that distress somehow be experienced by anyone who has performed a culpable action.

This is to be distinguished from the proposition that it is intrinsically good that such a person have a penalty in the standard sense imposed on him—where that is to say that it is intrinsically good that we do to him what typically causes distress, perhaps gaol him. The latter proposition—a fourth answer to our question, to be noticed only in passing—cannot usefully be given as a justification of what we do, since it itself *is* just to the effect that there is a justification of what we do. The *Petitio Answer*, as we can call it, produces only the useless argument that something has a justification because it has just that justification. The argument begs the question, by using the conclusion as its premiss, and is of course an instance of the fallacy of *petitio principii*.

The third and different answer, to repeat, is that there is intrinsic goodness in the state of affairs which consists in the distress of the culpable. That proposition offers the formal possibility of an argument, since it is not identical with some proposition which it can be taken to support, about our embracing the means to the good end, acting so as to bring about the distress. What we have, rather, is that the distress of the culpable does not have extrinsic or instrumental value, as a means to something else which is of value, but rather is something which is good in itself. We see or feel that the relation that holds between a man's culpability and his distress is that the two constitute an intrinsic good.

What this must come to or entail, in part, is that it is *better* that a man's culpable action be followed or accompanied by his distress than not be so followed or accompanied. There is, as just suggested, the further entailment that there exists *some* reason for our acting so as to bring about the given intrinsic good. This reason need not consist in a moral obligation to cause distress to the culpable man, in its being wrong not to do so, let alone an obligation which overcomes all other obligations not to act—perhaps the conflicting obligation precisely not to cause distress. It may be, rather, that what is taken to follow from the possibility of securing the intrinsic good is merely the absence of a certain moral obligation on us not to act—its not being wrong to act. Further, the initial claim as to intrinsic goodness, however construed, is presumably not merely in logical connection with some such judgement or judgements about the rightness of actions, but also, to remember our earlier account of morality (1.6), in logical connection with our judgements on agents as to their general standing and also our moral approval or disapproval of particular actions. Something follows, from your having so acted as to earn a kind of moral disapproval, about my somehow earning approval or disapproval for actions bearing on your subsequent distress or the lack of it.

Must the view as to the intrinsic good of the suffering of the guilty in fact involve the postulation of not one intrinsic good but rather an untold number of them? This is implied by the thought that a proponent of the view surely cannot suppose, with respect to a certain degree or sort of culpability, that *any* subsequent distress to the agent would make for an intrinsic good. That is, in line with the supposition that a petty offender does not deserve a long gaol sentence, it is natural to think that someone who gives the Intrinsic-Good Answer to our question cannot suppose that a *petty* culpability together with the distress of twenty years in gaol make for an intrinsic good. Rather, the possible intrinsic good will consist in the given petty culpability and some lesser distress. The Intrinsic-Good Answer, it seems, will therefore be that for each of the many degrees and sorts of culpability, there is a particular intrinsic good.

Is it possible to maintain against this that really there is but one intrinsic good, a general intrinsic good consisting in culpability and *some distress or other*, and that we are to use different considerations —perhaps the degree of need for prevention of a type of offence—to fix what particular distress ought to be imposed on an offender? That would be singularly uncompelling. It is *desert* that is being analysed by way of the idea of intrinsic good, and it is precisely desert that is used to justify particular penalties rather than others. The Intrinsic-Good Answer, then, must indeed involve the postulating of very many intrinsic goods.

This multitude of intrinsic goods is not reassuring, but entirely consonant with a larger fact of relevance. It is that there appears to be no logical or other effective barrier to the postulating of intrinsic goods in any area. In the history of moral philosophy, and in ordinary reflection, there are two categories of intrinsic goods. One of these, to say the very least, has immediate appeal. This is the category, to describe it very generally, which has to do with the satisfaction of desire, both amounts and distributions of satisfaction. Traditionally what has been spoken of is happiness. Perhaps it is happiness above all, whether conceived as satisfaction or differently, that has most often been taken to be a good in itself. The second category, which can be defined only negatively, contains intrinsic goods which are not a matter of satisfaction and its distribution. It has contained the intrinsic goods of promise-keeping, truth, truth-telling, beauty, certain intentions, a good will, personal autonomy in Kant's sense or a like one, and, as we know, the distress of the culpable. All of these, if they *are* in the category in question rather than the other one, are conceived wholly independently of satisfaction and its distribution. There appears to be no logical or other effective barrier to adding, say, the intrinsic good of persons of long family lineage having twice the income of others, or, for that matter, the intrinsic good of the colour mauve, or of Irish-Norwegians being arranged in straight lines.

Since there seems to be no logical or other barrier to the affirming of any intrinsic good, we cannot refute the claim that the distress of the culpable is such a good. (Cf. Kenny, 1978, p. 73) At the same time, the plethora of affirmable intrinsic goods of the second category seems to make each of them doubtful, and in fact all of them have been disputed. The contrast between intrinsic goods of the two categories is, in this very relevant respect, a sharp one.

To express it in one way, consider a person who denies that the fulfilment of desire is an intrinsic good. She feels there is no reason, in the frustration itself of the sick or the enslaved, to end that frustration. Her position is not, as is often true, that she sees reason in the frustration for ending it, but also believes that other reasons of whatever kind require its continuation. Rather she sees in the distress of the victim *no* reason of whatever weight for ending that distress. Such a person is less than human, and in danger of being assigned to some medical category. If she really does see or feel no difference between pressing the Distress Button or the Happiness Button in a case we can imagine—she knows *only* that pressing one will cause distress, and pressing the other will cause happiness—we shall, not to put too fine a point on it, regard her as insane. We have no such attitude to someone who denies the intrinsic good of, say, beauty which gives no satisfaction whatever, or a good-will in itself— or the suffering of the guilty.

All of this sceptical reflection, while persuasive, must be admitted to be inconclusive. It seems to remain a kind of possibility to maintain that the suffering of the guilty *is* an intrinsic good, as much so as the intrinsic goods of satisfaction or happiness, and that those who fail to see or feel this are somehow morally insensitive, and that the proponents of most other intrinsic goods in the second category are also such, and so on. There is the same possibility, if no more, of affirming more elaborate intrinsic goods of the same kind, including those which are bound up with kinds of knowledge on the part of the person punished and also with his reformation. (Nozick, 1981, pp. 363–97) Perhaps this possibility can somehow be closed off, but the attempt to do so, by way of a good deal of moral philosophy, will not be made here.

However, it is one thing to allow that there seems no strict refutation of the claim that the suffering of the guilty is good in itself, and another thing to allow that the desert-relation which we have been considering can in fact be construed as consisting in such a good.

In the first place, it seems settled, as much so as such facts ever are, that to claim a man deserves a certain distress for his culpable action, and somehow to use the claim to defend imposing the distress on him, is to depend on some *claim of fact*. It is to claim and to rely on something which is in the ordinary sense true or false. In defending ten years of imprisonment for a man by saying that he deserves the distress of it for a killing, people do not mean to argue merely that ten years is right since that conclusion follows from some other moral conviction, however logically independent, which thing *also* lacks a truth-value. This would be the conviction as to an intrinsic good. They would not accept that they are offering no reason of fact whatever. No doubt to say that he deserves ten years is ordinarily to imply that it is right that he have it, but to take that implication as the total content of what is said can safely be said to be simply mistaken.

There is a connected but more conclusive consideration, which applies as decisively to the other answers given so far to the question of the desert-relation—the Uninformative Answer, the Indifference Answer, and the Petitio Answer. As long as men have been punished, their punishments have been defended or justified, wholly or partly, as deserved. The defence has been given of very different institutions of punishment. It would be no less than bizarre if this tradition of desert-claims, defined and entrenched in law, had in it only an *obscure, uncertain, or yet weaker* argument. There may be no *finally effective* argument in the tradition—that question remains open—but it cannot be that the tradition has in it only an obscure or uncertain argument. (p. 204)

What was said before against the Intrinsic-Good Answer can perhaps be regarded as less than decisive. What is beyond question is that what we get from the Intrinsic-Good Answer at best gives us no more than an uncertain argument for punishment. We can then draw the conclusion that we have not arrived at the correct answer to the question of the nature of the desert-relation in connection with punishment. We need not consider the question of how the traditional answers we have stand to origination and hence to determinism. The correct answer will take us further forward, to various possible institutions of punishment, some of which do claim attention, and may enter into a response or indeed *responses* of affirmation with respect to punishment.

4.4 PUNISHMENT AND DESERT-CLAIMS——ANOTHER VIEW

Let us make another start, by way of a certain realism. Let us remember facts which are basic to at least much talk of desert in connection with punishment—and also remember, so to speak, their felt nature for us. Some of us are the victims of others, of their culpable offences. We are vilified and slandered, or terrified in the street and robbed, or maimed by the negligence or wilfulness of others. We are treated offensively and attacked for doing our jobs, or the colour of our skins, or for intervening to help others. We have our houses or rooms broken into and our things taken, are defrauded out of our property, or are led into vicious financial arrangements. We are victimized by employers, or assaulted and lied about by policemen. We suffer the ordeals of threat, harassment, extortion, and rape. Our children are ill-treated, molested, or corrupted. We have deformed children because some drug companies have too clear an eye to their profits. Our husbands and wives are tortured, or murdered, for gain or for political purposes.

When such things happen, we want the offender to *get what he deserves*. We may say just that, or something very like it—perhaps that we want him to get his *just deserts* or his *rightful deserts*. We also say, evidently with the same end in view, that we *want justice*, or to *have justice done*, or to *have the law take its course*, or to *have things put right*. We may say, more openly, but to the same end, that we want him *not to get away with it*, to *pay* or to *pay his debt*, to *get his punishment, get what is owing to him* or *coming to him*. We may say plainly that we want *satisfaction*.

Certainly this want, expressed in these various desert-claims and still more forcibly in more common speech, may not be our only want, or all that moves us. We may also demand compensation or restitution. We may be anxious about the prevention of more such injuries to ourselves and others. We may perhaps have some general concern for the public good. We may have kinds of understanding of those who have injured us. We may have an uncomfortable sense of circumstances of social injustice which lie in the background of the offences against us. Few or none of us, however, if we can have it at a tolerable or even bearable cost, and without danger, fail to have the desire which is variously expressed. It evidently is a desire which is in some way focused upon the culpable agent who injured us, and somehow also has much to do with ourselves.

Is what we want most clearly expressed when we say one of the mentioned things, that we *want justice*? As might be thought from that expression of our desire, is what we want just that the criminal law as it stands, in the judgement of its officers, and with the care or diligence they in fact bring to bear, be carried forward with respect to the offender? Do we, that is, want the fact of *legality*? This is often supposed, but cannot be right, since we may not get what we want when exactly what is legal happens. We do not get what we want when we disagree with the law as it stands or the course it takes, properly in its own terms but unsatisfactorily to us. This is the case when we take the law to be soft, unfair, or worse. On the other hand, we may get just what we want when we suppose the law to have been departed from in our favour, its officers to have exceeded their legal roles or rights. Here we take the law or its operation to have been improved upon, but not, so to speak, by having been made more legal.

It is clear from such considerations that when we are satisfied, and the law has been carried forward properly in its own terms, what we have got is not the satisfaction of legality, the satisfaction simply that the law has been observed. In fact the end in question, when separated from other things, is an elusive and abstract one, unlikely to move many of us. If we are moved by it, and do get the satisfaction in question when the law is carried forward, that is not the different satisfaction we get which is expressed in the various ways as focused on the culpable doer of injury but having much to do with us.

Is what we want most perspicuously expressed when we say we want our injurer to get his *rightful desert*, or we want to *have things put right*? That is, is what we want that the right thing be done, the *morally right thing* by our lights? Certainly we say and believe that, and we believe it with full confidence and without self-deception. But that is not to exclude another fact. Consider two persons. One is the victim of an offence, a man whose life has been wrecked, or has just been injured or suffered a loss about which he cares. The other is a person in no particular connection with the victim, and who does not identify with him for some particular reason—but a person of whom we can also truly say that he wants the right thing to be done. He thinks that the offender, like all such offenders, ought to be punished, for whatever reason or reasons.

The victim may indeed be described as wanting the right thing done. But his state of desire, if the words do fit it, is none the less not the state of desire of the disinterested person. We rightly hear a good deal more in the words of the victim when *he* says he wants the right thing done. We hear self-interest. We hear it, partly, because unlike the disinterested person, he says other things, or we can readily think of him saying other things, some of those noticed above. The most revealing is that he wants *satisfaction*.

It seems clear enough, despite several things that obscure the matter, that desert-claims about punishment are properly understood in terms of a certain fact. It is a fact from which we try to avert our eyes, which jurisprudents are keen to exclude from their subjects, and defenders of what might be called 'the moral realm' find intolerable. It is that when we want justice, or the man who has injured us wrongly to get what is owing to him, or satisfaction, what we want is that *he suffer a distress, of some degree or kind*. We have a desire for his distress, aimed at that itself. It is a desire that will be satisfied only through the belief that the person who has wrongly injured us has been subjected to an effective reprimand, a disgrace, deprivation, hurt, injury, or worse, and, no doubt, with a knowledge of why. We thus have a desire that, like any other, can be less than satisfied, or more than satisfied, or satisfied.

To come to the central proposition, it is that the indubitable if unwelcome fact of what can be named our *grievance-desires* is what is fundamental to at least many claims of desert in connection with typical institutions of punishment. The relation between an offender's culpability and a certain distress when the latter is taken as deserved for the former—the relation so unsuccessfully characterized in various face-saving ways—is essentially that the distress satisfies a desire to which the offender has given rise by his offence. It does no less and no more than satisfy it. The deserved penalty is in fact the satisfying penalty, or any rate that is the principal fact about it in so far as argument for the penalty is concerned.

This is a conclusion with some history behind it, despite its conflict with what have rightly been called the traditional analyses of desert. It has the inexplicit support, which is worth something, of many of those whose reflections on the law and punishment are most in touch with it—judges, policemen, and some legal theorists. Few of them are slow to say, whatever else they say of the law, that it stands in a certain relation to revenge, in the sense of satisfaction obtained by the repayment of injuries. The classical statement of the view is that of the Victorian judge James Fitzjames Stephen.

The benefits which criminal law produces are twofold. In the first place, it prevents crime by terror; in the second place, it regulates, sanctions, and provides a legitimate satisfaction for the passion of revenge. I shall not insist on the importance of this second advantage, but shall content myself with referring those who deny it is one to the works of the two greatest of English moralists, each of whom was the champion of one of the two great schools of thought upon that subject—Butler and Bentham. The criminal law stands to the passion of revenge in much the same relation as marriage to the sexual appetite.

Of these two advantages, the first—the prevention of crime by terror—must, from the nature of the case, be co-extensive with the criminal law. The second—the pleasure of revenge—is obtained in those cases only in which the acts forbidden by the law excite feelings of moral indignation. (Stephen, 1863, pp. 98–9; cf. Lotze, 1885, p. 98)

Mill is of a similar view, as the following two passages indicate, although he brings it together less than clearly with a good deal else.

. . . the two essential ingredients in the sentiment of Justice are, the desire to punish a person who has done harm, and the knowledge or belief that there is some definite individual or individuals to whom harm has been done. (1972c (1859), p. 47)

The sentiment of justice, in that one of its elements which consists of the desire to punish, is thus, I conceive, the natural feeling of retaliation or vengeance, rendered by intellect and sympathy applicable to those injuries, that is, to those hurts, which wound us through, or in common with society at large. This sentiment, in itself, has nothing moral in it; what is moral is, the exclusive subordination of it to the social sympathies, so as to wait on and obey their call. (1972c (1859), p. 48)

More needs to be said in explanation and qualification of the conclusion that at least many desert-claims in connection with typical institutions of punishment are somehow to be understood in terms of the fact of grievance-desires and their satisfaction. Certainly the conclusion is a long way from philosophical thought about the intrinsic good of the suffering of the guilty, declarations about wholly elusive or morally ineffectual factual relations involving only culpability and distress, and the like. It is no popular conclusion. Let me first enumerate reasons for it.

(i) It does indeed go against sense to suppose that desert-claims in connection with punishment do not provide or involve any clear and firm reason for it. That desert-claims are empty of relevant content has in fact been supposed by many philosophers, but it must go against sense to suppose that men have not seen and got some clear gain in the repetition, over millennia, of claims that others deserve penalties. As remarked above, particularly in connection with the Intrinsic-Good Answer to the question of the desert-relation, the tradition of desert-claims cannot have been directed to an obscure or uncertain good. (p.200) The account just given of desert-claims, the *Grievance Theory*, discovers in them an argument of the most fundamental kind, that something satisfies an existing desire, a persisting and strong desire. It is an argument, although more will be said of the matter, that depends on an unproblematical instrinsic good of the first category. No other analysis of desert in punishment passes this crucial test. (Cf. Kenny, 1978, Ch. 4; Mackie, 1982)

(ii) As already implied, it is clear that the analysis issues directly from the most entrenched and explicit ways of talking of desert, and is at least consonant with all of them, including theoretical and institutional usages and constructions. The entrenched and explicit usages are that the deserved penalty for the offender is the debt he is to be made to pay, what is owed by him, what is owed to him, what is coming to him, what gives satisfaction. The theoretical or institutional usages are that the deserved penalty is the equivalent, corresponding, proportional, commensurate, or reciprocal penalty.

With respect to these latter expressions, it is in fact unthinkable that in so far as they involve a reason for punishment, they have to do only with a bare equality taken for itself, like the equality of two things in length or weight. Rather, they have to do with a transaction, in which one party provides and one party receives something, which thing is in some or other relation of equality with something else. We do not put people into gaols with the aim of increasing the number of bare equalities in the universe. That is an aim, to have its pointlessness clear, which might be had by a dotty passenger who puts effort into trying to make all his bus journeys as many minutes long as there are passengers on the bus.

(iii) The Grievance Theory does of course give a factual reason for punishment, as theories about intrinsic goods do not. (p. 200) Whatever the final argumentative worth of the proposition that a penalty satisfies a grievance-desire, it is true or false in the ordinary sense, however much a matter of judgement. As with any other propositions about desire, incidentally, there are behavioural criteria as to truth or falsehood.

(iv) We do have a clear relation with respect to a man's culpability and a certain distress. The distress is so related to the culpability that it satisfies the desire deemed to be owed to that culpability. The distress is unlike any other in that it alone satisfies the grievance-desire deemed to have been brought into being.

(v) To come to something not so far anticipated, it can reasonably be asked of any account of desert and punishment that the account issues from, or at least fits, a defensible account of things more fundamental, out of which punishment mainly arises. These things are the resentful personal feelings, and morality, and in particular our moral disapproval of persons for particular actions. One kind of the resentful feelings, as was remarked in passing, have in them desires to return a hurt. So too with one kind of moral disapproval. (p. 65) With respect to the vicious husband, our feelings in part are that he should have a return for his action, that he should at least have the pain of moral criticism or condemnation.

To speak summarily, typical institutions of punishment are, in part, our resentment and moral disapproval carried into action on our behalf by others, not just the action of speaking out. Both kinds of resentment and disapproval enter into these institutions. The given account of desert in punishment, based on grievance-desires, is an account, in fact *the* account, which we can rightly expect to have, given the nature of one kind of resentful feelings and moral disapproval, and the fact that punishment is importantly a kind of product of them. We can be confident that we have a right account of a part of punishment since it is an account that fits sources of it. It might be replied that desert conceived in the way of the Intrinsic-Good Answer reflects the presence of certain judgements of intrinsic good in moral disapproval. Similar remarks might be made about other answers to the question of the desert-relation. These replies would not connect punishment with the very nature of the accusatory feelings and moral disapproval, in particular certain desires which are fundamental to them, whatever the content of the feelings in terms of this or that value, principle, or commitment.

As remarked, further explanation and qualification is needed of the general conclusion that when a certain distress is somehow said to be deserved for a certain culpability, the fact of importance is that the distress will satisfy what is deemed to be the grievance-desire created by the offence, and the argument for the distress is that the distress will satisfy the desire. This explanation and qualification of the Grievance Theory will be given by way of considering five objections to it.

(i) Some care has been taken, as may have been noted, to frame the theory in a limited way. It has been said that *the proper understanding* of many desert-claims about punishment is in terms of grievance-desires (p. 203); that they and their satisfaction are *fundamental to* desert-claims about punishment (p. 203); that the reason *provided by* or *involved in* many desert-claims is that penalties satisfy grievance-desires (p. 204), and so on. It has not been claimed, then, that when we say in this way that a certain penalty is deserved for a certain offence, *what we standardly mean* is that the penalty will satisfy the caused grievance-desire. Any objection to that effect is misdirected. It is perhaps arguable that some of the entrenched locutions, about the offender paying, or giving satisfaction, *can* have their meaning properly characterized in terms of grievance-desires, but I intend no general claim to that effect. It is perhaps proper to say that desert-claims about punishment, whenever made, do carry an implication about the satisfaction of grievance, but let us leave alone the parts of linguistics and the philosophy of language which are concerned with such matters.

It can be supposed without damage to the general conclusion that has been drawn that the desert-claims in question are properly to be understood as essentially vague, as suggesting some factual connection or other between offence and penalty, such that the connection justifies the penalty. It would not damage the conclusion if, as is unlikely, these desert-claims were claims as to indifference scales (p. 196), or if they were claims to the effect that a penalty was in accordance with precedent or a penalty-system—which view was passed over in our survey. Nor would it damage our conclusion if, as may be more likely, they were non-factual claims as to the intrinsic good—the fittingness—of the suffering of the guilty.

This is so since our conclusion is not essentially a piece of linguistic analysis but an answer to this question: What is the argument for punishment that is suggested by and involved in certain desert-claims about it? Does some doctrine of the philosophy of language resist the idea that what is *said* may not convey the essential argument of an enterprise? If that is so, then, to my mind, so much the worse for the doctrine. What is true here, of course, may not be true elsewhere. Elsewhere, as we shall see, desert-claims may call for a similar linguistic analysis but not involve the given argument.

(ii) It may be objected against the conclusion, simply enough, that it is in error to suppose that the satisfaction of grievance is what is offered in defence of punishment by any desert-claims: 'Nobody ... would say that a judge ought to sentence because the people outside in the street are baying for blood, and that's what it amounts to.' (N. Walker, 1983, p. 15) If the conclusion did amount to that, it would of course be absurd. It does not.

A first thing to be kept in mind here as well as elsewhere is that the conclusion does not include any proposition as to the relative weight of desert-claims or the given argument in connection with punishment, as against, say, considerations of prevention. We have not come to that matter. A second is that there is no doubt that a good deal of the law and punishment has little or nothing to do with desert, and is not defended by reference to it. Stephen makes such a point in the passage quoted above (p. 204), and it has more application to legal systems since his time. The conclusion that has been drawn here has to do with desert-claims where they do figure in punishment, and not with the extent to which they figure.

The objection, to repeat, is that the conclusion reduces criminal justice or the argument from desert to the mistaken proposition that a judge is or ought to be governed by the mob in the street. In reply to one thing that might be intended by the objection, something needs to be allowed. It is not proposed that the given desert-claims involve the argument that penalties satisfy *whatever* desires for satisfaction happen to exist in particular cases, for whatever reason. To restrict ourselves to the actual victims of offences, either persons harmed or persons close to them, who are of prime importance, it is not proposed that judges, in so far as they are influenced by matters of desert, are in fact attempting to gauge the actual desire for satisfaction of these individual victims, whether or not unreasonable, peculiarly vindictive, or inflamed. For a number of clear reasons, despite the fact of *some* attention paid to individuals, it is rather the case that a penalty system is to be seen as reflecting what can be called standard grievances.

One thing that determines a standard grievance is certainly a conception of a person of ordinary or average responses of feeling. Again, a standard grievance is conceived in relation to a particular culpability. It is not as if such a grievance were understood as a desire arising out of, say, popular hatred for some group of people, or a popular fear of some type of offender. There is also a consideration of another kind which touches on the idea of a standard grievance. It is evident that the institution of punishment is very subject to the principle of formal justice, that of treating like cases alike. With respect to penalties, this operates in much more than the obvious way: requiring a like distress for offenders of like culpability. The most relevant at the moment is its operation with injuries and grievance-desires. A like injury is to be taken as giving rise to a like grievance-desire.

What has been said so far, in answer to the simple objection, may well bring to mind certain other objections which will be treated below. To finish with the simple objection itself, it might be improved into this: Punishment by the state, in so far as it is governed or influenced by desert or by anything else, is rule-governed, a matter of principle, consistency, precedent, objectivity, specific resistances to kinds of partiality and feeling; this punishment, further, is independent in different ways of society generally, of parts of it, and of victims themselves; therefore it is mistaken to regard desert-claims in punishment as a matter of grievance-satisfactions for victims.

The premisses as they stand and a good deal more about the nature of the law, all of it in fact fundamental to Stephen's view (p. 204), can be granted. The conclusion nevertheless does not follow. The claim that a man deserves ten years for the rape is indeed a claim made within an institution, a claim shaped by and subject to a considerable number of kinds of constraint. This complexity, which has been little more than indicated, does not begin to defeat the proposition that desert-claims and arguments from desert are to be made sense of in terms of a ruling idea: that the distress of a man's penalty satisfies a certain desire. The objection is no better than conceivable ones about other institutions, say that of old-age pensions, whose aims are also in various ways defined and constrained, and whose categories are necessarily standard or general.

(iii) It may be objected very differently, that the given account of desert-claims and arguments from desert cannot be right because of the existence of a certain very settled custom. Theories about the justification of punishment, or different justifying considerations within theories, divide without much important remainder into two groups: those that attempt to justify it somehow by reference to agreement and desert, and those that attempt to justify it by reference to the prevention of future offences. The former group, by settled custom, are conceived of and spoken of as finding an argument for punishment in only the past offence, or only in a relation between it and a punishment, which relation does not bring in consequences of the punishment. They are backward-looking. By contrast, the second group of theories or considerations are forward-looking or consequentialist. The account that has been given here of desert-claims goes against this customary view. Desert-claims have been understood as having to do fundamentally with a forward-looking or consequentialist argument. It is that a penalty is defensible or has a recommendation because it has the consequence of satisfying desires.

One admirable philosopher who made this objection did unwittingly weaken it, and in effect point to its proper rejoinder, by also arguing something else. This is that traditional attempts to clarify and defend an argument from desert in connection with punishment have been failures. '. . . a retributive principle of punishment cannot be explained or developed within a reasonable system of moral thought. . . .' '. . . attempts to make sense of the principle of positive retributivism, as an independent principle with immediate moral authority, have signally failed.' (Mackie, 1982, pp. 3, 6) He went on to offer an *explanation* of the fact of desert-claims with respect to punishment, a persuasive explanation derived from biology and in particular evolutionary theory, but to persist in the position that they can involve no significant *argument*.

My answer to the objection can be anticipated, resting as it does on an argument already given. It is not enough to grant that there exists a causal explanation of the fact of desert-claims. What needs also to be granted is that the tradition of them and of punishment, entrenched over time, cannot be without effective rational content. (pp. 200, 204) It cannot be that in this continuing tradition men have not aimed at and got something of value and capable of clear enunciation. By way of brisk summary, offenders have always been seen as having debts of some kind to pay, and have been forced to pay them—*how could it be that no one received anything?*

One can reasonably have a certain readiness to be impressed by customary philosophical reflection, and in particular to be impressed by the customary philosophical idea that desert is not forward-looking or consequentialist. However, if a struggle over centuries to produce an argument of the supposedly right character has failed, and if an argument of a different but fitting character can be found, it is more reasonable to take that argument to be the one which has informed and does inform talk of desert. By an argument of a fitting character I mean, in part, one that is in accord with desert-claims and only with them.

(iv) Will someone say that the argument taken as fundamental to desert in punishment does not really fit because, at bottom, it defends penalties as giving satisfaction, and has little to do with equivalence or whatever between offence and penalty? Certainly, as has been granted, these desert-claims *are* claims as to some sort of equivalence. The objection needs only a brief reply, in two parts.

It is of course true that penalties are defended in the argument by the fact that they give satisfaction. But the clear idea of equivalence involved in the argument is bound up with or integral to that fact. The idea, to repeat, is that the penalty is equivalent to the offence in that it does not do less or more than satisfy the relevant grievance, but rather just satisfies it. That the penalty must not do less than satisfy it is simply entailed by the requirement of satisfaction. If the penalty were to do more than satisfy the grievance, the additional distress would be pointless—it would lack exactly the defence advanced by the argument for the distress of an equivalent penalty in the given case. The further distress would in fact be indefensible in terms of the argument.

(v) If the given argument is what is fundamental to desert-claims about punishment, then punishment is indeed like revenge. That is not to say that it *is* revenge, since, for one thing, punishment by proper definition is the work of an authority rather than the free-lance activity of the person harmed or those close to him. There are other differences. (Nozick, 1981, pp. 366–70) However, if the given argument is right, punishment is like revenge in involving desires for the distress of others. This conclusion cannot be said to be obviously false, to be a consequence of the Grievance Theory which in fact refutes it. Punishment, as already noticed, *is* often enough likened to revenge. (p. 204) What an objector to the theory must do is identify a respect in which the theory makes punishment like revenge, and show that punishment does not in fact have the supposed feature. Perhaps the theory gives to punishment a moral shortcoming had by revenge, and in fact punishment does not have that shortcoming. There is such a line of thought, as follows.

It may be held that desires for the distress of others, of all desires, are most evidently those which we ought not to have. They may be described as indecent, vicious, or degraded—such as to make revenge what it is, which is abhorrent. Therefore they are desires whose satisfaction should be absolutely ignored in considering the worth of any action. That an action gives rise to grievance-satisfaction is no recommendation whatever of it. Surely any such satisfaction should even count *against* the action. Thus it cannot be that the argument from desert, as it has been presented, is even a tolerable one. It cannot be that any institution can even in part be defended by saying that it satisfies such desires. On the assumption that there is an argument of some force pertaining to desert and punishment, this cannot be it. We have several times assumed in this inquiry, not that there must be a conclusive reason for punishment having to do fundamentally with a man's past action, but that there must be a clear and a significant or prima-facie reason, something of value which is capable of explicit enunciation. The objection now before us is that we have no such reason in the consideration having to do with grievance-desires. The consideration is clear, but, it is unique in its absolute want of value or significance, indeed in being abhorrent.

The objection must not be confused with something else to which we are coming. That is, what we have is not the inevitable proposition that while the satisfaction of grievance-desires is a significant and firm reason for punishment, it is outweighed by other things. Rather, the objection is that it is indecent or whatever to desire someone else's distress as an end in itself, and hence that any satisfaction of grievance-desires produced by a punishment counts as *no* reason for it, or even a reason against it.

This has nothing to do with opposition to taking the ordinary means to that satisfaction, the actual causing of distress to the person in question. If it were possible to satisfy a man's grievance-desire by a deception, such that no distress at all was caused to the person he has in mind, we would none the less have no reason to satisfy his desire and would perhaps have a reason to frustrate it. We ought perhaps to prevent him having the false belief that the person was or would be in distress, and hence prevent him having his grievance satisfied. This would not be on account of anything about truth and falsehood, but on account of the baseness of the satisfaction. Nor, incidentally, does any of this have to do with the possibility of certain undesirable consequences of the satisfying of grievance-desires, say the man's getting some abnormal or heightened sexual passion for the causing of suffering. It has to do with the nature of ordinary grievance-desires and grievance-satisfaction.

What is to be said of this? Certainly, when we are not ourselves the victims of the culpable actions of others, we find something pertaining to the fact of grievance-desires unattractive or worse. We may, when we are such victims, be less than happy with our having such desires ourselves. We may do a good job of concealing them from ourselves, at least some of the time, by diverting our attention from them to more elevated considerations, perhaps the supposed need to impose a punishment in order to prevent more offences. This disinclination is in the background of what can be called the *concealing* character of certain of the ordinary and entrenched ways of talking of desert, as when we say we want things put right. (p. 202) It is also in the background of the concealing theoretical and institutional usages mentioned earlier, whereby a penalty is said to be equivalent, corresponding, proportional, commensurate, or reciprocal. (p. 195)

The fact of disinclination, however, is not at all sufficient to establish the moral conclusion that grievance-satisfaction is to be ignored in considering the worth of an action or practice, let alone the stronger view that it counts against it. For one thing, it is possible to give an explanation of this disinclination which is consistent with the grievance-satisfaction itself having a positive value. The explanation of course has to do, in part, with our very naturally associating a man's grievance-desire with what is indubitably bad in itself, which is the proposed suffering he has in mind. Another part of the explanation has to do with the seemingly undeniable proposition that the world would be a better place if it were very different, perhaps unrecognizably different, such that our grievance-desires were replaced by desires with other effects, desires for the well-being of others.

A further and more conclusive reply to the objection is that in fact no clear reason has been given for the proposition that the possibility of grievance-satisfaction is to be ignored in considering the rightness of actions, let alone that it counts against rightness. We do not get a reason, as it seems to me, in the moralist's rhetoric about the indecent, vicious, base, or other nature of the desires and the satisfaction in question. What we get, surely, if we get something precisely to the point, is no more than an anticipation or a version of the conclusion for which we are looking for a reason. Further, while it is indeed possible to be in a frame of mind where condescension is possible, another frame of mind is also possible, and it certainly has a reasonableness about it. Is is, for what the point is worth, the frame of mind of judges, or very many judges, as they go about their work.

Consider again the extraordinary but simplifying case where it is possible to satisfy a man's grievance-desire by deception. He has been savagely treated, perhaps maimed. *What* reason do we have, aside from the obvious irrelevant reason of truthfulness, for thinking that whatever is to be said against, there is *nothing* to be said for giving the victim content in place of discontent, peace in place of bitter passion, and escape from a kind of wretchedness? To my mind, any reason that exists has never been brought into clarity. It is open to anyone to declare, of course, that grievance-satisfaction is simply intrinsically bad, as it is open to anyone to declare that the suffering of the guilty is intrinsically good. Few of us, however, are likely to be reassured or persuaded by these fiats. We want a *reason*, surely, for abandoning what seems to be the reasonableness of replacing discontent by content, bitterness by peace, and so on.

It can be allowed that we might think better of the maimed victim if he had escaped or risen over his grievance. But even if we would think better of him if he were quite different, that does not entail that when we consider him as he is, we have a reason for leaving him in his self-mortifying passion. We might think better of a man in some quite different situation if he were willing to forgo an absolutely indubitable moral right which he has to something, but it does not follow at all that we are not obliged to respect his right. That he might become Christlike does not dissolve our obligations to him as he is. Nor, in fact, might our obligations be dissolved if he did become Christlike, since his renunciation would certainly leave intact many of our obligations to him.

It was remarked earlier in connection with the idea that the suffering of the guilty is an intrinsic good, that in the history of moral philosophy two categories of intrinsic goods can be distinguished. (p. 199) The first has to do with quantities and distributions of satisfaction—very roughly, well-being and fairness. The second has to do with the other postulated intrinsic goods. The goods of the first category, despite the fact of great disagreement about their proper characterization and ordering, are in some way beyond any serious question. In no substantial inquiry do we stop to ask whether pain or frustration considered in itself might be good, or pleasure or satisfaction in itself bad. Nor do we stop to ask, of the situation of which we know only that there is enough food for two equally starving people, whether we ought to give all to one and none to the other, or most to one and little to the other. By contrast the goods of the second category, although some of them certainly appeal to us, are open to doubt. All, as I remarked earlier, have in fact been doubted.

No reason has been given, and in my view none exists, for excluding grievance-satisfactions from the first category. In themselves—and we are wholly concerned with them themselves, rather than any costs, concomitants, or effects of them—they are satisfactions like any others. They are open to a range of descriptions inseparable from the descriptions we apply to other satisfactions. For example, they may be said to consist in, or to give, contentment. Like other satisfactions, they are struggled for, and, like other satisfactions, their denials or frustrations can be a torment and an affliction. They have just the properties or character which give satisfactions generally the place which they have in our lives.

Like very nearly any goods, there can most certainly be countervailing reasons against having them or providing them. By way of a random example of another equally vulnerable good, there is perhaps no moral view which can take a hold on us which does not allow *any* conceivable circumstance in which there would be countervailing reasons against the good of preserving an innocent life. That grievance-satisfactions can for good reasons be denied is one truth. That they do, despite that, provide a clear and firm reason for punishment, is another truth. It cannot successfully be objected that an argument based on grievance-desires cannot be the argument from desert since an argument from grievance-desires is insignificant. It is not.

4.5 THE THEORIES OF PUNISHMENT

We now have an understanding of the clear and firm argument for punishment, the argument based on grievance, which is involved in desert-claims about it. We need now to deal with two further questions, as anticipated earlier. (p. 180) The first is the bearing of determinism on the argument from desert. The second is that of the relative weight of the argument, as against other justificatory propositions about punishment, and hence the relative importance of certain features or a certain character, having to do with desert, of our actual institution of punishment and also possible institutions.

There is the possibility, among others, that determinism does affect the argument from grievance—in fact we already have grounds for thinking so—but that the argument is not of great relative weight. In particular, the argument is not of great importance within justifications attempted of our actual institutions of punishment.

The answer to the first question is in accordance with findings in earlier stages of this inquiry. One kind of our personal feelings of the resentful kind, as noted again recently (p. 33), have within them desires to return the hurt done to us by those whose actions give evidence of bad feelings towards us or bad judgements on us. Moral disapproval of one kind, to turn to it, also has within it at least an inclination to the discomfiture or worse of persons whom we take to have acted wrongfully. (p. 65) It was said of the latter desires, and implied of the former, that they could not survive our actually coming to believe that persons lack the power to originate different actions than those they perform (pp. 67, 39) Our desires against others on account of their actions could not hold up if we came to believe of them that *they could not have done otherwise,* in the specific sense of the words having to do in part with origination. One argument for the vulnerability of these desires was that in certain circumstances we do now resist any doubt or denial of origination, taking it as a threat to our resentment and disapproval. (p. 67)

The feelings had by victims of offenders, expressed in desert-claims, are perhaps best regarded as being within the class of the given kind of resentful personal feelings, rather than the like feelings of moral disapproval, although an argument could be attempted for assigning them to the latter class. The feelings had by victims of offenders are the strongest of the given resentful feelings, involving enlarged and dominant retributive desire, such desires as rightly have the name of grievance-desires. (p. 203)

The true argument from desert, to repeat, is to the effect that a penalty will satisfy grievance-desires. The desires, and hence the argument, are vulnerable to a determinism. The argument, if determinism is taken as true, depends on desires that will not survive if determinism comes to be accepted. However, in so far as determinism is not generally accepted, and grievance-desires persist, the argument keeps its basis. Admittedly, as we know, it cannot be said that grievance-desires owed to an action do logically presuppose the proposition that the action could have been otherwise in the sense just mentioned. It cannot be that the expression of the desire, perhaps a prescription, *entails* the proposition that the agent was not only voluntary in his action but might have originated a different action. That does not matter. Just as we are so constituted to take the fact of suffering as *a* reason against an action, so we are constituted to take grievance-desires as requiring the reason of an originated action. That our grievance-desires depend on our ideas of actions as originated is indeed a brute fact. (p. 111)

The remaining and culminating issue is that of the relative importance of desert or grievance with respect to a number of possible theories of punishment and possible institutions of punishment into which it enters, above all our actual institutions. Among the theories are a certain family of theories commonly presented as justifying our actual institutions. This family, *Mixed Theories* as they will be called, can be set out most effectively by contrasting them with others. In specifying these other theories, *Pure Retribution Theories, Utilitarian Theories*, and *Fairness Theories*, we shall in passing deal with the further question of the bearing of determinism on them and hence on the associated possible institutions of punishment. Some of the latter were perhaps actual institutions in the past, and some may be actual in the future.

(i) *Pure Retribution Theories* have been curiously persistent despite the fact that it is very arguable that the possible institution of punishment they propose, if it was actual once, has ceased to be. Certainly it is not the institution found in societies with which most of us are familiar. Pure Retribution Theories depend or purport to depend entirely on considerations of desert in justifying punishment. All else is excluded. Some, like Kant's, are to the effect that we are not merely justified in punishing offenders purely on grounds of their deserts, but are obliged to do so.

Even if a Civil Society resolved to dissolve itself with the consent of all its members—as might be supposed in the case of a People inhabiting an island resolving to separate and scatter themselves throughout the whole world—the last Murderer lying in prison ought to be executed before the resolution was carried out. This ought to be done in order that everyone may realize the desert of his deeds. . . .' (Kant, 1887 (1797), p. 198)

There has been speculation on Kant's own understanding of desert-claims, and hence the particular argument from desert on which he depends, and the questions remain open. Let us proceed on the basis of the conclusion we have, that there is but one clear and firm argument from desert in connection with punishment, the argument based on grievance-desires. Pure Retribution Theories, conceived in terms of this argument, are no more defensible than they have generally been taken to be when otherwise conceived. It is morally unthinkable that we can disregard all else about punishment, above all what can be said against it, or that we can suppose that the satisfaction of grievance by itself outweighs all of what can be said against it. It is unthinkable that we are obliged to engage in punishment solely because it satisfies grievance. Our present actual practice of punishment is certainly not owed to this. The theory would be destroyed by a general acceptance of the truth of determinism, since such an acceptance would dissipate the desires which are the theory's subject-matter. This, at least from the moral point of view just expressed, is of little matter.

Pure Retribution Theories have often been taken, rightly or wrongly, to have a certain virtue despite their indefensibility. They are said to respect the claims of individuals. This has to do with the fact that they do not merely seek to justify punishments, but also to prohibit and limit them. They in certain ways prohibit what can be called, if improperly, punishment of the innocent, and they limit the punishment of the guilty. That is, only those who deserve it may be punished, and no one is to be punished more than he deserves. These features, whatever their worth—we shall look at the question later in another connection (p. 220)—are to some extent preserved when Pure Retribution Theories are conceived in terms of grievance-satisfaction. So conceived, they are to the effect that no punishment is justified which does not satisfy grievance-desires—whether punishment of non-offenders or offenders. Non-offenders, since they do not give rise to grievance, are at least in general not to be punished, and offenders are not to be punished more than satisfies grievance. A general acceptance of determinism, issuing in the decay of grievance-desires, would of course affect these prohibitions. In the absence of grievance-desires, the given distinction between offenders and non-offenders, that the former do and the latter do not give rise to them, would no longer exist. Similarly, in the general absence of grievance-desires, the given limit on punishment would no longer exist.

Pure Retribution Theories conceived in terms of grievance-satisfaction are of course different in character from such theories conceived traditionally in terms of some other idea or image of desert. To the objection that to conceive them in our different way is too resolute, or even cavalier or pointless, since it is not to consider such theories as they have been understood and advanced, there is the reply that will be anticipated. As our inquiry into the desert-relation indicates, it is only by conceiving them in terms of grievance-satisfactions that we do have something firm and significant to consider. It has generally been assumed that determinism conflicts with Pure Retribution Theories traditionally conceived. The uncertain grounds for this assumption (p. 177) can continue to go unconsidered. It is a merit of the interpretation of desert in terms of grievance-satisfaction that it makes clear why desert in connection with punishment is affected by determinism.

(ii) *Utilitarian Theories* of the justification of punishment have typically contained dismissals of talk of desert, and been to the effect that punishment is justified when it is economically preventive of offences. The prevention may be the result of incapacitation, as when a man is prevented from many offences by being in gaol, or deterrence in several forms, or the creation and reinforcement of habitual, unreflective obedience to law. There are of course many difficulties here, of a factual kind. The theories in question, to state them more generally, are to the effect that punishment is justified when, in whatever way, it produces a greater total balance of satisfaction or a lesser total balance of dissatisfaction than any alternative to punishment. What is dismissed by Utilitarian Theories, in so far as desert is concerned, has been traditional argument which makes use of desert-claims but does *not* have to do with the satisfaction of grievance. Utilitarians have been rightly disparaging about such items as the instrinsic good of the suffering of the guilty.

The argument from desert in justification of punishment, as it has been conceived here, is the argument from grievance. In fact it could and in consistency should enter into any Utilitarian justification for imposing punishment, for the reason that grievance-satisfactions are among satisfactions produced by punishment. (Bentham's general enumeration of the kinds of pleasures and pains in fact includes 'the pleasures of malevolence', those 'resulting from the view of any pain supposed to be suffered by the beings who may become the objects of malevolence'. (1970 (1789), p. 44))

It is not the case, however, that a recognizably Utilitarian theory could in consistency use considerations of desert, understood in terms of grievance-satisfactions, to prohibit the punishment of the innocent and the over-punishment of the guilty. A theory could not consistently defend punishment by consequences of satisfaction having to do with prevention, and prohibit it, despite *any* such consequences, on grounds of absence of grievance-satisfactions. If satisfactions having to do with prevention were of a certain magnitude, it would be inconsistent to prohibit some particular punishment of an offender on the ground that it did more than satisfy existing grievance-desires.

Utilitarian Theories of punishment have in fact long been objected to on the ground that they somehow ignore the claims of individuals. It is a consequence of the theories, it has been claimed, that the innocent may or must be treated as offenders in conceivable circumstances where this would be called for by a comparative judgement of satisfaction and dissatisfaction. Further, it is a consequence of Utilitarian Theories that offenders may or must be punished excessively. Both objections have been advanced on the basis of some or other principle of desert.

However, it is very far from being the case that the only way of ignoring the claims of individuals is by ignoring considerations of desert, however conceived. The claims of individuals are ignored when we treat them, as we say, *unfairly or unequally*. Utilitarianism can be argued to conflict not with Retributive Justice but with Distributive Justice. Utilitarian Theories of punishment as we have defined them, which are approximate to Bentham's, and hence do not themselves incorporate elements of Distributive Justice, can be argued to be untenable for reason of that conflict.

These theories, to the effect that punishment is justified when it produces a greater total balance of satisfaction or a lesser total balance of dissatisfaction than any alternative practice, face no obstacle based on determinism. This is so since the theories so understood, if some of them rightly take grievance-satisfaction into account, do not *depend* on the existence of grievance-satisfaction. In so far as determinism is concerned, then, the situation with Utilitarian Theories may be argued to be in an important way like that with Pure Retribution Theories. Although the retribution theories necessarily are vulnerable to determinism and the Utilitarian Theories as naturally understood are not, neither fact, it may be argued, is of much importance. This is so since theories of both kinds are open to objection not having to do with determinism—in the case of retribution theories, overwhelming objection. The retribution theories fail without help from determinism, so to speak, and the Utilitarian Theories are not to be saved by their consistency with it. Let us not attempt to draw a firm conclusion about the worth of Utilitarian Theories. More can be said in defence of some of them than is often supposed.

There is another conclusion that *is* to be drawn. Utilitarian Theories, if they are not judged to be intolerable, offer the possibility of *a* response of affirmation with respect to punishment, the first possibility we have encountered in these reflections. It is a possibility for someone who supposes that the Utilitarian Theories *can* be saved from the mentioned objections. *He* can seek to free himself from commitment to whatever is inconsistent with determinism by relying on a Utilitarian institution of punishment. This is one of several possible responses of affirmation that will be noticed. As will have been anticipated, the essential features of the response of affirmation are consistent with different moral views.

(iii) *Mixed Theories* of the justification of punishment make up a majority of contemporary theories. They are at bottom amalgamations of what are taken to be the virtues of the theories of the first two categories, perhaps with further additions. Pure Retribution Theories, as noticed, do have the feature of placing a certain limit on what can be done to individuals—the limit of their desert, somehow conceived. Utilitarian Theories do have the virtue of recommending punishment on the basis of an indubitable good, at bottom the prevention of offences. Mixed Theories are fundamentally to the effect that punishments are justified only when they are both preventive and deserved. These theories thus escape what appears to be the pointlessness of theories of the first category when desert is conceived not as we have, but traditionally, and also escape the bizarre concentration on satisfactions of one category, which is the principal fact about Pure Retribution Theories when conceived as we have, in terms of grievance. Mixed Theories are also supposed to escape the general objection to Utilitarian Theories having to do with the claims of individuals.

There are very many theories of this general kind, the work of philosophers, jurisprudents, less theoretical legal writers, and others. They differ very considerably in emphasis and detail, and many of them, at least to a philosophical eye, are sadly inexplicit, above all about desert. It will be best not to attempt any further unitary summary of them, but, at the risk of too much complication, instead provide models of three varieties of them.

(iiia) Mixed Theories on the first model require of any justified punishment that (1) it be no more than deserved. This first requirement can be expressed, as typically it is in jurisprudential and legal writing, by some choice from the plethora of desert-locutions noticed earlier. (p. 195) The punishment must be no more than 'proportional', 'commensurate', or whatever. If we give satisfactory content to the requirement, it is that a punishment must not do more than satisfy grievance, which allows either that it does satisfy it or does less than that. (2) It is also required on these theories that a justified punishment must have a certain preventive effect. That is to say, precisely, that it prevents what are in fact fixed as criminal offences in the society. That as it stands may be regarded as insufficient, since it sanctions punishments whose preventive effect is trivial. It is then to be added (3) that the punishment must be economical: prevent more distress than it causes. It may be added, further, that (4) if the punishment is one of a number which can be judged to have the same preventive effect, it is the least severe of them.

It is possible to object to such a justification of punishment. To be brief, and despite what has been supposed by many about desert, such a justification may be argued to issue in an unacceptable denial of the claims of individuals. There is in fact no guarantee in the four requirements, it can be said, that individuals *will* be *fairly* treated, no guarantee that their treatment will be according to an acceptable principle of Distributive Justice. To consider the first of the four requirements, it is possible that a penalty will not do more than satisfy grievance, and yet be in a sense unfair. That it does to some extent satisfy grievance does not ensure its fairness. Nor, it may be said, does any of the other three requirements ensure its fairness.

There is also a wholly different difficulty. As already remarked, developed legal systems punish those who cannot be said to deserve it. (p. 194) These are offenders convicted under statutes of strict liability, or statutes interpreted as requiring only strict liability. There is also the fact of exemplary punishments, imposed when it is believed that there is a particular need of deterrent examples. Both matters are to some extent controversial, but it appears necessary to allow exceptions to the first requirement of the justification we are considering, that all punishments be deserved. It is unclear what lesser thing is to be put in place of the absolute requirement.

What determinism here affects, then, as of course it does, is not an indubitable justification of punishment. As for the effect, a general acceptance of determinism and hence the decay of grievance-desires would make pointless the first requirement of the justification. In the absence of grievance-desires, there could be no distinction between punishments that do more than satisfy them, and punishments that either satisfy them or do less than that.

(iiib) A second model of Mixed Theories of punishment differs from the first only in its preventive part. It does not require that punishment prevents what in fact are in part fixed as criminal offences in the society. Rather, punishment must prevent actions which are such that they give rise to such grievance-desires as can be satisfied only by distress of the extent which is caused by punishment. It is not a conceptual or other necessity that the class of actions which theories on the first model seek to prevent will be identical with the like class of actions in the second model. There are the same possible objections to this second mixed justification of punishment, the main one having to do with Distributive Justice, and the same situation with respect to determinism. In fact this second mixed justification, given its greater reliance on desert, would be more undermined than the first by an acceptance of determinism.

(iiic) A third model of Mixed Theories, in a way harsher, does not require of any justified punishment only that it be *no more than* deserved. It specifies, rather, that any such punishment be no more and *also no less than* deserved. In clear terms, what is required is that a justified punishment does no more and no less than satisfy grievance. There are added certain requirements as to prevention. These cannot simply be to the effect that there be economical prevention, since a fully deserved punishment may not be economical, and an economical punishment may be less than deserved. The difficulty is often overlooked or ignored in Mixed Theories, but we shall not consider it further. Mixed Theories on this third model are also open to the objection having to do with the claims of individuals and Distributive Justice. The consequence of an acceptance of determinism is also of the same kind as with the previous two models.

It is evidently the Mixed Theories which can be taken as providing a kind of general characterization of punishment by the state as we have it in our societies. That punishment is, so to speak, an effect of mixed theories. It is a difficult matter of judgement which of the three models of Mixed Theories or a related one is closest to our practice. It may be that our practice in one part or feature is a kind of realization of one of these models, in another part or feature a realization of another. (Hart, 1968) Whatever is to be said of these secondary questions, it is evidently one or more of the mixed justifications which can be taken as telling us of our practice. (N. Lacey, 1988)

Let us not try to draw a firm conclusion about the defensibility of Mixed Theories. What is rather to be concluded is that they stand in some considerable conflict with determinism, given their content having to do with desert. That is to say, since one or more of them does give us our actual institutions of punishment, that our actual institutions are in some considerable conflict with determinism. Change is required. That change, a response of affirmation, is the keeping of what can be kept, and the giving up of what must be given up. This can be conceived not as necessarily involving a commitment to some different theory and institution of punishment, the Utilitarian or another, but as involving a valuing of and a choice from the elements of Mixed Theories. Their desert-element, conceived as we have conceived it, must be abandoned. Other elements, most importantly the element of prevention, can be maintained. More can be said than that, since Mixed Theories may have more to them than has been indicated in the quick summary given. In particular, although this complication has so far been suppressed, they may involve matters of desert so far unconsidered, desert where it is *not* vulnerable to determinism. (p. 227)

(iv) Finally, and briefly, there is a further category of theories of punishment, different from the Utilitarian but like them in facing no serious threat from determinism. The category, which has but few announced members, although more are implied by certain political philosophies and ideologies, consists in theories which rest on some principle of Distributive Justice. They are the *Fairness Theories*. One is the theory which I myself take to provide the only defensible justification of an institution of punishment. It is, in essence, that an institution of punishment is justified if it is in accordance with the Principle of Equality. That principle requires of any social institution that it have a certain function, which is to say that it contributes to making well off those who are badly off. The well off and the badly off are defined in terms of satisfaction or the lack of it with respect to certain fundamental desires. (4.7; Honderich, 1981c, 1983a, 1984c) There can be no objection to the Principle of Equality taking account, although necessarily it will be slight account, of existing grievance-desires. It is in this respect vulnerable to determinism. However, like the Principle of Utility, the Principle of Equality does not depend on the existence of grievance-desires, and can of course be stated without reference to them. Like Utilitarianism, although the fact was not mentioned before, it has the consequence, on consequentialist grounds, that we should try to diminish them. Shall we ever have a practice of punishment in accordance with this justifying theory? That can be no more than a matter of less than confident hope. The given theory, evidently, can enter into a response of affirmation different from those so far noticed. As in the case of the other responses, it will involve the support, so to speak, of what can be taken as a fundamental principle of morality.

4.6 OTHER SOCIAL FACTS

It was remarked at the beginning of this discussion of the social and political consequences of determinism that our wide use of talk of desert, across many contexts, does not entail that we are advancing a single argument, or a single kind of argument, whenever anyone or anything is said to deserve something. Talk of what is deserved is in this respect like talk of what is just or fair, which is also diverse in intention and content. Thus it cannot be supposed that since much talk of desert in connection with punishment has to do with a certain argument about grievance, so too does *all* talk of desert with respect to persons, let alone other animals and inanimate things. Still, to turn now to the first of the remaining social institutions, practices, and habits listed earlier (p. 175), it is to be expected that there will at least be a similarity, having to do with determinism, between punishment and *moral blame and praise, moral condemnation and commendation.*

The similarity between punishment and blame, in so far as determinism is concerned, is indeed that desert-claims typically made about both are vulnerable to an acceptance of determinism. More particularly, just as our grievance-desires which are fundamental to desert-claims about a man's punishment cannot survive our coming to believe that his action was not originated, so there cannot be survival of certain related desires or inclinations somehow involved in typical claims that a man deserves blame or condemnation. That is not to say, as we have seen, that punishment must come to an end. There is more to be said for punishment than that it gives grievance-satisfaction, indeed much more. To see clearly how matters stand with blame, let us recall certain essential distinctions already made or implied.

Moral disapproval, the source of blame, consists in two complexes of elements. Each complex is properly described as an attitude or feeling. One complex carries a belief or idea as to an agent's origination of a wrongful action, and our own related retributive desires to act against him. Moral disapproval when it is different has in it, in so far as ideas as to the initiation of action are concerned, only beliefs as to voluntariness, and does not include retributive desires. It does have in it, as the first complex also does, feelings of repugnance, and forward-looking desires as to the prevention of further actions of the kind in question, and perhaps restitution.

Our *blaming or condemning* is an activity, usually linguistic, not an attitude. It is evidently to be characterized, however, by reference to moral disapproval. To reprove, upbraid, or accuse a man or a group may or may not be to convey or presuppose ideas or beliefs about his origination of wrongful action, and may or may not be to convey or imply retributive desires. Thus blaming may or may not be an analogue to punishment in the latter's backward-looking character.

Thirdly, there is our *desert-claim that a man deserves blame or condemnation.* The claim, perhaps 'He deserves a reprimand', has to do with the effect of the activity of blaming him. We have in mind some kind or degree of distress. The desert-claim also has to do with his initiation of his wrongful action. It may have to do in part with his presumed origination of his wrongful action, or only with his voluntariness. There is also the matter of the relation or connection which is claimed to hold between the wrongful action and the distress. This requires attention.

As with punishment (p. 207), it is unlikely that a single relation is always asserted. Sometimes what is asserted is no more than the fact that by some precedent or rule, such wrongful actions get such blame. This is analogous to speaking of an offender's penalty as deserved, and meaning that it is the penalty according to a certain penalty-system in the law as it stands. Sometimes what is asserted is the moral judgement that it is fitting or right that such a wrongful action bring such pain or discomfiture on the agent. That is, the action and the distress form an intrinsic good. This is no claim of fact, but it can serve as a kind of premiss for the conclusion that someone was right to speak as he did. Such a point was noticed with the Intrinsic-Good Answer to the question of the nature of the desert-relation with punishment. (p. 200) Sometimes, finally, what is asserted *may* be partly that the blameworthy agent's pain or discomfiture satisfies desires on the part of the victim or victims of the blameworthy action, desires for just that pain or discomfiture.

Be all that as it may, it can hardly be doubted that our desert-claims about blame, even when they do not convey it, may involve desires or inclinations which we ourselves have for the pain or discomfiture of those we take to have behaved badly, wrongly, treacherously, or viciously. That this is true of our claims that blame is deserved cannot be surprising, given the fact that moral disapproval, so to speak, is a source of or enters into such desert-claims.

The contention that our desert-claims about blame may involve such desires on our part must not be confused with a related one, which is unacceptable. What was said of punishment and desert-claims, centrally, was that such claims *involve a single clear and firm argument* having to do with the satisfaction of the grievance-desires. Blame is different. It cannot be said of blame that in so far as we speak of it as deserved, there is involved a significant argument for it based on the satisfaction of retributive desires of either victims or ourselves. With punishment, there *is* the argument based on grievance, but it can hardly be said that there is a counterpart argument for blame. At any rate, to say so would be to engage in overstatement. Consider my claim that the moral condemnation by someone of the husband anticipating his divorce was deserved. It would at least be unpersuasive to say that the desert-claim involves something properly called the argument that the condemnation satisfies certain desires of either his wife or myself.

There are clear explanations of this discontinuity. One is that we can engage in blaming persons, and very often do, without their knowing it and hence without their being adversely affected by our activity. We also blame the dead. In neither case is there any possibility of satisfaction of the relevant kind for anyone. Punishment is different. Secondly, it is the case that desires for others' distress in connection with punishment give rise to demands or claims in a way that such desires in connection with blame do not, since punishable actions are more serious than actions which merit only blame. A third difference is that blame gives less satisfaction than punishment. A fourth, although not a simple one, is that the distress or frustration of persons blamed is less than the distress or frustration of persons punished. With blame, therefore, on the whole, there is less need for justification.

These latter reflections adequately explain the absence, with blame said to be deserved, of an argument analagous to the argument from grievance. They also serve, incidentally, to defeat a certain belated sceptical thought about our earlier conclusion about deserved punishment and the fundamentality to it of the argument from grievance. The sceptical thought is that that conclusion is put in doubt by the want of analogy with what is related to it, blame.

As for the main question before us now, the answer already suggested is not affected by what we have. That is, the absence of an argument analagous to the argument from grievance, and the reflections which explain the absence, do not put in doubt what was said about the consequence of determinism for moral blame: one kind of moral blame *is* vulnerable to an acceptance of determinism. This is so, to sum up, partly because the claim that blame is deserved itself may involve retributive desires or inclinations on the part of the claimer, which desires or inclinations rest on an idea of origination. Further, such desert-claims may involve assertions having to do with related retributive desires on the part of victims. However, another kind of blame is not vulnerable to determinism. It has to do only with voluntariness. It may involve, among other things, forcing a self-awareness upon a wrong doer, an awareness of his moral standing or rather the lack of it. This blame is a kind of analogue to institutions of punishment that are untouched by determinism.

So—an acceptance of determinism would not leave blame as it is, or leave us with nothing worth the name. This is the response of affirmation. The circumstance is essentially the same with moral praise or commendation. Consider, in this regard, a woman attracted to a comfortable position in her social world. Her life is lived among people prone to be embarrassed or worse by activities of a certain moral or political character. She none the less carries forward such a campaign, of which we approve, at some cost to herself. We take praise of her to be deserved.

Our doing so may rest on the idea that she could have done otherwise—that what she did was a matter of her own origination—and our praise does involve our desire or inclination to benefit her on this account. To attempt to deny this pair of facts, as some philosophers have, is simply to escape for a moment, usually in the pursuit of theory, from an awareness of entirely common feelings intimately connected with an idea as common, the origination idea. To come to see that origination is a fiction is to be unable to persist in the given desire. We may well feel attracted to her and thus inclined in a certain way to favour her over others. We may take ourselves to have reason to reward her, having to do with the future. But these are matters distinct from the feelings that get their nature from the belief that an agent in a fundamental sense could have done a lesser thing, but did a greater. Like blame, then, praise is necessarily affected but not demolished by an acceptance of determinism.

That is not the end of the story about blame and praise. Let us notice a large complication which so far has been suppressed, but also has relevance to punishment and blame. It is relevant too to the social institutions and the like still to be surveyed.

Punishment, moral blame, and moral praise, as we have seen, have grounds which are affected and grounds which are not affected by determinism. These grounds give rise to parts of the nature or features of different possible institutions and practices. The grounds and the natures or features which are affected have been spoken of in terms of desert. As for the grounds and features which are not affected, it has been said that they have to do not with origination of actions, but with their voluntariness. This is so with the preventive or like features of each of punishment, blame, and praise, and also their feature of involving feelings such as those of repugnance which are not intimately connected with origination.

In each of punishment, blame, and praise, certainly, talk of desert *does* most importantly have to do with origination, although to different degrees, and this fact has been reflected in our inquiry. However, as already emphasized, desert-locutions are put to very varied uses. To come to the main point, the large complication, desert-locutions *can* in fact be used to speak of the grounds and the nature or features of moral blame and praise, and perhaps punishment, which are *not* vulnerable to determinism.

Return to the worldly woman who nevertheless carries forward the estimable moral or political campaign. It is entirely natural to say that she deserves praise for her character, or for her good and firm intentions. That may be to say that she deserves praise on the ground of estimable actions, which, considered from the point of view of their initiation, are taken only as voluntary. Consider the vicious husband anticipating his divorce. It is, despite all that was said above, entirely natural to say that he deserves blame for his despicable intentions, and to conceive of them as no more than voluntary. All that is required here, it seems, for him to deserve blame, is for him to have acted as he did out of his own intentions, rather than for him to have been somehow ignorant of what he was doing, or to have acted in some other way involuntarily. (Cf. Parfit, 1984, pp. 323–6)

There are uncertainties and obscurities here, but the main point is clear. Not all talk of our desert, of persons' deserving things, is welded to the idea of origination and what goes with it. If more reason for this conclusion is needed, some can be had from the fact already noticed, that pictures, other artefacts, and also natural objects, can be said to deserve attention, approval. It would be odd if this were so, but admirable human properties unconnected with origination were excluded from discourse in terms of desert.

None of this affects the conclusions that have been drawn about punishment, blame, or praise. These conclusions can as well be stated in a way which takes into account what has belatedly been allowed, the fact of the different uses of desert-locutions. Let us divide these uses into two categories, those which take origination as a condition of what is said to be deserved, and those which do not. We can label the first and main category of uses as having to do with origination-desert. Our conclusions are then essentially as follows. Each of punishment, blame and praise depends in part on, and has a nature or features in part owed to, considerations of origination-desert. Each stands in the same way to other considerations, including other considerations of desert. In so far as each depends on and is affected by origination-desert, it is vulnerable to determinism. In so far as each depends on and is affected by other considerations, including other considerations of desert, it is not vulnerable to determinism. Affirmation consists in part in eschewing origination-desert and embracing the other considerations.

To proceed now with the remaining five social institutions and the like, having to do with (ii) reward for obedience to law, (iii) income, (iv) wealth, (v) power, and (vi) kinds of rank or standing, the first of these is different from the rest. This is so partly because the reward in question, a life untroubled by policemen, judges, and gaolers, is in a way the same for all law-abiders. In the case of income and the other things, there is great variation in what is received or possessed. Also, reward in the given sense is also different in that the ground for getting it is in a way single and simple: obedience to law. Both points need qualification but let us not pause.

If we ask our principal question, whether an acceptance of determinism would somehow affect the given ground for reward, a certain answer may be attempted—no. This is the case, it may be said, since obedience to law is not necessarily something dependent on origination. In particular, if the reward of an untroubled life is taken as deserved by those who keep the law, the desert-claim is not to be taken as vulnerable to determinism. The desert-claim is to be characterized, perhaps, in terms of an idea not so far mentioned, that of compensation. We do commonly speak of compensation as deserved in many contexts. To say law-abiders deserve an untroubled life in the given sense is to say, or mainly to say, that such a life is a kind of compensation for the obedience to law, and more precisely for the restraint or self-denial of keeping to the law. The self-denying in question is to be understood, roughly, not as denying oneself goods in an ordinary sense, but as denying oneself all but the legal means of coming to possess or enjoy them. The self-denial consists in denying to oneself short-cuts to things we all desire. (Honderich, 1984b) To think of the self-denial as deserving the given reward, it may be said, is not to think of something affected by determinism. The self-denial is a matter of voluntariness.

Things may not be so simple, as can perhaps be shown by a piece of imagining. Imagine we were to come to believe in what can be called partial determinism. That is, there are two kinds of persons. Some of us are subject to determinism, and some of us have the capability of origination. In particular, the law-abiders contain some of the determined and some of the originative. Do all of the law-abiders deserve the same? To return to something like strict liability (pp. 194, 221), suppose further that we believe there are grounds for infringing ordinary expectations of some law-abiders, grounds having to do with the need for prevention. If we could, would we be inclined to choose from the class of the determined rather than from the class of the originative? It is possible to conjecture that we should take those who are law-abiding but subject to determinism as *less* deserving of the given reward than those who are law-abiding, but, in the requisite sense could have been otherwise.

Thus there is the thought, which might be supported in other ways, that our present situation, in which we do not believe in either partial or total determinism, is one where we take the general reward for obedience to law to rest in part on origination-desert. Let us move on to consideration of the remaining social facts, however, and draw a general conclusion at the end.

In the societies with which most of us are familiar, inequality in the distribution of *income* and what goes with it is great. Some idea of it can be had from the facts that the lowest tenth of families in terms of income in Britain and the United States receive something less than 3 per cent of the total income after tax, and the highest tenth receives upwards of 23 per cent. (Honderich, 1984b, p. 192) The justifications offered of the spread of incomes may be divided into three classes, those which have to do with desert of whatever kind, those which have to do with agreement-claims, and those which have to do with claimed economic and other effects of income-inequalities. (Cf. Dick, 1975)

Of justifications of the third class, to begin with it, the most familiar has to do with incentive. The possibility or the actuality of earning more, it is said, gives rise to a greater social total of material and other goods. This, it may be said, is to the benefit of all, including those who earn less or nothing. It is possible to believe, as certainly I do myself, that the argument is greatly weaker than it is taken to be, and consists largely in unreflective habit and perhaps self-deception. It involves ignoring the conceivability and indeed the actuality of productive societies not organized by the income-incentive principle, whatever else is to be said of them. It is true, however, that in many societies some form of the income-incentive argument is accepted by many members. The argument, taken as having whatever weight, can of course be detached from Utilitarianism and also from doctrines of Conservatism, to which it is sometimes connected. It can figure, and does, in social and political philosophies whose principles of distribution are neither Conservative nor Utilitarian.

The second class of justifications, having to do with agreement-claims, is evidently of importance. It is with income above all, perhaps, as against other social institutions and the like, that agreement-claims are significant and of weight. Employers and employees agree that a certain salary or wage is to be paid for certain work. Here, despite considerable difficulties about degrees of voluntariness of agreements, and difficulties of other kinds, there is no need for the kind of speculativeness and unpromising struggle that goes into the idea of which we know, that offenders agree to their punishments, or the idea that we all somehow contract to abide by social arrangements.

The remaining class of income justifications in itself illustrates the diversity of talk of desert. A man is said to deserve higher pay or other financial benefits on one or more of many grounds: ability, skill or talent; effort, energy, or industriousness; productivity or profit-making; qualifications and the time it took to get them; a burden of responsibility or the danger or disagreeableness of a job; contribution to general economic well-being; popularity or simply demand for services. He may be said to deserve higher pay not for present attributes of these kinds but for his past history of effort, profit-making, or whatever. With respect to each of these attributes, he may be compared both to others in his own line of life, say the civil service, and to others in other lines of life.

Let us postpone consideration of the character and implications of these agreement-claims and desert-claims, and turn now to *wealth*. It is yet more unequally distributed than income, and the effect of this distribution on society is greater than that of income. As with income, a general idea of the distribution of wealth in many societies can be had from the shares of total personal wealth of the bottom and top deciles of families in terms of such wealth in Britain and the United States. The bottom decile of families has less than 1 per cent. The top tenth has roughly 80 per cent in Britain and 60 per cent in the United States. (Honderich, 1984b, p. 193) The attempted justifications of the distribution perhaps fall into roughly the same three classes as with income, partly for the reason of the connection between income and wealth. A part of a man's personal wealth may be saved or invested income, earned wealth.

The class of attempted justifications in terms of certain general *economic and social effects* includes the familiar idea that wealth concentrations are essential to provide capital for investment and economic advance. The claim in itself is false, as the existence of socialist societies demonstrates. Samples of other different arguments of this class are the argument from incentive, the argument that concentration of wealth allows for the patronage essential to art and the preservation of certain traditions of culture, and the argument, if it can be taken seriously, that such concentrations give a power to some which is important in the preservation of personal liberties generally. At least the first two arguments, whatever their worth, have a considerable acceptance. Both, perhaps like most arguments for wealth-concentration, can be offered in defence of inherited as well as earned wealth.

The second class of arguments offered by or on behalf of the wealthy is that their situation is the outcome of certain *agreements*. So too can the situations of others be presented as outcomes of agreements. It can be maintained, with earned wealth, that it is the outcome of the explicit agreements already mentioned in connection with income. The claim enters into a larger one covering inherited wealth as well. It is that the wealth distribution is the outcome of voluntary transfers between individuals. It is the outcome of exercises of defensible liberties. (Nozick, 1974b) The argument is at the very least open to question, essentially because it is incomplete. It is far from tolerable to suppose that *all* voluntary transactions between two individuals, whatever the effect on others, are anything like sacrosanct. Also, it is plainly insufficient to *declare* something to be a defensible liberty. Others can be as declarative. Substantial argument is required. Again, however, the argument from voluntariness and liberty has a considerable acceptance and a wide effect.

To come to the class of *desert-arguments*, what is said of deserved income evidently applies to the earned part of personal wealth. Desert-arguments surely have a kind of summation in one seemingly fundamental part of the most famous of justifications of private property, that of Locke. (1960 (1690)) A man's private property is partly justified by the fact of his having *mixed his labour* with something, perhaps a plot of land or raw materials. Too many inheritors of Locke's idea, for several reasons, do not attempt to explain why it is that mixing one's labour with something should give one a right to it or to some product. It is hard to resist the view that what is in question is fundamentally the claim that a man deserves something in virtue of his labour, effort, industriousness, or the like. Whatever the obscurity of talk of desert, that view of Locke is clearer and more effective than the idea, say, that a man has some sort of right to his labour and so comes to own the thing with which it has become inextricably mixed. (Cf. Becker, 1977)

The last two of the array of social facts, more difficult to characterize briefly, are those of power and rank. With *power*, what is of most interest to the present inquiry are the many systems, hierarchies, and relations of relative power within societies: the devolution of authority in national and local political systems; pyramidal control in business, industry, the civil service and so on; chains of command in the military and the police; the organization of the judiciary; ordinary relations of overseeing and the like with respect to jobs. These are to be seen as effective decision-making systems, and the power of positions in them is perhaps well judged in terms of the number of people affected, according to the rules, by decisions taken at the positions.

In so far as these systems are true to a predominant theory of them, persons within them have the position, as it is said, to which they are suited. They have positions that suit their abilities, these being open to tests and judgements of various kinds. That is, the rationale is effectiveness in terms of the goal of the enterprise. None the less, judgements of desert are common, and often acted upon. Whatever the character and implications of such judgements, men and women are said to deserve to be made judges, drivers, editors, clerks. It is not merely that of two equally qualified candidates for a post, the more deserving in some sense may be appointed, but that a more deserving candidate may be appointed rather than a somewhat more able. Still, it is perhaps safe to say that in so far as relative power is distributed or possessed on grounds at all, as distinct from coming to someone through friends, social connection, and the like, it is effectiveness in terms of the goal of the endeavour that is paramount.

Positions of *rank, standing, respect, and the like*, by very rough definition, are desired positions which none the less are not positions of power. They do not, at any rate, involve defined relations of decision-making. Almost all of those which are hereditary, say aristocratic rank, are now but weakly defended by uncertain considerations. In the main these defences actually have more to do with what commonly goes with hereditary rank, which is to say wealth or power. Non-hereditary positions of rank and the like are various, but many are of the nature of awards or prizes. They are therefore very different from hereditary positions. Here there are memberships of orders of merit, prizes for books, tributes for long service. There are also more informal practices of respect. Certainly it can be said of all of these non-hereditary positions that they have the recommendation of encouraging achievement and excellence. Of all the seven social institutions, practices, and habits, however, it is the practice of according rank, standing, or respect to individuals that somehow is most governed by desert.

To look back and draw a general conclusion, it seems evident that reward for obedience to law, and the facts of income differences, wealth differences, power, and rank, all have grounds having to do with origination as well as grounds having only to do with voluntariness. Some of the grounds of the first kind are of origination-desert. Others, it can be argued, have to do with agreement-claims that do bring in origination. What we have is the conclusion that the given social institutions and the like are or will be *significantly affected* by determinism. Each of the institutions and the like makes *a* distinction between people having to do with origination, although a uniquely general one in the case of reward to law-abiders.

With the gradual acceptance of determinism, we shall have one less kind of reason for distinguishing as we do between people. The upshot, to the extent to which our existence is subject to rationality, a significant extent, must be a lesser difference between what people enjoy, possess and have imposed on them. That human life will change in this way does not involve the conclusion, as hardly needs saying, that it will change out of all recognition, or anything of the sort.

The proper response, less difficult to make with these public matters than with the more internal matters of life-hopes and the like, is again properly described as the response of affirmation. It is that change is forced upon us, not destruction, and that the change is better than tolerable. It may be aided by being perceived, as it can be, as having quite independent moral recommendations.

4.7 POLITICS

Let us finally speculate about something related, determinism and politics. What are, or will be, the political consequences of determinism, its consequences for the principal ongoing political traditions? These traditions include attitudes to and judgements on the social nstitutions and the like just considered, but are open to general characterization. Fundamentally they give encompassing if often veiled answers to the central question of political philosophy, that of the principle or principles on which our societies ought to be organized. The question, at bottom, is about the distribution of the things we all desire. The traditions, which make up what can properly be called the spectrum of politics, despite occasional and certainly misguided scepticism about that idea, are those of the Left, Centre, and Right. More particularly, let us get a view, although necessarily an impressionistic one, of the Left, Liberalism, and Conservativism.

The Left in politics has in it diverse principles, movements, parties, and national states, including opposed ones. It includes social democracy and democratic socialism, various ideologies of an egalitarian kind, the Eastern Communist states, other somehow Marxist states, some national liberation movements, and also labour or workers' movements, terrorist organizations, and the weak tradition of anarchism. Despite the range of ends and means exemplified, it is possible to bring the Left under a general description, by way of certain pervasive features, and so to distinguish it from the rest of the political spectrum.

(i) It is traditional and correct to take the Left as committed to various ideas and ideals of *equality*, and correct to see it as having, in some places, partly realized some of them. Social democracy and democratic socialism, the latter giving more place to socialism, defend what is called social justice. 'We need to persuade men and women who are themselves reasonably well off that they have a duty to forgo some of the advantages they would otherwise enjoy . . .' (Jenkins, 1972) Many national movements are opposed to racial inequality and to the great imbalance in conditions of life between the world's rich and poor societies. The Eastern Communist states have acted to a considerable extent on Marx's declaration, 'From each according to his ability, to each according to his needs'. Marxist and Trotskyist ideologies which concentrate on the fact of what is called exploitation are in part protests against the unequal use of people by people, and also resulting inequalities.

(ii) A second large feature of the tradition of the Left, as is illustrated by good accounts of it (Berki, 1973), has consisted in demands and struggles for *freedoms* of many kinds. Democratic socialists and some social democrats have in effect sought greater democratic rights than those supported in the tradition of Liberalism. That is not to say they have been more zealous about the individual's right to vote and related political rights, but that they have been more committed to extending the reach or extent of governmental power, and hence, it can be argued, the worth of individual political rights. Democratic socialists and social democrats, in their support of such rights, distinguish themselves from the other part of the Left, more influenced by Marx.

It has defended political freedoms of a different and in a way a lesser kind, those of citizens of the one-party state or proletarian democracy, thereby producing a great divide in the Left. This more Marxist part of the Left, however, has pursued and in large part secured what is called freedom from economic oppression and distortion within politics. It can further be argued, with some success, that a fundamental Marxist commitment is to an ideal of freedom that has to do with the full development of individuals. (Brenkert, 1979, 1983; cf. G. A. Cohen, 1978) Finally, with respect to freedom and the Left, anarchism has traditionally taken the impulse of personal autonomy to an extreme degree.

(iii) There can be no doubt that *fraternity and community* have a considerable importance among ideals of the Left. In place of each of us being moved by kinds of self-concern, we are to have societies where each identifies with others and in an effective way with his or her society as a whole. Rousseau requires, if obscurely, not only that 'each of us puts his person and all his power in common under the supreme direction of the general will', but that 'in our corporate capacity, we receive each member as an indivisible part of the whole'. (1973 (1762)) China and Cuba have in ways been realizations of this.

To come to several related and more particular doctrines and practices, (iv) the capitalist system has been and continues to be condemned or questioned by the Left, to a greater or lesser degree, for its presumed injustice, inefficiency, waste, and irrationality. (v) Policies of public ownership or social control of the means of production, or at any rate of greater governmental entry into the economy, have derived from this condemnation and also from the various ideas and ideals of equality and freedom. (vi) The great divide in the Left in the matter of government, with the more Marxist part opposed to the traditional democracy of the multi-party state, is of course accompanied by a divide on other political means. There has remained a Marxist acceptance, not merely formal, of the means of armed revolution.

This slight sketch of the Left in politics, as does a fuller picture (Honderich, 1982b), suggests what can be taken as its fundamental commitment. It is a commitment to effective means to the end of **making well off those who are badly off**. The conditions of being well off and badly off may be defined in terms of fundamental human desires: for a decent length of life; an enlargement of life dependent on more material goods than merely enough to sustain a decent length of life; freedom and power in larger and smaller contexts; respect and self-respect; personal and wider human relationships; the goods of culture. The effective means to the end, making well off those who are badly off, include many crucial practices of equality, of which 'One man, one vote' is one, but not of overwhelming importance. The principle of the Left, that we should adopt effective means to the end of making well off those who are badly off, is partly for reason of these crucial practices properly named the Principle of Equality, mentioned earlier in several connections. (pp. 52, 223; Honderich, 1981c)

The first of the defining features of the Left specified above, a concern with various ideas and ideals of equality, is of course in accord with this view of the fundamental commitment of this part of the political spectrum. The concern for freedoms is a concern both for a part of the end of the principle of Equality and also for effective means to that end. Related remarks are to be made about the remaining features.

It is necessary to allow, certainly, that the Principle of Equality is no more than the *fundamental* commitment of the Left. It is true that other commitments and impulses are evident in both its past and its present. It is most relevant to ask this question: do considerations of desert of whatever kind play a significant part? Certainly what seem to be voices of desert have often been heard. Socialists have commonly claimed that those who toil must have their just reward. It needs to be allowed, and also for the reason that retributive impulses are a part of all our natures, that ideas of desert have been significant in the tradition of the Left. That they are secondary to the fundamental commitment is beyond question.

To turn now to the Centre in politics, if one seeks to characterize it, as is reasonable, as being other than an assortment of compromises between Left and Right, the most promising tradition is that of *Liberalism*. It can be described, although clarification is needed, as having two principal and connected ideals, those of political freedom and individualism.

(i) Liberalism has been an opposition to constraint by the state. (Ryan, 1970, Ch. 13; Manning, 1976) In the eighteenth and nineteenth centuries, in its assertion of political freedom against monarchical, sectional, and other unrepresentative government, it advocated what can be called balanced democracy, such as gives a certain general political freedom. This advocacy of political freedom has subsequently issued in opposition to movements and ideas of the Left. Liberalism has been opposed not only to systems of proletarian democracy, which does not much distinguish it, but also to increasing egalitarianism in the traditional democracies. It has had a fear of the increasing democratic power of the working classes. It has often enough seemed to be somewhat more concerned with Left than Right as enemy of the political freedom it defends, which tendency may be a true reflection of its character.

(ii) As for individualism, liberals of the eighteenth and nineteenth centuries were to the fore in seeking and defending rights of individuals in the matters of economic life, religion, thought and discussion, and private life. Mill's *On Liberty* (1972c (1863)) is the *locus classicus* of much of this individualism. The essay's clear intention, in which it does not notably succeed, is to state a clear, single principle of individual liberty, to specify a large part of life where individuals are to be left to govern themselves, free of interference by both state and society. The main idea or at any rate declaration is that individuals are to be free of interference in their lives so long as they do not harm others, although the essential definition of harm is far from evident and has been a matter of persistent controversy. (Honderich, 1974, 1982c)

Already in *On Liberty* there is evident another Liberal proposition with respect to individual life, one which has been more prominent since. It has to do with the state's interference, as it may somewhat controversially be called, to support and help citizens. Mill not only prohibits state interference in the lives of individuals if they do not somehow harm others, but also prohibits interference in their lives to help them. By inference at least, he also prohibits interference in the lives of some individuals in order to help others. The first group are not to be made to contribute to the second. He is opposed to the end of what we now know as the Welfare State, and at any rate by implication to its essential means. We are all to be responsible for ourselves, self-supporting and self-reliant, and indeed are to be constrained to do this. Liberalism, like all political traditions, has had to make some accommodation with history, and does so at this point, but its impulses are in a line of descent from Mill's.

If these are perhaps the principal features of Liberalism, there are other related ones worth distinguishing. (iii) Unlike much of the Left, and like Conservatism, Liberalism has in various ways defended the institution of private property and related rights. (iv) Both political freedom and those freedoms which enter into individualism are to be secured by way of, and to be rooted in, the rule of law. There is in Liberalism a greater attachment to the rule of traditional law than is evident on the Left. (v) Political and social change is to be gradual and democratic in nature. There is in Liberalism, also, a persistent tendency to call for the scrutiny of social and political change in terms of what is called rationality, reasonableness, enlightenment, or judgement. Liberals have taken themselves to be well placed with respect to such virtues. (vi) Mill was in no way atypical in his very considerable faith in the possible development of individuals, partly through education. The hope for individuals within Liberalism has perhaps sometimes been a quite general one, but perhaps more often not. Some are capable of worthwhile advance, the mass of individuals not so capable.

As shown in a fine account of Liberalism, it is not much more uniform than other political traditions, and certainly shows national differences. (Cranston, 1967) As with the Left, however, let us attempt a judgement as to the fundamental commitment or commitments of Liberalism, initially by way of a reflection on its two principal features, having to do with freedom and individualism. The political freedom defended by Liberalism has necessarily been a matter not only of one vote for each person, and of like political rights, but of the scope of political decision-making, the effective power of the elected government. The political freedom defended by Liberalism therefore becomes clearer, as does the associated idea of balanced democracy, when one brings to mind Liberalism's other principal feature, individualism. Individualism of the given kind sets a limit, whether or not a defensible one, to whatever political freedom is advocated along with it. Indeed, this has been clearly enough indicated in the Liberal tradition. Sir Henry Maine provides but one early example of this in his rooted opposition to

the omnipotent democratic state ... which has at its absolute disposal everything which individual men value, their property, their persons, and their independence, ... the state which may make laws for its subjects ordaining what they shall drink or eat, and in what way they shall spend their earnings ... and which, if the effect on human motives is what it may be expected to be, may force us to labour in it when the older incentives to toil have disappeared. (Maine, 1886, p. 156)

It is difficult to resist the idea, since a large part of what the doctrine of individualism defends has to do with personal achievement—the same personal achievement not to be impeded by the given political freedom—that Liberalism includes a considerable commitment to ideas of desert. More particularly, what is it that justifies constrained individualism, the doctrine that people are to be left to fend for themselves? Is it in part that they are to have no more than their earned deserts? What supports the related right of others to keep what they have gained by their own efforts? It is clearer here that desert of some kind is essential to the explanation. Further, ideas of desert are consonant with the secondary features of Liberalism, and to the fore in several of them, notably those having to do with private property and the development of more gifted individuals.

The tenor of many Liberal pronouncements are of relevance to this contention. To hinder the farmer from sending his goods at all times to the most profitable market, according to Adam Smith, 'is evidently to sacrifice the ordinary laws of justice to an idea of public utility, to a sort of reasons of state: an action of legislative authority . . . which can be pardoned only in cases of most urgent necessity'. (1844 (1776), p. 354) Under socialism, according to Maine again, 'no man is to profit by his own strength, abilities, or industry, but is to minister to the wants of the weak, the stupid and the idle.' (1886, p. 158)

In *On Liberty*, Mill announces that his Liberalism rests wholly on the Principle of Utility, but adds what he does not explain, that he means 'utility in the largest sense, grounded on the permanent interests of man as a progressive being'. (1972c (1863), p. 74) His subsequent defence and celebration of individuality is so relentless as to obscure matters further. Still, it is to be allowed that Mill's Liberalism does stand in some connection with some principle of utility, perhaps one whose end is no more precise than the general good. This is true as well of Liberalism generally. It needs to be allowed, also, that Liberalism has been and is informed by certain ideas and ideals of equality. This particular collection of such things is not identical with the related collection which distinguishes the Left and is not such as to allow summary by way of the Principle of Equality. It is such as to distinguish Liberalism from Conservatism.

It is reasonable to allow, then, that Liberalism has fundamental commitments to other than ideas of desert. The commitment to desert somehow conceived, however, is indubitable, and indubitably greater than the commitment of the Left.

Conservatism is sometimes characterized as resistance to fundamental social and political change, but misguidedly. Even if it is conceived in a restricted way, so as not to include all of the Right, and in particular not to include Fascism, which did advocate and in ways produce great and terrible change, Conservatism has often enough not resisted change but sought to secure it, change in the direction of the past, a Golden Age. As good accounts of Conservatism illustrate, Edmund Burke has in this respect had successors. (O'Sullivan, 1976) However, a more fundamental objection to characterizing Conservatism as resistance to change—which is *a* truth about it—is that this is to fail to get hold of what is basic. In fact, if Conservatism were no more than general resistance to change, it would be no less than wholly irrational. General resistance to change itself, on the *sole* ground that it is change, like general support for change in itself, is indeed wholly irrational.

There is some diversity in Conservatism, but evidently not so much as in the Left, or in all of the Right. Still, it is certainly possible to see social and political ideals, convictions, and practices that Conservativism in its continuing history has favoured, and certain that it has opposed. Most of these features do not openly reveal its fundamental commitment or nature, and none reveals all of it. However, they do point to that commitment or nature.

(i) Conservatism as we now recognize it came into existence as a response to the French Revolution, and it is indubitably a part of its nature that it is anti-egalitarian. It has been against almost all ideas and movements that can reasonably be called egalitarian. It has defended and continues to defend actual élites, and has occasionally aspired to the creation of new ones. Coleridge in his advocacy of a new spiritual leadership for English society, a clerisy, provides an example. (1972 (1830))

(ii) A very great deal of Conservatism has involved some ideal of an organic, hierarchical, ordered, or balanced society. An organic society is one of spiritual unity, or unity of feeling. It depends on authoritative institutions, above all strong government, and on a general acceptance of a certain ideology, insufficiently described as an ideology of a traditional state, an orthodox or pure culture, and perhaps an orthodox church. (Cf. Scruton, 1980) All of this is most notable in German thought, including that of Fichte, Novalis, Muller, Treitschke, and, in his way, Hegel. It was Novalis who recommended that a citizen should pay his taxes to the state in the spirit in which a lover gives presents to his mistress. Carlyle provides an English variation in his vision of an industrial society united by a deep sense of community and of mutual responsibility between social classes. (1888 (1843))

(iii) A defence of private property, including private ownership of the means of production, and also a defence of related structures of law and power and systems of morality, have always been features of Conservatism. It has been more encompassing and unyielding in this regard than Liberalism.

(iv) As already remarked, political traditions do necessarily accommodate themselves to history. Conservatism has done so with democracy. It is none the less not by impulse or conviction democratic. It remains opposed to the further democratization of democracy, as might be secured, say, by constraints on the financing of political parties, and also to the further democratization of institutions and practices within democracy.

(v) Conservatism has been very committed to restricting certain roles of the state and government in society, to preserving in certain ways a separation between state and society. The English *laissez-faire* economists will come to mind, as will American Conservatives of this century, sometimes dedicated above all to the proposition of limited government in so far as business and welfare services are concerned. In connection with limitations of the first kind, it has been common to speak of the defence of individual liberties.

(vi) Conservatism has tended to a low or pessimistic view of human nature, such that no great improvement in human affairs is possible. What has been delivered to us by the past has stood the test of time and is superior to any new order that could be the product of our own limited rationality, knowledge, and our strong passions. We ought to eschew *theory*. One related line of thought is that we are of very limited fellow-feeling, such that the more able will use their abilities only if they are given certain greater rewards, at bottom, economic rewards. A further related line of thought is that we are such that any tolerable society must be one where we are subjected to traditional constraints of an external kind. It is not conceivable that a tolerable society could count on fraternity, community, or anything other than law as we know it, police, judges, and prisons, in order to preserve itself.

(vii) It needs to be mentioned that the inequalities Conservatism defends or prescribes have sometimes been defended by the claim that they are to the benefit of all. In English politics the idea is perhaps owed to Disraeli (1835). It is the idea, put in plain form, that the rich must be as rich as they are so that the poor are not poorer. The claim is related to ideas of paternalism, social obligation, and stewardship.

(viii) It needs to be mentioned too that Conservatism, despite much philistinism, has in several of its forms had connections with the defence of cultural excellence and its advance. T. S. Eliot provides an example. (1939) It has sometimes condemned the vulgar materialism of commerce and industry.

Anti-egalitarianism, the first of these features, is indeed fundamental to Conservatism. However, this is no more than a negative side. We require an enlightening positive characterization of Conservatism in order to have a true grasp of it. This is implied by its defence of élites but not made explicit. Is an enlightening positive characterization to be found in the second feature, having to do with a kind of society?

Hardly, since there are in fact many possible societies, including societies of the Left, which could fall under the description of being organic, hierarchical, ordered, balanced, or unified. The additional idea of a traditional ideology calls out as much for clarification. It is some particular *nature or character* of our traditional ideology that is fundamental and needs to be made clear. Certainly Conservatism is not committed to *any* conceivable traditional ideology.

The third feature, having to do with private property, has often issued in the perception of Conservatism as being no more than the self-interest of the well-placed. There is no doubt that Conservatism *is* an ideology of self-interest, but it can hardly be distinguished by that. It is as true that movements of the Left have an impulse of self-interest. It is quite as persuasive, also, to regard Liberalism as being moved in part by the self-serving inclinations of a bourgeoisie or middle class. For our purposes the relevant question about the third feature of Conservatism, like the others, is that of what positive principle or commitment, of a fundamental kind, can be offered in justification of private property and its accompaniments.

Nor does the fourth feature of Conservatism, its disinclination to democracy, being of a negative character, take us far foward. It is of course in intimate connection with the anti-egalitarianism. Like anti-egalitarianism, the disinclination to democracy does point to a conclusion which is left inexplicit. So with the fifth feature, a limited role for government in certain prescribed areas. What is the recommendation of limiting the activity of governments with respect to business and the welfare services? It may be thought that things are made plainer by the proposition that Conservatism is devoted to and defends individual liberties. But what liberties, in terms of their basis, are in question? To approach the same point differently, a liberty is evidently a power or want of constraint, which thing is in some way justified. What is the justification with the particular liberties defended by Conservatism?

The remaining features are no more revealing. With respect to the sixth, what *is* the recommendation of the ordering of things that has stood the test of time? It is certain that some characterization is assumed by Conservatives. If there were none, then of course the unavoidable response would be to try to mend or improve human nature, or to try to alter circumstances so as to take better account of our limited rationality, knowledge, and fellow-feeling, and our strong passions.

With the seventh feature, we do indeed come to an explicit claim as to the commitment or nature of Conservatism. It is, we are told, the political tradition moved by the proposition that the inequalities it defends are the means to the betterment of all, without exception. The proposition is false, as is the claim that it is anything like the mainspring of Conservatism. Both consist in what of course is no distinguishing feature of Conservatism, which is to say false propaganda. It is the most rebuttable of propositions that the rich must be as they are in our societies so that the poor are not poorer. Many counterparts of the proposition, pertaining to earlier wealth-distributions, social orderings, and a good deal else, are now accepted by all as having been no more than fictions.

Finally, the connection of Conservatism with cultural excellence is by no means general. The defence of such excellences, where it does exist, is wholly subordinate to such other features as the defence of private property.

All or most of these reflections can be encapsulated in a single question. What is the fundamental commitment or nature of Conservatism, which is in accordance with the defence of élites and opposition to egalitarianism and democracy, which recommends societies somehow unified by the particular traditional ideology of which we all know, which issues in defences of private property, of the restriction of government in so far as individual initiative or responsibility is concerned, and of our societies such as they are, and which is at least consistent with views as to our fallen nature and perhaps a certain aestheticism?

The answer, to repeat, cannot be that Conservatism is resistance to change, a pure principle of traditionalism. It would not be a service to Conservatism, either, to take it as no more than some congeries of intimations, intuitions, and unreflective feelings, as is done by defenders, without the approval of others. (Oakeshott, 1962, p. 168; Kirk, 1982, pp. xi ff.) What cannot be said cannot be a defence, and cannot reasonably be taken to have informed a political tradition of great strength. Nor could Conservatism be characterized as no more than an acceptance of what has been produced by a history of transactions or transfers, with little more said of the transactions than that they were somehow voluntary. (Nozick, 1974b) Certainly, it cannot be that Conservatism is at bottom informed by a Utilitarian principle, as may be suggested by the seventh feature, the mistaken claim that inequalities serve the well-being of all. That is not to deny, as can be added, that it has involved a certain sense of obligation to some of those in need. That falls entirely short of a Utilitarian commitment, or a commitment to anything like the Principle of Equality.

The only answer to the question of the fundamental commitment or nature of Conservatism is that it consists in a body of desert-claims. It is not too much to say, despite the misleading suggestion as to unity and simplicity, that Conservatism must be taken as founded upon the Principle of Desert, that each of us is to have what he or she deserves.

It is this which is very nearly in view with its defence of élites and its opposition to what are in effect refusals to go by desert—egalitarianism and democracy. It is this commitment which accords with its defence of our societies as they are, in which desert plays so considerable a part. So with its defence of private property in particular, and of the limitation of government in such ways as to leave room for or to compel individual initiative. The answer is supported, as well, by considering feelings with respect to the seven social institutions, practices, and habits. What feelings are identified with Conservatism? There is little possibility of disagreement. Conservatism stands in peculiar connection with retribution in punishment, and with defences in terms of desert of the general practice of reward, our income and wealth distributions, and positions of power and standing.

It would be a large task, and not greatly rewarding, to attempt to analyse meanings with respect to the body of desert-claims which are fundamental to Conservatism. Some tolerable idea of this body of desert-claims, of course, can be had from the reflections on punishment and the other institutions and the like, and of course on the identifying features of Conservatism. Some of the desert-claims in question are best seen in terms of the argument from grievance, others in terms of an image of a factual relation of proportionality or whatever, others in terms of an intrinsic good or of compensation.

What we have in sum, then, is that the commitment of the Left is to the Principle of Equality, and the commitment of Conservatism to desert. Inevitably there are other things to be said of Conservatism, but it is not to be regarded as having several distinct commitments in the way of Liberalism.

Desert-claims, by our earlier distinction, divide into two categories: those which take the origination of an action as a condition of what is deserved, and those which do not. The first are directly vulnerable to an acceptance of determinism. Our conclusion here, since Conservatism does to some significant extent rest on origination-desert, more so than any other political tradition, must therefore be that it is peculiarly vulnerable to determinism. The gradual acceptance of determinism, to the considerable extent that political traditions are rational, will peculiarly affect this political tradition. It will do less to Liberalism, and little to the Left. I leave to Conservatives the matter of reflecting on a response of affirmation.

4.8 RETROSPECT

It has not been part of this book to provide it, but we can come to have a clear conception of the connection between a causal circumstance and an effect, got from our experience of the natural world. On this conception there can rest a philosophy of mind and action, free of ancient and modern mystery. It, or something not fundamentally different from it, is likely true. It makes our choices and decisions, and our actions, into certain necessitated events. They cannot then derive from what is named origination. To be inclined to accept this is to have a problem of feeling, which one can attempt to resolve by a certain affirmation. That response first involves the main category of possible consequences of determinism, which includes life-hopes, personal feelings, knowledge, moral responsibility, the rightness of actions and the moral standing of persons. These great things are affected by determinism, but persist, and our lives do not become dark, but remain open to celebration. This response can also be made with a second category of possible consequences of determinism, more of the order of necessities than great things. These have to do with our social lives. It was Schopenhauer's view, perhaps, that our existence is to be mourned, that we would decline the gift of life if we could anticipate its nature beforehand. Nietzsche, in his way also a determinist, said differently, that we may affirm life. It is Nietzsche with whom we can and must agree. (1883 (1818), 1962 (c. 1840); 1954 (c. 1880), 1966 (c. 1880))

Notes

Notes to Chapter 1

1. This conception of a mental event, as consisting in interdependent subject and content, is fundamental to Mental Realism, defended in the companion volume to this one, *Mind and Brain*, pp. 77 ff.
2. The conviction is discussed in *Mind and Brain*, pp. 91 ff.
3. These are discussed in *Mind and Brain*, pp. 175–206
4. *Mind and Brain*, pp. 216 ff.
5. *Mind and Brain*, Ch. 1
6. *Mind and Brain*, pp. 360–73
7. *Mind and Brain*, pp. 209–44

Notes to Chapter 3

1. *Mind and Brain*, pp. 175–206

References

ADLER, M. J., 1958, *The Idea of Freedom: A Dialectical Examination of the Conceptions of Freedom.* Garden City, Doubleday.

ALEXANDER, P. P., 1966, *Mill and Carlyle: An Examination of Mr John Stuart Mill's Doctrine of Causation in Relation to Moral Freedom.* Edinburgh, Nimmo.

ALSTON, W., 1967, 'Emotion and Feeling', in Edwards, 1967.

ARISTOTLE, 1915 (c.350 BC), *The Works of Aristotle: Ethica Eudemia,* trans. W.D. Ross. Oxford University Press.

—— 1953 (c.350 BC), *The Ethics of Aristotle: the Nicomachean Ethics Translated,* trans. J.A.K. Thomson. Hardmondsworth, Penguin.

AUSTIN, J. L., 1956, 'Ifs and Cans', *Proceedings of the British Academy.* Reprinted in Austin, 1961.

—— 1961, *Philosophical Papers,* ed. J. O. Urmson and G. J. Warnock. Oxford, Clarendon.

—— 1961a, 'Unfair to Facts', in Austin, 1961.

AYER, A.J., 1936, *Language, Truth and Logic.* London, Gollancz.

—— 1964, *Man as a Subject for Science.* Auguste Comte Memorial Lecture. London, Athlone.

—— 1976, *The Central Questions of Philosophy.* Harmondsworth, Penguin.

—— 1980, *Hume.* Oxford University Press.

—— 1984, *Freedom and Morality and Other Essays.* Oxford University Press.

—— 1984c, 'Freedom and Morality', in Ayer, 1984.

AYERS, M. R., 1968, *The Refutation of Determinism.* London, Methuen.

BAKUNIN, M., 1895, *Œuvres.* Paris.

—— 1953, *The Political Philosophy of Bakunin: Scientific Anarchism,* ed. G.P. Maximoff. New York, Free Press.

BECKER, L. C., 1977, *Property Rights.* London, Routledge and Kegan Paul.

BENNETT, J., 1980, 'Accountability', in van Straaten, 1980.

BENTHAM, J., 1950 (1840), *The Theory of Legislation,* trans. R. Hildreth, London, Routledge and Kegan Paul.

—— 1970 (1789), *An Introduction to the Principles of Morals and Legislation,* ed. J. H. Burns and H. L. A. Hart. London, Athlone Press.

BERKI, R. N., 1973, *Socialism.* London, Dent.

BERLIN, L.,1969, *Four Essays on Liberty.* Oxford University Press.

BEROFSKY, B., 1966, ed., *Free Will and Determinism.* New York, Harper.

BOSWELL, J., 1934–64 (1791), *Boswell's Life of Johnson,* ed. G. Birkbeck Hill and L.F. Powell. Oxford, Clarendon.

BOYLE, J. M. JR., GRISEZ, G., TOLLEFSEN, O., 1976, *Free Choice: A Self-Referential Argument.* Notre Dame University Press.

BRADLEY, F. H., 1927, *Ethical Studies*. Oxford University Press.

BRAMHALL, J., 1676, 'A Defence of True Liberty', in his *Works*. Dublin. Passages quoted in Hobbes, 1839–45a.

BREITMEYER, B. G., 1985, 'Problems With the Psychophysics of Intention', *Behavioural and Brain Sciences*.

BRENKERT, G., 1979, 'Freedom and Private Property in Marx', *Philosophy and Public Affairs*.

—— 1983, *Marx's Ethics of Freedom*. London, Routledge and Kegan Paul.

BUDD, M., 1985, *Music and the Emotions*. London, Routledge and Kegan Paul.

CAMPBELL, C.A., 1951, 'Is Free Will a Pseudo-Problem?', *Mind*.

CARLYLE, T., 1888 (1843), *Past and Present*, London, Routledge.

CAWS, P., 1979, *Sartre*. London, Routledge and Kegan Paul.

CHURCHLAND, P. S., 1986, *Neurophilosophy: Towards a Unified Science of the Mind/Brain*. Cambridge, Mass., MIT Press.

COHEN, G. A., 1978, *Karl Marx's Theory of History: A Defence*. Oxford University Press.

COLERIDGE, S., 1972 (1830), *On the Constitution of Church and State*. London, Dent.

COMTE, A., 1875–7, *System of Positive Polity*, trans. J. H. Bridges. London, Longman Green.

—— 1905, *Positive Philosophy*, trans. H. Martineau. New York, Calvin Blanchard.

CRANSTON, M., 1967, *Freedom: A New Analysis*. London, Longman.

DANTO, A. C., 1975, *Jean-Paul Sartre*. New York, Viking.

DAVIDSON, D., 1980, *Essays on Actions and Events*. Oxford, Clarendon.

—— 1980e, 'Mental Events', in Davidson, 1980.

DAVIES, L. H., 1972, 'They Deserve to Suffer', *Analysis*.

DAVIS, W. H., 1971, *The Freewill Question*. The Hague, Nijhoff.

DENNETT, D. C., 1979, *Brainstorms: Philosophical Essays on Mind and Psychology*. Hassocks, Harvester.

—— 1984, *Elbow Room: The Varieties of Free Will Worth Wanting*. Oxford, Clarendon.

DICK, J. C., 1975, 'How to Justify a Distribution of Earnings', *Philosophy and Public Affairs*.

DIOGENES LAERTIUS, 1925 (c. AD 225), *Lives of Eminent Philosophers*, trans. R. D. Hicks. London, Heinemann.

DISRAELI, B., 1884 (1835), *Vindication of the English Constitution*. London, Field and Tuer.

EARMAN, J., 1986, *A Primer of Determinism*. Dordrecht, Reidel.

EASTERBROOK, J. A., 1978, *The Determinants of Free Choice*. New York, Academic Press.

EDWARDS, P., 1961, 'Hard and Soft Determinism', in Hook, 1961.

—— 1967, *The Encyclopedia of Philosophy*. New York, Macmillan and Free Press.

—— 1967a, 'The Meaning and Value of Life', in Edwards, 1967.

ELIOT, T. S., 1939, *The Idea of a Christian Society*. London, Faber and Faber.

ENGELS, F., 1978 (1934), *Anti-Dühring*, trans. E. Burns. London, Lawrence and Wishart.

EPICTETUS, 1928 (*c.* AD 100) *Discourses*, trans. W. A. Oldfather. London, Heinemann.

EPICURUS, 1926 (*c.*300 BC), *The Extant Remains*, ed. C. Bailey. Oxford.

FEINBERG, J., 'Justice and Personal Desert', in *Doing and Deserving*. Princeton University Press.

FICHTE, J.G., 1873, 'The Closed Commercial State', in *Fichte's Works*, ed. W.S. Smith. London, Trubner.

FLETCHER, G., 1978, *Rethinking Criminal Law*. Boston, Little, Brown.

FOOT, P., 1957, 'Free Will as Involving Determinism', *Philosophical Review*.

—— 1978, *Virtues and Vices*. Berkeley, University of California Press.

FRANKFURT, H., 1969, 'The Principle of Alternative Possibilities', *Journal of Philosophy*.

—— 1971, 'Freedom of the Will and the Concept of a Person', *Journal of Philosophy*.

FRENCH, P.A., UEHLING, T.E., and WETTSTEIN, H.K., 1979, eds., *Midwest Studies in Philosophy IV: Studies in Metaphysics*. Minneapolis, University of Minnesota Press.

—— 1981, eds., *Midwest Studies in Philosophy VI: The Foundations of Analytic Philosophy*. Minneapolis, University of Minnesota Press.

—— 1982, eds., *Midwest Studies in Philosophy VII: Social and Political Philosophy*. Minneapolis, University of Minnesota Press.

—— 1984, eds., *Midwest Studies in Philosophy IX: Causation and Causal Theories*. Minneapolis, University of Minnesota Press.

GEACH, P., 1957, *Mental Acts*. London, Routledge and Kegan Paul.

—— 1969, *God and the Soul*. London, Routledge and Kegan Paul.

GETTIER, E., 1963, 'Is Justified True Belief Knowledge?', *Analysis*.

GLOVER, J., 1970, *Responsibility*. London, Routledge and Kegan Paul.

—— 1987, *I*. Harmondsworth, Penguin.

GOLDMAN, A. H., 1979, 'The Paradox of Punishment', *Philosophy and Public Affairs*.

GOLDMAN, A. I., 1967, 'A Causal Theory of Knowledge', *Journal of Philosophy*.

GRUNBAUM, A., 1953, 'Causality and the Science of Human Behaviour', in Feigl and Brodbeck, 1953.

—— 1971, 'Free Will and Laws of Human Behaviour', *American Philosophical Quarterly*.

HALL, J., 1960, *General Principles of Criminal Law*. 2nd edn. New York, Bobbs-Merrill.

HAMPSHIRE, S., 1951, *Spinoza*. Harmondsworth, Penguin.

—— 1972a, 'Freedom of Mind', in *Freedom of Mind and Other Essays*. Oxford, Clarendon.

HARE, R. M., 1952, *The Language of Morals*. Oxford, Clarendon.

HEGEL, G. W. F., 1929 (1840), *Science of Logic*, trans. W. H. Johnston and L. G. Struthers. London, Allen and Unwin.

—— 1942 (1840), *Philosophy of Right*, trans. T. M. Knox. Oxford, Clarendon.

—— 1944 (1840), *The Philosophy of History*, ed. J. Sibree. New York, Wiley.

HINTZ, H. W., 1961, 'Some Further Reflections on Moral Responsibility', in Hook, 1961.

HOBART, R. E., 1966, 'Free Will as Involving Determinism and Inconceivable Without It', in Berofsky, 1966.

HOBBES, T., 1839–45 (c.1650), *Works*, ed. W. Molesworth. London, Bohn.

—— 1839–45a (c.1650), *Of Liberty and Necessity*, 1830–45 (c.1650).

—— 1839–45b (c.1659) *Leviathan*, 1839–45 (c.1650).

HONDERICH, T., 1969, *Punishment, The Supposed Justification*. London, Hutchinson. Revised edition, 1984b. Harmondsworth, Penguin.

—— 1970, 'A Conspectus of Determinism', *Supplementary Proceedings of the Aristotelian Society*.

—— 1973, ed., *Essays on Freedom of Action*. London, Routledge and Kegan Paul.

—— 1973a, 'One Determinism', in Honderich, 1973.

—— 1974, 'The Worth of J. S. Mill's *On Liberty*', *Political Studies*.

—— 1975, 'The Use of the Basic Proposition of a Theory of Justice', *Mind*.

—— 1980a, *Violence for Equality: Inquiries in Political Philosophy*. Harmondsworth, Penguin.

—— 1981c, 'The Problem of Well-being and the Principle of Equality', *Mind*.

—— 1982b, 'Determinism and Politics', in French *et al.*, 1982.

—— 1982c. '*On Liberty* and Morality-Dependent Harms', *Political Studies*.

—— 1983a, 'The Principle of Equality Defended', *Politics*.

—— 1984b, See Honderich, 1969.

—— 1984c, 'The Principle of Equality: Reply to Nathan', *Mind*.

—— 1984e, ed., *Philosophy Through Its Past*. Harmondsworth, Penguin.

—— 1990, *Mind and Brain*. Oxford University Press.

—— and BURNYEAT, M. F., 1979, eds., *Philosophy As It Is*. Harmondsworth, Allen Lane.

—— and BOTTOMS, A., EDMUND-DAVIES, E., FLOUD, J., GOSTIN, L., GUNN, J., TAYLOR, L., WALKER, N., 1983, 'Symposium: Predicting Dangerousness', *Criminal Justice Ethics*.

HOOK, S., 1961, ed., *Determinism and Freedom in the Age of Modern Science*. New York, Collier.

HSOPERS, J., 1961, 'What Means This Freedom?', in Hook, 1961.

HUBY, P., 1967, 'The First Discovery of the Freewill Problem', *Philosophy*.

HUME, D., 1888 (1739), *A Treatise of Human Nature*, ed. L. A. Selby-Bigge. Oxford, Clarendon.

—— 1902 (1748), *An Enquiry Concerning Human Understanding*, ed. L.A. Selby-Bigge. Oxford, Clarendon.

—— 1938 (1740), *An Abstract of a Treatise of Human Nature*, ed. J.M. Keynes and P. Straffa. Cambridge University Press.

—— 1963 (1748), *An Enquiry Concerning Human Understanding*, ed. L.A. Selby-Bigge. Oxford, Clarendon.

JAMES, W., 1909, 'The Dilemma of Determinism', in *The Will to Believe and Other Essays*. New York, Longman.

JENKINS, R., 1972, *What Matters Now*. London, Fontana.

KANT, I., 1887 (1779), *Philosophy of Law*, trans. W. Hastie. Edinburgh, Clark.

—— 1943 (1781), *Critique of Pure Reason*, trans. J. M. D. Meiklejohn. London, Bell.

—— 1949 (1788), *Critique of Practical Reason*, trans. L. W. Beck. University of Chicago Press.

—— 1950 (1781), *Critique of Pure Reason*, trans. N. Kemp-Smith. London, Macmillan.

—— 1959 (1785), *Foundations of the Metaphysics of Morals,*trans. L. B. White, Indianapolis, Liberal Arts.

KENNY, A., 1975, *Will, Freedom and Power*. Oxford, Blackwell.

—— 1978, *Freewill and Responsibility*. London, Routledge and Kegan Paul.

—— 1979, *Aristotle's Theory of the Will*. London, Duckworth.

KIRK, R., 1982, *The Portable Conservative Reader*. New York, Penguin.

KLEMKE, E. D., 1981, ed., *The Meaning of Life*. Oxford University Press.

KRAUT, R., 1986, 'Feelings in Context', *Journal of Philosophy*.

LACEY, N., 1988, *Punishment and Political Principles*. London, Routledge and Kegan Paul.

LAMETTRIE, J. O., de, 1974 (1748), *Man a Machine*. La Salle, Open Court.

LEHRER, K., 1966. ed., *Freedom and Determinism*. New York, Random House.

LEIGHTON, S. R., 1985, 'A New View of Emotion', *American Philosophical Quarterly*.

LOCKE, D., 1986, REVIEW OF DENNETT, 1984, *Philosophical Books*.

LOCKE, J., 1960 (1690), *Two Treatises of Government*, ed. P. Laslett. Cambridge University Press.

LOTZE, H., 1885, *Outlines of Practical Philosophy*, trans. G. T. Ladd. Boston, Ginn.

LYONS, W., 1980, *Emotion*. Cambridge University Press.

MACINTYRE, A., 1967, *A Short History of Ethics*. London, Routledge and Kegan Paul.

—— 1971, *Against the Self-Images of the Age*. London, Duckworth.

—— 1971a, 'The Antecedents of Actions', in McIntyre, 1971.

—— 1971b, 'Psychoanalysis: The Future of An Illusion', in MacIntyre, 1971.

—— 1971c, 'Emotion, Behaviour and Belief', in MacIntyre, 1971.

—— 1972, ed., *Hegel: A Collection of Critical Essays*. Garden City, Doubleday.

—— 1984, 'Hegal: On Faces and Skulls', in MacIntyre, 1972, and Honderich, 1984e.

MACKIE, J. L., 1976, *Problems From Locke*. Oxford University Press.

—— 1977, *Ethics: Inventing Right and Wrong*. Harmondsworth, Penguin.

—— 1982, 'Morality and the Retributive Emotion', *Criminal Justice Ethics*. Reprinted in 1985b.

—— 1985, *Logic and Knowledge*, ed. J. Mackie and P. Mackie. Oxford, Clarendon.

—— 1985b, *Persons and Values*, ed. J. Mackie and P. Mackie. Oxford, Clarendon.

MAINE, H., 1886, *Popular Government*. London, Murray.

MANNING, D. J., 1976, *Liberalism*. London, Dent.

MARX, K., 1971 (1859), *A Contribution to the Critique of Political Economy*. London, Lawrence and Wishart.

MILL, J. S., 1924 (1873), *Autobiography*. New York, Columbia.

—— 1961 (1843), *A System of Logic*. London, Longman.

—— 1972a (*c*.1860), *Utilitarianism, Liberty and Representative Government*, ed. H.B. Acton. London, Dent.

—— 1972b (1863), *Utilitarianism*, in Mill, 1972a (*c*.1960).

—— 1972c (1859), *On Liberty*, in Mill, 1972a (*c*.1860).

—— 1979, *Collected Works of John Stuart Mill*, ed. J. M. Robson. University of Toronto Press and London, Routledge and Kegan Paul.

—— 1979a (1865), *Examination of Sir William Hamilton's Philosophy*. In 1979.

MOORE, G. E., 1912, *Ethics*. London, Williams and Norgate.

MORGENBESSER, S. and WALSH, J., 1962, eds., *Free Will*. Englewood Cliffs, Prentice-Hall.

MULLER, A., 1955, excerpts in H. S. Reiss, ed., *The Political Thought of the German Romantics*. London, Macmillan.

MURPHY, J.G., 1971. 'Three Mistakes About Retributivism', *Analysis*.

—— 1973, 'Marxism and Retributivism', *Philosophy and Public Affairs*.

NAGEL, T., 1979, *Mortal Questions*. Cambridge University Press.

—— 1979a, 'What Is It Like to Be a Bat?', in Nagel, 1979.

—— 1986, *The View From Nowhere*. Oxford University Press.

NIETZSCHE, F., 1954 (*c*.1880), *The Portable Neitzsche*, ed. W. Kaufman. New York, Viking.

—— 1966 (*c*.1880), *Basic Writings of Nietzsche*, ed. W. Kaufman. New York, Viking.

NINO, C., 1983, 'A Consensual Theory of Punishment', *Philosophy and Public Affairs*.

—— 1987, 'Consenting to be Punished: A Reply to Professor Honderich'. Forthcoming.

NOVALIS, 1891, *The Thought of Novalis*, ed. M. J. Hope. London, Stott.

NOWELL-SMITH, P. H., 1954, *Ethics*. Harmondsworth, Penguin.

NOZICK, R., 1947b, *Anarchy, State and Utopia*. Oxford, Blackwell.

——1981, *Philosophical Explanations*. Oxford, Clarendon.

OAKESHOTT, M., 1962, *Rationalism in Politics and Other Essays*. London, Methuen.

OLAFSON, F., 1967, 'Jean-Paul Sartre', in Edwards, 1967.

O'SULLIVAN, N., 1976, *Conservatism*. London, Dent.

PARFIT, D., 1984, *Reasons and Persons* Oxford, Clarendon.

PEARS, D., 1963, ed., *Freedom and the Will*. London, Macmillan.

—— 1972, *What Is Knowledge?* London, Allen and Unwin.

—— 1973, 'Rational Explanation of Actions and Psychological Determinsm', in Honderich, 1973.

—— 1975b, *Questions in the Philosophy of Mind*. London, Duckworth.

POPPER, K.R., 1982a, *Quantum Theory and the Schism in Physics*, ed. W.W. Bartley III. London, Hutchinson.

—— 1982b, *The Open Universe*, ed. W. W. Bartley III. London, Hutchinson.

—— and ECCLES, J. C., 1977, *The Self and Its Brain*. Berlin, Springer.

RAWLS, J., 1972, *A Theory of Justice*. Oxford, Clarendon.

ROUSSEAU, J. J., 1973 (1762), *The Social Contract and Discourses*, trans. G. D. H. Cole. London, Dent.

RUSSELL, B., 1917, *Mysticism and Logic*. London, Allen and Unwin.

—— 1917b, 'A Free Man's Worship', in Russell, 1917.

RYAN, A., 1970, *The Philosophy of John Stuart Mill*. London, Macmillan.

SANTAYANA, G., 1930, *The Realm of Matter*. London, Constable.

SARTRE, J.-P., 1957 (1943), *Being and Nothingness*, trans. H. Barnes. London, Methuen.

SCHLICK, M., 1956, 'When is a Man Responsible?', in his *Problems of Ethics*, trans. David Rynin. New York, Dover.

SCHMITT, F. O. and WORDEN, F. G., 1974, eds., *The Neurosciences Third Study Program*. Cambridge, Mass., MIT Press.

SCHOPENHAUER, A., 1883 (1818), *The World as Will and Idea*, trans. R. B. Haldane and J. Kemp. London, Routledge.

—— 1962 (c.1840), *The Will to Live—Selected Writings of Arthur Schopenhauer*, ed. R. Taylor. Garden City, Doubleday.

SCRUTON, R., 1980, *The Meaning of Conservatism*. Harmonsworth, Penguin.

SEARLE, J.R., 1984, *Minds, Brains and Science*, Reith Lectures. London, BBC.

SLOTE, M., 1980, 'Understanding Free Will', *Journal of Philosophy*.

SMART, J. J. C., 1959, 'Sensations and Brain Processes', *Philosophical Review*.

—— 1963, *Philosophy and Scientific Realism*. London, Routledge and Kegan Paul.

—— and WILLIAMS, B., 1973, *Utilitarianism: For and Against*. Cambridge University Press.

SMITH, A., 1844 (1776), *An Inquiry Into the Nature and Causes of Wealth of Nations*. London, Nelson.

SOLOMON, R. C., 1986, 'Emotions, Feelings and Contexts', *Journal of Philosophy*.

SORABJI, R., 1980, *Necessity, Cause and Blame: Perspectives on Aristotle's Theory*. London, Duckworth.

SPINOZA, B., 1910 (1678), *Ethics*, trans. W. Hale White. Oxford University Press.

—— 1949 (1678), *Ethics*, ed. J. Gutmann, New York, Hafner.

SPRIGGE, T. L. S., 1983, *The Vindication of Absolute Idealism*. Edinburgh Universty Press.

STEPHEN, J. F., 1862, *A General View of The Criminal Law of England*. London, Macmillan.

STRAWSON, G., 1985, review of Dennett, 1984, *Times Literary Supplement*.

—— 1986, *Freedom and Belief*. Oxford University Press.

STRAWSON, P. F., 1962, 'Freedom and Resentment', *Proceedings of the British Academy*. Reprinted in Strawson, 1968.

—— 1968, ed., *Studies in the Philosophy of Thought and Action*. Oxford University Press.

—— 1985, *Skepticism and Naturalism: Some Varieties*. London, Methuen.

TAYLOR, R., 1966, *Action and Purpose*, Englewood Cliffs, Prentice-Hall.

TREITSCHKE, H. VON., 1963, *Politics*, trans. B. Dugdale and T. de Bille. New York, Harcourt Brace.

TRUSTED, J., 1984, *Freewill and Responsibility*. Oxford University Press.

VAIHINGER, H., 1924, *The Philosophy of 'As If'*, trans. C. K. Ogden. New York, Hacourt Brace.

VAN INWAGEN, P., 1974, 'A Formal Approach to the Problem of Freewill and Determinism', *Theoria*.

—— 1975, 'The Incompatibility of Freewill and Determinism', *Philosophical Studies*.

—— 1983, *An Essay on Free Will*. Oxford, Clarendon.

VONWRIGHT, G. H., 1971, *Explanation and Understanding*. Ithaca, Cornell.

WALKER, N., 1983, Comments in Honderich *et al.*, 1983.

WALKER, R., 1978, *Kant*. London, Routledge and Kegan Paul.

WARNOCK, G. J., 1971, *The Objects of Morality*. London, Methuen.

WARNOCK, M., 1965, *The Philosophy of Sartre*. London, Hutchinson.

—— 1973, 'Freedom in the Early Philosophy of J.-P. Sartre', in Honderich, 1973.

WATSON, G., 1979/80, critical notice of Kenny, *Will, Freedom and Power*, *Journal of Philosophy*.

—— 1982, ed., *Free Will*. Oxford University Press.

—— 1986, review of Dennett, 1984, *Journal of Philosophy*.

WESTERMARCKE, E., 1932, *Ethical Relativity*. London, Kegan Paul, Trench, and Trubner.

WILLIAMS, B., 1960, 'Man As Agent: On Stuart Hampshire's Recent Work', *Encoter*.

—— 1963, 'Postscript', in Pears, 1963.

—— 1973, *Problems of the Self*. Cambridge University Press.

—— 1981, *Moral Luck*. Cambridge University Press.

—— and SMART, J. J. C., 1973, *Utilitarianism: For and Against*. Cambridge University Press.

WILLIAMS, G., 1961, *Criminal Law, The General Part*. London, Stevens.

Index